D0351077

Defending the Filibuster

★ ★ ★ ★ ★

DEFENDING
the
FILIBUSTER

THE SOUL OF THE SENATE

Richard A. Arenberg and
Robert B. Dove

FOREWORD BY
SENATOR MARK UDALL AND
SENATOR TED KAUFMAN

INDIANA UNIVERSITY PRESS

Bloomington and Indianapolis

This book is a publication of

Indiana University Press
601 North Morton Street
Bloomington, Indiana 47404-3797 USA

iupress.indiana.edu

Telephone orders   800-842-6796
Fax orders   812-855-7931

⊖ The paper used in this publication
meets the minimum requirements
of the American National Standard for
Information Sciences—Permanence
of Paper for Printed Library Materials,
ANSI Z39.48-1992.

Manufactured in the
United States of America

Cataloging information is available
from the Library of Congress.
ISBN 978-0-253-00191-7 (cloth : alkaline
paper)
ISBN 978-0-253-00698-1 (e-book)

1 2 3 4 5   16 15 14 13 12

TO BERNIE ARENBERG
$(1922-2011)$

*No president or Red Sox manager
ever quite met his standards*

.

CONTENTS

Senator Mark Udall and Senator Ted Kaufman

As two U.S. senators who served during the 111th Congress, we often encountered the perception that the 2009–2010 Senate was a dysfunctional body. As we traveled in our home states and across the country, voters, commentators, pundits, and academics all lamented governmental "gridlock," laying most of the blame on the Senate's rules—in particular the "filibuster," which requires a 60-vote supermajority to overcome even a single member's objection to consideration of a bill, nomination, or final vote.

At a time when many Americans are casting doubt on the viability of their institutions of government, it's easy to dismiss the Senate as "broken." In recent years, senators used the filibuster to block consideration of virtually every bill, executive appointee, and judicial nomination. While the filibuster has helped define the Senate through history, statistics show that in the past 2 years, senators used the filibuster more often than any time previously. The famed institution—already known as the "world's greatest deliberative body"—appeared to have become perpetually tied in knots with "debate over the debate."

Yet, it would be inaccurate to say that the filibuster prevented the Senate from passing meaningful legislation. On the contrary: although it's true that the filibuster made it incredibly difficult to get anything done, senators still enacted legislation at a historic pace during the same 2-year period. Starting with the American Recovery and Reconstruction Act, the 111th Congress passed major pieces of legislation, including health insurance reform, Wall Street reform, credit card reform, repeal of "Don't Ask, Don't Tell," and ratification of the New START treaty. While many federal judicial nominees lingered in political purgatory for months due to "holds," many of those same nominees were confirmed unanimously when the Senate finally held an up-or-down vote. Eminent congressional scholars Tom Mann and Norm Ornstein deemed the legislative record of the 111th Congress greater than any recent Congress and on par with the historic Congresses resulting from the landslide elections of FDR in 1932 and LBJ in 1964.

And so the arrival of *Defending the Filibuster* is particularly timely. Two extraordinarily well-qualified Senate veterans—Richard A. Arenberg and Robert B. Dove, who represent both parties and over 65 years of Senate experience—lead the reader through the hallways and back rooms of the Senate. They are uniquely qualified to explain the history of the Senate filibuster and more. By illuminating one of the basic principles undergirding the U.S. government since its founding, the co-authors provide a blueprint for how it should function in the twenty-first century. They explain the form and function of the Senate filibuster and why it is required if we wish to maintain our stable and secure form of government. They also show how it has been distorted over the years and what should be done to put it back on course.

One important lesson we learned from the 111th Congress is that even though the filibuster has been used more often recently—so much one could even argue it has been abused—it hasn't prevented action; rather, it has accomplished what it was ostensibly created to do: allow meaningful debate. When crafting a bill, senators must consider opposition, and they must compromise to accommodate others' interests and concerns in order to avoid a fight that stalls or even kills legislation. Thus, the filibuster encourages senators to work to find consensus whenever possible. Throughout history, that has been the case. For every important initiative that has been blocked, delayed, or squashed by the use or abuse of the filibuster, there is an opponent who lauds its use to prevent an insidious change to the law. Take the Alaska National Interest Lands Conservation Act, which protects the Arctic National Wildlife Refuge (ANWR). The act was filibustered, yet eventually was signed into law. And while proponents of protecting ANWR might decry the use of the filibuster in that case, those same conservationists have also repeatedly used it to prevent oil drilling in ANWR.

We agree with many of the criticisms raised by leaders of the filibuster reform movement; the Senate should deal with them in a constructive manner. But eroding the institution by drastically changing Senate rules is not necessary or wise. The recent agreement between Senate Majority Leader Harry Reid and Republican Minority Leader Mitch McConnell, which eliminates secret holds, limits procedural abuses, and decreases the number of government appointments requiring Senate confirmation, was an important step. However, if the Senate were to employ a majoritarian way of doing business and adopt new rules by a simple majority vote at the beginning of each new Congress—as was suggested during the 111th Congress by a frustrated faction of our colleagues—we fear that it would trigger major and destabilizing changes in the role and nature of the Senate as a body.

We believe in evolutionary—not revolutionary—changes. The history of the Senate is one of struggle between compromise and intransigence. The Senate is a place that protects political minorities from being run over roughshod. During the Senate's long history, members on both sides of the aisle have upheld certain traditions. Whenever anyone moves to change one of those traditions in a way that diminishes comity—the grease for the Senate's wheels—they should do so carefully. "Unintended consequences" result from dramatic rule changes. And on a practical level, a senator who, while in the majority, votes to limit the filibuster will one day live with the "intended" consequences when in the minority.

In too many countries around the world, the political majority has used its electoral victory as a rationale to crush its opponents. Winning an election in the United States has never been a license for a slim majority to disregard the rights of political minorities. Without our safeguards, including the filibuster, elected majorities could govern inured to the voice of minorities or important regional considerations. In U.S. history, the presidency, House, and Senate have several times been held by one single party. In those times especially, the filibuster has been a key ingredient in America's formula for maintaining political stability.

We recommend this book to all who care deeply about American political institutions. Robert Dove is a former parliamentarian, whose decades in the Senate chambers cemented his bona fides as a keeper of the rules. Richard Arenberg has spent 30 years in the thick of history, procedure, and protocol in the Senate as a venerated advisor. Their collective experience and observations have been distilled here in a clear exposition of one of the staples that define the Senate, and it is well worth the read for any student of this deliberative body. With its wisdom, we are confident that America and its elected leaders—out of the frustrations of some and the stubbornness of others—will eventually find their way toward the next great compromises that will keep America moving forward to its ever-brighter future.

This house is a sanctuary; a citadel of law, of order, and of liberty; it is here—it is here in this exalted refuge—here, if anywhere, will be resistance made to the storms of political frenzy and the silent arts of corruption. And if the Constitution be destined ever to perish by the sacrilegious hands of the demagogue or the usurper, which God avert, its expiring agonies will be witnessed on this floor.

—*Vice President Aaron Burr, Farewell to the Senate, March 2, 1805*

We had met on several prior occasions, beginning in the 1970s. Bob Dove began in the Senate as an assistant parliamentarian in 1965. He would go on to become the Senate parliamentarian in 1981. Rich Arenberg came to Capitol Hill with Paul Tsongas, who was part of the new class of "Watergate babies" elected to the House of Representatives in 1974. Four years later, Tsongas upset an incumbent senator and Arenberg moved with him to the Senate. As parliamentary advice was required from time to time to prepare Senator Tsongas for deliberations on the Senate floor, including the epic battle over the Alaska lands issue, Arenberg would seek out Dove. But it was in April of 1982 that our friendship was forged.

The scene was Ocean City, Maryland. The Congressional Research Service was conducting its Graduate Institute for Legislative Staff, known as the "CRS Congress." Bob Dove, then the Senate parliamentarian, was asked to play the role of the vice president of the United States, the presiding officer of the Senate. CRS asked Rich Arenberg, Senator Tsongas's legislative director, to play the role of the Senate majority leader.

As the mock Congress deliberated, we, building on our shared love of the U.S. Senate and the adrenaline of parliamentary maneuver under fire, playfully attempted to stump each other, exploring the most arcane parliamentary situations we could muster up. Arenberg, imitating the real majority leader, Senator Robert Byrd, even delivered a long speech on Senate history invoking the lessons of ancient Rome. Byrd was in the midst of such long lectures on the Senate floor, which later became his famous book on Senate history. At the conclusion, Arenberg, to honor Dove for his good humor and skill in presiding, led the CRS Senate in adopting a resolution pursuant to a standing order in the U.S. Senate which provides for marble busts of Vice Presidents to be placed in the niches in the Senate gallery. Sent to the podium with the Arenberg resolution was a little yellow rubber duck with the label "VP" emblazoned on its chest.

Over the years, we continued to work together on many occasions. Arenberg, while working for Senator Tsongas, Majority Leader George Mitchell, and Senator Carl Levin, sought the advice of Dove on numerous parliamentary matters. In recent years, we have lectured in each others' classrooms at Brown University and George Washington University.

In November of 2009, we came together to begin writing *Defending the Filibuster*. We wrote this book for many audiences. At one level, we wrote this book for ourselves. We are two longtime Senate staffers who love the institution, its critical role in American democracy, and its unique history. We share the conviction that the existing view of the Senate and its rules, particularly the filibuster, is negative in the eyes of much of the public, popular media, and academia. Inevitably, those who have not served Burr's "exalted refuge," Madison's "great anchor" of the government, fail to adequately take into account the impacts of the filibuster on the unique characteristics of the Senate. These include discouraging unchecked majority control, fostering deliberation and compromise, moderating extreme outcomes and avoiding precipitous decision making, protecting the rights of minorities, discouraging more populated states from dominating the congressional process, ensuring the role of the legislative branch in oversight of the executive branch, and assuring the role of the Senate as a check and balance of the majoritarian House of Representatives in the legislative process. At the basic level, we wanted to explore the history and lay out our analysis and advocate for our view.

We also wrote this book for the senators themselves and the staffs that serve them. We hope that our long experience and insight into the workings of the Senate might convince those intent on radically changing the Senate's character to reevaluate. And, we seek to reinforce the conviction of those who seek to defend the Senate's historic role, including the rights of senators to debate and amend.

We hope this book will be of use to the federal employees, contractors, lobbyists, and other advocates who together keep the capital city cauldron in which the Senate operates boiling. Filibuster critics are fond of saying, "Elections have consequences." The implication is that once a majority is elected, it should be able to work its will. The minority should debate but then get out of the way. Some of these folks are deeply committed to public service and the efficiency of government. Others toil tirelessly in the political arena, working toward those ends but sometimes caring foremost about who is winning or losing. We think all are better served by a clearer understanding of how the Senate fits into that process.

We also seek to address those in the academic community who study the Senate. Political scientists, historians, and professors of public policy have contributed a great deal to the understanding of that body. However, there is a different perspective that grows out of the experience of participant-observers. We hope to contribute some of that broader perspective to the academic debate on the filibuster.

We believe this book will be a valuable resource for students, activists, and others who need a concise and accessible introduction to the filibuster and related aspects of the history and workings of the U.S. Senate. A balanced view of the filibuster is essential to any educated understanding of the way the Congress works. As adjunct professors, we have used much of the material in our teaching and recognize the need for a text of this sort.

And finally, we wrote this book for the citizens of our great democracy, the constituents of the Congress, the voters, the American people. Some have only a passing interest in public affairs, others are more engaged. We seek to inspire at least a few of the former to join the latter by shining a light on more than 200 years of Senate history. If we accomplish nothing more than helping a few to better understand the importance of some arcane Senate rules and practices for the course of events in our nation now and in the future, we will have done a great deal.

This book could not have been written without the encouragement, support, and assistance of our families and many friends and colleagues. We received a highly competitive 2010 Congressional Research Award from the Dirksen Congressional Center. We are grateful for this early support, which made possible interviews and much of the research necessary for this book. We are indebted to our literary agent, Leah Spiro, who embraced this project and guided two rookies through the publishing world. This is a better book because of the hard work, dedication, and wisdom of Rebecca Tolen, our editor, and the people at Indiana University Press. Our copy editor, Sarah Brown, discovered and helped us correct our many distortions of the English language.

A number of people read chapters as they were developed and suggested improvements along the way. This book could not have been written without the careful editing and constructive criticism of longtime friend and colleague Dennis Kanin. Governor Michael Dukakis, while disagreeing with the central theme of support for the filibuster, nonetheless enthusiastically supported the effort all along the way. Senate Historian Donald Ritchie provided us with the confidence of knowing our sense of Senate history was not wildly off target and contributed valuable suggestions along the way. Harvey Boulay often provided a fresh insight when it was most needed. Kaye Meier was usually the first to read each new chapter, and it was her words of praise that encouraged us to begin sharing each chapter with others. Brent Segal read with a fine eye for detail. We were buoyed too when Marty Paone, who served the Senate as secretary of the majority, himself an expert on Senate rules, was supportive of what we had written. Colleagues at Brown, Northeastern, George Washington, and Suffolk Universities were kind with their time, advice, and support, including Jim Morone, Ethan Pollock, Marion Orr, Wendy Schiller, Chris Bosso, Dan Urman, Chris Deering, and Rachael Cobb.

We are also grateful to Senators Tom Udall, Mark Udall, Carl Levin, Jack Reed, and Ted Kaufman for the interviews they granted that were so valuable to us in adding freshness and immediacy to our understanding of the current reform debate. One of the most engaging and thoughtful interviews was with former Congressman Lee Hamilton, now the director of the Indiana University Center for Congress.

Senators Mark Udall and Ted Kaufman accepted our invitation to write the foreword for this book. We chose them because they are among the most thoughtful and articulate voices for reforming the filibuster without destroying its critical role in the Senate and our system of government. We could not have asked for a more articulate, timely, and relevant opening to our book than they have provided.

There are many others who contributed time, effort, and moral support in large ways and small that we want to acknowledge: Roy Jones, Alex Harman, Neil Campbell, Anita Jensen, Eric Kingson, Ned Arenberg, Nancy Altman, Max Wertheimer, Josh Arenberg, Bob Barbera, Jack Danielson, Stan Sloss, Meg Arenberg, Tara Andringa, Mitch Tyson, Georgina Segal, Judy Schneider, Colin McGinnis, Jeremy Hekhuis, and others.

In the end, the most important encouragement and steadfast support, which sometimes required their great perseverance and patience, which always reliably came, was from our beautiful and insightful wives, Linda Arenberg and Linda Dove.

We served the Senate in various positions for more than 65 years combined. We love and revere that institution. The Senate is a unique body, unparalleled in human history. We firmly believe that the right to virtually unlimited debate lies at its heart. The filibuster is truly the soul of the Senate.

We began this preface with the words of Aaron Burr to the Senate in his farewell address. Nearly a hundred years later, in 1897, Vice President

Adlai Stevenson gave his farewell address, which summarizes much of what we hope to say in this book:

> It must not be forgotten that the rules governing this body are founded deep in human experience; that they are the result of centuries of tireless effort in legislative halls, to conserve, to render stable and secure, the rights and liberties which have been achieved by conflict. By its rules, the Senate wisely fixes the limits to its own power. Of those who clamor against the Senate, and its methods of procedure, it may be truly said: "They know not what they do." In this Chamber alone are preserved without restraint two essentials of wise legislation and good government: the right of amendment and of debate. Great evils often result from hasty legislation; rarely from the delay which follows full discussion and deliberation. In my humble judgment, the historic Senate—preserving the unrestricted right of amendment and of debate, maintaining intact the time honored parliamentary methods and amenities which unfailingly secure action after deliberation—possesses in our scheme of government—a value which cannot be measured by words.

Defending the Filibuster

★ ★ ★

ONE

Soul of the Senate

Headlines in recent years scream out: "Senate's Abuse of Filibuster Rule Threatens Democracy,"[1] "A Dangerous Dysfunction,"[2] "Filibuster Abuse: Founding Fathers Didn't Plan It This Way,"[3] "Filibuster, Gone Rogue: A Senate Rule That Cripples Our Democracy,"[4] and a *Harvard Crimson* op-ed proclaims, "Tyranny of the Minority."[5]

The 2009–2010 Republican filibuster of the healthcare reform proposals of President Obama and the congressional Democrats and the struggles to reach the 60-vote supermajority necessary to overcome this tactic moved the filibuster and associated Senate parliamentary maneuvers again to center stage. As has occurred from time to time in the Senate's history, frustrated majorities and their constituencies, as well as observers in academia, the media, and the Congress itself, have demanded the elimination of "unlimited debate" in the Senate.

Lawyer Thomas Geoghegan in a *New York Times* op-ed fumed, "The Senate, as it now operates, really has become unconstitutional." He declared that the filibuster is "a revision of Article I itself; not used to cut off debate, but to decide in effect whether to enact a law."[6] Lloyd Cutler, who was White House counsel under both President Jimmy Carter and President Bill Clinton, asserted "a strong argument can be made that its requirements of 60 votes to cut off debate and a two-thirds vote to amend the rules are both unconstitutional."[7] And the *New York Times,* in a 1995 editorial, called it "an archaic rule that frustrates democracy and serves no useful purpose."[8]

The leader of the U.S. House of Representatives, Speaker Nancy Pelosi (D-CA), in a July 2010 interview with the *Huffington Post,* attacked the Senate filibuster as "the 60-vote stranglehold on the future." She demanded, "The Senate has to go to 51 votes, and not 60 votes . . . Getting from where the nation is, to a sustainable place would require doing away with the filibuster." She continued, "It's very doable. It's just a decision. And one of the decisions that has to be made is that the Senate has to go to 51 votes and not 60 votes. Otherwise, we are totally at their mercy."[9]

In the Senate itself, young senators in their first term like Tom Udall (D-NM), Jeff Merkley (D-OR), and Mark Udall (D-CO) began working seriously on filibuster reform. Veteran senator Tom Harkin (D-IA) dusted off a proposal he offered in 1995 to more or less sweep the filibuster away and began pressing for its consideration once again.

There can be little argument but that the right to filibuster in the Senate is being abused. It has been by both parties. It has become the fashion in the public media, academia, and in some quarters of the Congress itself to view the filibuster as strictly a tactic of obstruction and as an affront to majority rule. Nearly forgotten or simply dismissed is the role that extended debate has played in giving voice to minorities, protecting the moderating role of the Senate and the Senate's place as the intended counterweight to an otherwise unchecked executive. In these times of extreme partisan polarization, this role is more, not less, important.

THE SENATE AS "COOLING SAUCER"

Amusingly, it sometimes seems as though no one on any side of the issue can explain or analyze the filibuster without mentioning three figures—two Jeffersons and a Washington. Nearly all descriptions of the practice reference the probably apocryphal story of George Washington explaining to Thomas Jefferson, just back from France, that the Senate was included in the federal design to serve the same function as the saucer into which he poured his hot tea to cool.[10]

The Senate's smaller size, longer terms, and state-wide constituencies all predispose it to be a more moderate, measured body than the House of Representatives, less impacted by the shifting winds of public opinion. The filibuster, although not created by the Framers themselves, grew out of the independent precedents and procedures evident in the Senate from the outset, which themselves grew out of the constitutional design for the Senate. For example, the very first Senate assured that its presiding officer, the vice president of the United States, would be weak in contrast to the powers of the presiding officer of the House, the Speaker.

At least as often when the filibuster is discussed, it is not Thomas Jefferson who is invoked, but Jefferson Smith, the fictional senator played by the great Jimmy Stewart in his romantic portrayal of the filibuster in the 1939 film *Mr. Smith Goes to Washington*. In that film, the naïve newly appointed senator champions a bill to construct a national boys' camp. Nearly defeated by the cynical powers in Washington, he launches a 23-hour filibuster in defense of the bill, declaring, "I've got a few things I want to say to this body . . . And as a matter of fact, I'm not gonna leave this body until I do get them said." The public rallies to his side and the heroic senator wins in the end. When the film was released, Senate Majority Leader Alben Barkley called it "silly and stupid" and asserted that it made the Senate look like "a bunch of crooks." According to the official Senate website, "Years later, producer Frank Capra alleged that several senators had actually tried to buy up the film to prevent its release."[11]

Even the most renowned academic examination of the filibuster, the landmark *Politics or Principle? Filibustering in the U.S. Senate,* written by Sarah Binder and Steven Smith in 1997, couldn't get past the second sentence of chapter 1 without referring to *Mr. Smith Goes to Washington.* And, a mere six paragraphs later, Jefferson and Washington are cooling their favored beverage.[12]

Senator Harkin, in February 2010, when introducing S Res. 416, his rules change proposal aimed at squashing the filibuster, invoked Jimmy

Stewart's character on the Senate floor only seven paragraphs into his speech.[13] And Washington and Jefferson, sipping their coffee from the saucer, popped up a few short minutes later. A large blowup image of Stewart, exhausted and near collapse, filibustering on the Hollywood mock-up Senate floor was even actually displayed on the real Senate floor during the debate on filibuster reform in January of 2011.

Gridlocked and perhaps dysfunctional as it sometimes is, failing to overcome the extreme partisan political polarization that plagues it today, the Senate nonetheless remains unique among the world's legislatures. Nineteenth-century British prime minister William Ewart Gladstone is often cited by those seeking to describe the nature of the U.S. Senate. He called the body "the most remarkable of all the inventions of modern politics."[14] While few outside of the Senate itself would still label it the "world's greatest deliberative body," it remains a symbol of respect for the rights of the minority in a democratic system of government. In the Senate, no minority can be silenced for long. The views of a minority, even a minority of one, can be heard, and it can, at the very least, have its legislative proposal raised and voted upon. Most importantly, the majority in the Senate is not handed the "keys to the bulldozer."

SENATE'S RULES ESTABLISH ITS CHARACTER

The Senate is most clearly characterized by two features, the right of its members to unlimited debate and their right to offer amendments practically without limit. This is on occasion misunderstood or misstated. The right of unlimited debate in the Senate is not contained in the Constitution, nor is any prescription for cloture (the ending of debate). The Constitution does, however, in Article I, Section 5, state that, "Each house may determine the rules of its proceedings." In setting "the rules of its proceedings," pursuant to this constitutional provision, the Senate adopted Rule XIX, which states: "When a Senator desires to speak, he shall rise and address the Presiding Officer, and shall not proceed until recognized, and the Presiding Officer shall recognize the Senator who shall first address him. No Senator shall interrupt another Senator in debate without his consent." This rule combined with the absence in the Senate rules of a "previous question motion"—that is, a motion to end debate and vote on the matter before the body in normal parliamentary procedure—means that senators have the right of unlimited debate.

The Senate's original rules did contain a motion for the previous question.[15] The 1789 rules stated, "The previous question being moved and seconded, the question for the chair shall be: 'Shall the main question now be put?' and if the nays prevail, the main question shall not be put."[16] In other words, a majority vote on the previous question motion would end debate on the matter and a final vote would then occur. The rule, seldom used, was eliminated in 1806, at the suggestion of outgoing Senate president Aaron Burr.[17] From that point on, the perceived "unlimited debate" of the Senate became a fact and along with it the possibility of the use of that right for purposes of obstruction.

Speaking on the Senate floor in 1893, Senator Orville Platt (R-CT) said, "There are just two ways under our rules by which a vote can be obtained. One is by getting unanimous consent—the consent of each senator—to take a vote at a certain time. Next comes what is sometimes known as the process of 'sitting it out,' that is for the friends of a bill to remain in continuous session until the opponents of it are so physically exhausted that they cannot struggle any longer."[18]

In a potentially momentous procedural development in 1917, the Senate adopted Rule XXII, which for the first time provided for a process known as cloture and created a way in which debate in the Senate could be brought to an end, allowing a vote on a bill, motion, or amendment to take place. The rule required a two-thirds vote to end debate. Each senator "post-cloture" would be allowed to speak for up to and no more than 1 hour and any amendments proposed after that point must be germane. Yet the principle of unlimited debate was so entrenched that over the next 46 years, the Senate managed to invoke cloture on only five occasions.[19]

In 1975, after years of efforts by the Senate's liberals to change the filibuster rules, as part of a compromise offered by Senator Robert Byrd (D-WV) and supported by the party leadership on both sides of the aisle, the number of votes required to invoke cloture was reduced from two-thirds of senators voting to three-fifths of all senators "duly elected and sworn." This is the famed 60-vote supermajority required to end debate in the current Senate. As part of the compromise, however, the two-thirds threshold for ending debate was retained for changes in the Senate rules. This difference very significantly raises the bar for changing rules in the Senate, because it requires 67 votes (if all senators are voting), not just 60, when a change in the rules is sought.

This rule in particular makes it easy for minorities in the Senate to slow things down. Majorities are frequently frustrated by the pace of the Senate and the difficulty of enacting their agenda. With that frustration sometimes comes a demand to eliminate the filibuster. The forces on the attack against the filibuster and in its defense have a way of switching sides as the majority power shifts from one political party or coalition to another. That is not to say that there are not principled adherents on both sides. In recent years, such as 2005, for example, in the face of Democratic filibusters of ten of President Bush's federal circuit court nominees, most Republicans were prepared to eliminate the filibuster in order to get their way and confirm the nominations. Most Democrats opposed that effort and rose to defend the filibuster.

The influential liberal voice the *Nation* argued editorially at the time:

> If the [filibuster is eliminated], Congress will become an altered branch of government. In the absence of rules that require the consideration of minority views and values, the Senate will become little different from the House, where the party out of power is reduced almost to observer status . . . This is a moment when we decide whether this country will remain a democracy in which those who govern must play by the rules, or will become a winner-take-all system where the gravest fear of the Founders— tyranny of the majority—will be the lasting legacy of George W. Bush, Tom DeLay and Bill Frist.[20]

Fast-forward to 2009–2010 and a series of Republican filibusters against the major elements of President Obama's legislative agenda. Now, the voices demanding an end to filibusters are on the Democratic side of the aisle, and there are no takers among the Republicans. They are defending the right to unlimited debate.

ROLE OF THE FILIBUSTER

There can be little argument but that the right to filibuster in the Senate has been abused by both parties. Vice President Joseph Biden, a long-time member of the Senate, has observed, "Most people would agree that the United States Senate has never acted as consistently as they have to require a supermajority, which is 60 votes, to get anything done. That's a fundamental shift. I was there for 36 years. I don't ever recall it being abused and used as much as it has now."[21]

It has become the fashion in academia and the popular media, as well, to view the filibuster as strictly a tactic of obstruction and as an affront to the sacrosanct majority rule. Nearly forgotten or simply dismissed is the role that extended debate has played in fostering the moderating role of the Senate as intended by the Framers in order to ensure minority participation in the legislative process and serve as a counterweight to an otherwise unchecked executive.

James Madison wrote in *The Federalist* No. 51[22] that

> if men were angels, no government would be necessary. If angels were to govern men, neither external nor internal controls on government would be necessary. In framing a government which is to be administered by men over men, the great difficulty lies in this: you must first enable the government to control the governed; and in the next place oblige it to control itself. A dependence on the people is no doubt a primary control on the government; but experience has taught mankind the necessity of auxiliary precautions.[23]

The Founders established a series of Madison's "auxiliary precautions" as checks and balances, many of which do not strictly adhere to majority rule precepts. They feared unfettered majorities. For example, the Connecticut Compromise itself set up a Senate that disproportionately represents the smaller states without regard to "one man–one vote ideals," and the Electoral College created in the Constitution fails to assure that a majority elects the president of the United States.

Lindsay Rogers in *The American Senate* expresses it well: "One must understand clearly the nature of the system [the Framers] desired in order to appreciate the present-day importance of the Senate. This importance is quite different from that contemplated by the architects of the Constitution, but it results, nevertheless, from their arrangements to prevent 'an unjust combination of the majority.'"[24]

In this book, we trace the history of the filibuster in the Senate and the struggle to reform abusive uses of the filibuster and associated tactics. We outline the dangers that arise as frustrated majorities seek to make the legislative process more "efficient" in order to adopt their legislative agenda. We defend the historic role of the filibuster as a protection of minority rights and a force for consensus building. We lay out a series of proposed reforms to reduce the incidence of filibuster abuse and we track the outcomes of the current effort to rewrite the Senate rules. We argue not only that the filibuster is a feature of the Senate rules that should be retained but that it is a part of the Senate's fundamental character.

Former vice president Walter Mondale, who had played a prominent role in the efforts to reform the filibuster during the 1960s and 1970s, delivered a special address to senators in 2002. He expressed his seasoned (and changed) view of the value of the right of unlimited debate in the Senate:

> One of the first things we learn in the Senate is the rules that govern the closure of debate. It is the essence of the stature and the power of each Senator and, I believe, of the Senate itself.
>
> When I came to the Senate, I thought a simple majority should be enough to end debate. I had seen the cloture rule abused in the past, especially on civil rights. The old rules permitted virtually endless talk. In recent years, many Senators had developed a . . . strategy where, even after a successful cloture vote, they could still carry on forever, reading and amending the Journal, reading and amending the Chaplain's prayer—as we did for several days—filing hundreds of amendments, with no end in sight.
>
> It had to be changed, and it was . . . but to end a filibuster still requires 60 votes, and I believe that is about right. It is a balancing act. You need to be able to close off debate, but you also need to give an individual Senator the power to stop everything in the country and to rip open an issue in a way that no other institution in America can.
>
> It can't happen in the House. Their rules of debate are very different. It can't happen in news conferences. It can't happen on talk shows. That is entertainment, not debate. Only the Senate can stop the nation in its tracks, and it is the only body in the world that allows it.[25]

In 2011, Mondale was back on the other side, arguing on the op-ed pages of the *New York Times* that the Senate should employ parliamentary tactics, known as the "constitutional option" (see the epilogue), which if successful would overturn the Senate's rules and allow changing the Senate's filibuster rule by a simple majority vote. This would soon lead to a majoritarian Senate.[26]

But we agree more fully with Vice President Mondale's testimony in 1993 before the Joint Committee on the Organization of Congress. He said, "If Members continue to use the filibuster to fight over issues that are most appropriately resolved through simple majority vote, the body may soon find itself under pressure to get rid of this important protection, and I believe that would be a tragedy."[27]

★ ★ ★

TWO

Filibuster, Cloture, and Unfettered Amendment

The tactical use of rules to obstruct the plans of legislative majorities is as old as legislatures themselves. Plutarch told of a request of ancient Rome's senate by Julius Caesar: "He applied to the Senate for permission to stand [as a] candidate [for consul]." Cato strongly opposed the request. He "attempted to prevent [Caesar's] success by gaining time; with which view he spun out the debate till it was too late to conclude upon anything that day."[1]

THE FILIBUSTER

In his 1940 classic, *Filibustering in the Senate*, Franklin Burdette points out that "obstruction which newspapers of today would call filibustering was certainly known in our colonial legislatures. George Mason of Virginia said in the debates upon the Constitution of the Federal Convention of 1787 that beneficial results might come from systematic 'quorum breaking,' refusing to vote so as deny the majority the quorum necessary to do business, practiced by members of the legislature."[2]

The term probably is taken from the Dutch word meaning "pirate."[3] According to the *Oxford English Dictionary,* during the mid-nineteenth century, the English label "filibusterer" was applied to Americans inciting revolution in Central America. Not long after, the word was popularly used to describe tactics used to delay or defeat legislation in the U.S. Senate.

The Senate's famed filibuster is largely the consequence of the *absence* of a rule. The missing rule is a previous question motion to bring a matter to a vote. The previous question motion in most legislative bodies, the U.S. House of Representatives included, can be adopted by majority vote, bringing debate to a close and the matter to a final vote. After the U.S. Senate abandoned its previous question rule in 1806, debate became unlimited, except after 1917 by the use of the cloture procedure under Rule XXII.

Although filibuster is commonly thought of as long dilatory speeches on the Senate floor, the term encompasses a variety of tactics. This might entail a long stream of motions and/or amendments or simply the refusal to permit leadership to move legislation along by unanimous consent. All of these steps have the effect of extending the debate and preventing the Senate from reaching a final vote on a matter.

THE RIGHT TO AMEND

Another defining feature of the Senate, one that goes hand in glove with unlimited debate, is senators' virtually unfettered ability to offer amendments. This right also derives, at least in part, from the absence of a rule. Under most circumstances, there is no germaneness rule in the Senate requiring that an amendment be relevant to the legislation under consideration.[4] This means that a senator can offer an amendment on virtually any subject to most bills regardless of the subject of that bill. Therefore, senators have not only the power to take and hold the floor and prevent a vote from taking place, but they may also raise whatever issue they choose and in most cases get a vote on it. This combination assures that a persistent minority of any number can be a formidable force to be reckoned with in the Senate. Any senator seeking recognition, under most circumstances, will be recognized by the presiding officer. Once that senator assumes his or her right to the floor, there is no limit to the duration of the member's speech.

CLOTURE AND THE THREAT TO FILIBUSTER

In the modern Senate, with its heavy agenda of complex issues, time for the body to deliberate, amend, and act is limited and valuable. This creates unrelenting pressure to keep legislative business going. In this environment, the impact of a senator's right to filibuster or even just to threaten to filibuster is magnified. Even if the threat to filibuster comes from one "lone wolf" senator, or a small group, and the majority leader knows he has the votes necessary to invoke cloture, the threat is problematic. This is because the process of invoking cloture itself is very time consuming. It is the role of the Senate's majority leader to manage the Senate's agenda and to keep legislation flowing. In the best of times, the majority leader's tools for accomplishing this are limited. Under the added time stress and uncertainty created by threatened filibusters, the task becomes even more difficult.

To initiate the process, the majority leader must file a cloture petition signed by sixteen senators. This starts the clock running. If no other arrangement is made by unanimous consent, the cloture vote will automatically occur 1 hour after the Senate convenes on its second day of session after the filing of the petition. Then, even if cloture is invoked, an additional 30 hours may be used up post-cloture. This means that the mere process of getting cloture, even when it is not seriously in doubt, can take 3 or 4 days. Add to this delay the fact that the motion to proceed—the motion just to take up a piece of legislation for consideration—may be filibustered, and then the bill itself can also be filibustered, and the challenge of ending debate becomes formidable. In fact, on any single piece of legislation, there are, in theory, up to six filibusters that could be carried out: on the motion to proceed; on the bill itself; on any of the three motions necessary to get the bill to a conference committee with the House, normally adopted by unanimous consent—the motion to insist on the Senate's amendments (or disagree to the House's amendments), the motion to request or agree to a conference with the House, and/or the motion to appoint conferees; and finally, on return of the bill to the Senate from a conference for final consideration.

As a result, just the threat of a filibuster can alter the majority leader's decision about whether to bring a bill to the Senate floor and may force changes in the language of the bill itself or other compromises simply to avoid a filibuster. This impacts legislation in the Senate at every stage and may affect how a bill is shaped from its very inception.

THE HOLD

The implied threat of a filibuster, often expressed in the form of a "hold," shapes legislative outcomes in the contemporary Senate. A hold, on its face, is a letter (or other communication) from a member of the Senate to his or her party leadership requesting delay in the Senate's consideration of a matter. Such holds may be public or anonymous. As Walter Oleszek of the Congressional Research Service writes, "Holds are a potent blocking device because they are linked to the Senate's tradition of extended debate and unanimous consent agreements. Party leaders understand that to ignore holds could precipitate objections to unanimous consent requests and filibusters."[5]

In other words, although there may be a whole range of reasons why a senator has requested a hold, it is most often understood to carry the implication that the senator will not grant unanimous consent to proceed to the matter and may, if necessary, launch a filibuster. While this all remains unspoken, the request for a hold, in most all instances, is honored by the leadership, at least for an undefined period of time.

THE SUPERMAJORITY REQUIREMENT—
IS IT ALWAYS A FILIBUSTER?

Above and beyond actual filibusters, threatened filibusters, and indirect threats through holds, the mere existence of the supermajority requirement to end debate creates a presumption in the Senate that 60 votes will be necessary for anything of significance to succeed. This itself greatly affects the shaping of legislation and the calculations that senators make, even before they engage on the issues involved.

While working in the Senate, we frequently encountered the question "Who's our lead Republican sponsor?" from Democratic senators at the very first stages of drafting amendments or bills. Similarly, Republican senators asked about Democratic cosponsors. If the first answer was a centrist senator who often crossed party lines, there might be pushback. "Can't we approach [for example] Hatch or Stevens or Inouye or Dole?" The idea was that the further down the other party's ideological spectrum your legislative partner stood, the better chance to achieve that needed supermajority of the 60 votes to defend against a filibuster. Frequently, this leads to consensus-building efforts and redrafting legislative language acceptable to a critical mass of senators long before a bill even sees the light of day.

One common point of confusion arises from the reference to cloture votes and filibusters as if the terms were interchangeable. Analysts will often cite the number of cloture votes as a tally of filibusters, for example. However, even when opponents of a measure resort to extended debate or other tactics of delay, supporters may not decide to seek cloture. In recent times, conversely, the Senate leadership has increasingly utilized cloture as a routine tool to manage the flow of business, even in the absence of any apparent filibuster. For these reasons, the occurrence or absence of cloture attempts cannot be taken as a reliable guide to the presence or absence of a filibuster. Since there is no enactment or announcement required, the question of whether a filibuster is occurring, in many instances, is a matter of judgment in the end. Senators when engaged in filibustering are sometimes very coy about acknowledging that a filibuster is under way. The minority leadership may just inform the majority leader that it is not ready to vote on a matter because members of its caucus are working on amendments or are studying the matter further. At such times, it is only with the passage of time that the fact that a filibuster is occurring is inferred. Senator Tom Harkin (D-IA) described this on the Senate floor, "Sometimes, in the fog of debate, it is hard to determine who is responsible for slowing something down. It is like the shifting sand."[6] Senate rules expert Martin Gold discussed the difficulty in identifying and quantifying filibusters in his 2004 oral history interview with Senate Historian Donald Ritchie:

> GOLD: I'll put it like this: you can have filibusters without cloture, and you can have cloture without filibusters. I think it's very hard to develop statistics on that, particularly if you get to this question: what constitutes a filibuster in the first place? After cloture has actually failed, you can probably say there's a filibuster going on. But beyond that, you can never quantify it.
>
> RITCHIE: Yes, because senators don't stand up and say, "Now we're going to begin a filibuster."
>
> GOLD: No, of course not.
>
> RITCHIE: It's really a pejorative term that applied to it. Those who are filibustering just say that they're conducting an extensive debate over an issue of national concern.
>
> GOLD: Exactly.[7]

On the other hand, the majority sometimes purposely conflates filibusters with the incidence of cloture votes in order to make the case that the minority is obstructing Senate business. For example, in December 2010, near the end of the 111th Congress, Majority Leader Harry Reid (D-NV) complained, "Senate Republicans need look no further than themselves in casting blame for the predicament we are in right now. In this Congress ... Republicans have waged 87 filibusters. They have used every procedural trick in the book to delay legislation that is important to the American people."[8] In Congresses of the past decade, the high incidence of obstructionism in the Senate, especially by whichever party is in the minority, has resulted in a more tactical use of cloture by majority leaders.[9] But majority leaders may also seek cloture votes for reasons not at all directly related to filibusters or even threatened filibusters.

Cloture imposes a requirement of germaneness, meaning all amendments must be strictly related to the subject matter of the bill, thus limiting amendments. Under most normal circumstances, when an amendment on a different subject is added to a bill, its passage may be rendered much more difficult. On occasion, such amendments are deliberately intended to kill the bill. Such amendments are referred to as "poison pills."

The minority party often proposes amendments that, although virtually certain to be defeated, raise issues that the minority wishes to highlight or on which they want to force senators in the majority to go on record with a roll-call vote. Such votes can play very prominently on 30-second TV commercials during political campaigns. On occasion, amendments can be motivated just by the desire to delay the legislative progress that the majority is making with its agenda. In the Capitol Hill jargon, this, along with other delaying techniques, is referred to as "slow-rolling."

Occasionally, the majority leader will file a cloture motion prior to the beginning of consideration of a bill. Since cloture will bring with it a germaneness requirement, under Rule XXII, the majority leader can, by invoking cloture, block many of the "message amendments" that the minority may want to raise and limit the minority's ability to change the subject. This strategy speeds up the process and greatly increases the majority leader's control over it. Of course, it is only successful if he or she has the 60 votes to back it up.

Frequently, a negotiation occurs between the majority and minority leadership about reaching a unanimous consent agreement to control the number of amendments and perhaps even to circumscribe which amendments would be in order. Because of the supermajority requirement and other difficulties imposed by the rules, much of the Senate's business is conducted through such agreements requiring the approval of all senators. When these negotiations are slow or the majority concludes that the minority is not negotiating in good faith, the filing of a cloture petition is often used as a stick in the closet to spur reaching an agreement. That cloture vote may or may not actually take place.

At times, filibusters are not aimed at delaying or defeating the bill before the Senate. There may simply be reluctance by one party or the other to allow a roll-call vote on a matter that it views as politically uncomfortable. This frequently results in negotiations between the party leaders and/or the floor managers. By filing for cloture and bringing the motion to a vote (it comes up automatically 2 days after the petition is filed), the majority leader can force minority members to cast a public roll-call vote on an issue that might otherwise, due to minority obstructionism, not come to a vote.

For these reasons, it is difficult to accurately quantify filibusters and draw conclusions about obstruction from their frequency. That said, no one who has closely observed the Senate over the past 30 years or so could deny the explosive increase over that period in the use of the filibuster as a partisan tactic. Of course, the steady and accelerating increase in the number of cloture votes is even more evident. But, if the central concern is the obstruction, delay, and imposition of a supermajority requirement on a matter that might otherwise be decided by simple majority vote, it may be less relevant whether we are focused on filibuster increases or on an increase in the use of cloture procedures.

Barbara Sinclair, who has done pioneering work on tracking filibusters, writes, "To be sure, the data must be regarded with some caution. Exactly when lengthy debate becomes a filibuster is in part a matter of judgment. Furthermore . . . filibusters have changed their form, and threats to filibuster have become much more frequent than the actual talkathons. As a consequence, cloture is sometimes sought before a filibuster manifests itself on the floor. Nevertheless, experts and participants agree that the frequency of obstructionism has increased."[10]

MINORITY RIGHTS AND CONSENSUS BUILDING

Senate Judiciary Committee Ranking Member Senator Orrin Hatch (R-UT) has noted that "A lot of people object to filibusters, arguing that the procedure unnecessarily impedes the passage of legislation and frustrates the ability of the Senate to function efficiently . . . New arrivals to the Senate, especially former members of the House, often propose eliminating the procedure entirely. Senator Trent Lott (R-MS) raised the issue again just a few years ago when he grew frustrated with repeated threats by the Democrats to filibuster a wide variety of bills."[11]

Senator Hatch suggests that this would be a mistake, arguing, "Although I have been a victim as well as a beneficiary of filibusters, I hope the procedure remains intact. It is, in many ways, the fundamental parliamentary power available to the minority in Congress. Unlike the rules in the House of Representatives, where a simple majority can always force the passage of any bill, in the Senate the filibuster or the threat of one ensures that the majority must give some consideration to the interests of the minority, or risk losing control of the legislative process."[12]

But even beyond the importance of protecting minority rights, the filibuster, in our view, serves to encourage a search for consensus in the Senate. Senator Hatch points to this as he concludes, "Its presence has guaranteed that American law does not reflect the will of only one side."[13] Senator Carl Levin (D-MI), speaking on the Senate floor against the efforts in 2005 to eliminate the filibuster for judicial nominations, said, "The enduring strength and beauty of the U.S. Senate is that we not only operate by rules, but that those rules provide protections for the minority. More than 200 years of Senate rulings have affirmed that this body stands against the 'tyranny of the majority' that our Founding Fathers cautioned us about."[14]

Former Senate Majority Leader George Mitchell (D-ME), speaking in the Old Senate Chamber to the members of the Senate as a part of the Leaders' Lecture Series used his experience in forging the Good Friday Agreement in Northern Ireland to dramatize his view:

> The discussions were long, very contentious, and repetitious. Some of the delegates grew impatient with me for not imposing time limits and for not limiting speakers when they strayed off the subject, as they frequently did. I rejected their protests and I refused to impose any time limits until the very end of the process when I established overall a final, firm deadline. And every time I refused to cut speakers off, I explained my decision that I acquired my political training in the United States Senate where the rules permit unlimited debate.
>
> But I must admit now that when I was majority leader, I didn't always enjoy unlimited debate. There were times when I was frustrated by the ease with which the Senate rules can be used for obstruction. But with time and distance comes perspective.
>
> So my first point is that the right of unlimited debate is a rare treasure which you must safeguard. Of course, it can be, and it is, abused. But that is the price that must be paid, and the privilege is worth the price.[15]

★ ★ ★

THREE

History of the Filibuster

The very first Senate rules adopted in 1789 provided for a previous question motion. Today we understand such motions as requiring an end to debate and an immediate vote on the pending matter. Most legislative bodies have such a motion in their rules. In the House of Representatives the motion to cut off debate requires only a simple majority vote. While the early Senate rules included a previous question motion, the evidence is that it served a different purpose. The best study, a scholarly essay by Harvard professor Joseph Cooper, concludes that the previous question as it existed in the early Senate of 1789–1806 "was not designed to operate as a cloture mechanism . . . it was not in practice used as a cloture mechanism" and "it is even improbable that the Senate could have used the previous question for cloture."[1] It had the effect in the Senate of delaying consideration of a question until a later time. It seems clear that it was seldom, if ever, employed. Cooper details the ten instances that he was able to find; in none of these cases did the rule function to curtail debate.[2] The Senate met behind closed doors in its early years and debates apparently ended only by consensus.

AARON BURR AND THE ELIMINATION
OF THE PREVIOUS QUESTION MOTION

On March 2, 1805, outgoing vice president Aaron Burr delivered his farewell speech to the Senate. It is considered one of the great speeches of Senate history. He called the Senate "a sanctuary" and asserted that it would be in the Senate, because of its character and its rules, that, if anywhere, there would be "resistance to the storms of political frenzy."[3] John Quincy Adams, then a senator, leaves us a firsthand account in his diary of Burr's farewell address to the Senate: "He mentioned one or two of the rules . . . and recommended the abolition of that respecting the previous question, had in the four years been only once taken, and that upon an amendment. This was proof that it could not be necessary, and all its purposes were certainly much better answered by the question of indefinite postponement."[4]

When the next year the Senate recodified its rules at the suggestion of Vice President Burr, the virtually never used previous question motion rule was simply dropped. From 1806, when it was eliminated, until 1917, when the cloture rule was adopted, a period of 111 years, debate in the Senate was truly unlimited.

EARLY FILIBUSTERS

Although early filibusters are difficult to identify, the first true filibuster in the Senate, according to the Congressional Research Service, although unsuccessful, did not occur until 1841 at the start of the 27th Congress. The issue was largely a patronage battle over the appointment of its official printers. The minority Democrats, in an ongoing partisan battle over the hiring of local firms to print the *Congressional Globe*, a precursor to the *Congressional Record*, were attempting to block the Whig appointments by denying the Senate a quorum. This lasted for 6 days. The debate was intense and marked by bitterness and personal accusations aimed at the fired incumbent official printers. Whig senator Henry Clay, as reported by the *Globe*, fumed that "he believed the *Globe* to be an infamous paper and its chief editor an infamous man."[5] He went on to characterize Senator William King of Alabama, with whom he was debating, as "false, untrue and cowardly."[6] In fact, the confrontation became so heated that Senator Clay challenged Senator King to a duel. The duel was averted when both senators were arrested, but the Whigs survived the filibuster and prevailed.[7]

A few short months later, a more organized and extended filibuster arose. At issue was Senator Henry Clay's bill for the establishment of a national bank. Senator John C. Calhoun (D-SC), another giant of the Senate, was among those who led the opposition. Senator Calhoun delivered a 2-hour attack on Clay's bank bill that was so dramatic that the reporter of debates added a highly unusual editorial comment in the *Congressional Globe* calling the speech "one of the finest, clearest and most impressive arguments which he has delivered."[8] In frustration, Clay threatened to offer a measure to allow a simple majority to control the business of the Senate.

Senator King of Alabama, whom Clay had challenged to a duel during the earlier filibuster over the Senate printers, demanded of Clay whether he really proposed to carry out such an unthinkable action, what King referred to as a "gag" measure. When Clay confirmed that he would, King thundered, "I tell the senator then that he may make his arrangements at his boarding house for the winter"[9] Calhoun vigorously opposed Clay's effort, calling it "a palpable attempt to infringe the right of speech."[10] When Clay, on July 12, 1841, did attempt to "move the previous question," Calhoun promised an extended battle in defense of the minority's "undoubted right to question, examine and discuss those measures which they believe in their hearts are inimical to the best interests of the country."[11] He promised that if this "gag-law" was attempted that he would "resist it to the last."[12]

Clay, who had himself exercised extended debate in the Senate, backed down.[13] Senate Historian Emeritus Richard A. Baker observes that "for the first time, the principle of minority rights was applied in defense of extended debate."[14] He writes that the principle that "the only limit on debate should be a member's sense of decorum" had become so deeply ingrained in the Senate's culture that in 1865, the Senate quickly killed a proposal to require that debate on the floor be germane "to the question under debate" and consistently defeated such efforts over the years.[15]

This episode has been seen by some scholars as characteristic of the Senate of that era. Minorities used the filibuster to slow the majority's agenda but did not expect to kill it in the end. Gregory Wawro and Eric Schickler argue that "the majority tolerated rules allowing considerable leeway for obstruction so long as filibusters were not pushed to the extreme of killing priority bills favored by a clear floor majority."[16]

THE BIRTH OF CLOTURE

By the 1850s, the term "filibuster"—derived from a Dutch word meaning "pirate" or "freebooter"[17] was being used to describe efforts to delay or block matters in the Senate. But it wasn't until February 1917 that the issue of obstruction by filibuster came to a head. In response to Kaiser Wilhelm II of Germany's declaration of unrestricted submarine warfare, President Woodrow Wilson sought authority from the Congress to arm merchant ships. Earlier, he had asked for and received an overwhelming endorsement of his decision to cut off diplomatic relations with Germany. Although the House of Representatives, responding to surging public sentiment against Germany in the wake of the sinking of several American vessels, endorsed President Wilson's measure, opposition from a group of isolationists in the Senate led to a 23-day filibuster until the end of the congressional session.[18] The battle was led by Robert "Fighting Bob" La Follette, a Republican senator from Wisconsin who was one of the Senate's "Famous Five,"[19] and another great Republican senator from Nebraska, George Norris. The enraged majority demanded that the Senate remain in session throughout the night (a demand of majorities in response to filibusters that we frequently hear now). The filibustering senators asserted what they viewed as their right under the Senate rules to require full discussion of a measure that seemed likely to bring the nation to the brink of war. Senator Norris declared, "If it is filibustering to try to find out about something, to do the best you can—when it all comes at once, you cannot do much—then I am guilty of filibustering."[20] He read Woodrow Wilson's own words from *Congressional Government: A Study in American Politics,* Wilson's doctoral dissertation, first published in 1885. Wilson wrote, "It is the proper duty of a representative body to look diligently into every affair of government and to talk much about what it sees."[21]

The effectiveness of the filibuster by such a small band of senators rested on the fact that the session was about to end. At the time, presidential inaugurations occurred on March 4 and the 64th Congress would expire at noon on that day. As the filibuster ran into the early morning hours of March 4, 1917, Senator La Follette sought to speak against the bill. By this time, feelings were running so high, however, that the Democratic majority leadership seized the floor and would not yield it. La Follette inquired of the presiding officer "whether I am to have an opportunity on this floor." Democratic senator Joseph Taylor Robinson of Arkansas raised a point of order to prevent La Follette's parliamentary inquiry. La Follette raged, "I will continue on this floor until I complete my statement unless somebody carries me off, and I should like to see the man who will do it."[22] The Senate sided with Robinson (by a 52–15 vote) and Democrats held the floor until noon, when the Senate was adjourned sine die.[23] In the words of Franklin Burdette, "Filibusterism, practiced both by a minority and by the majority, had been victorious."[24]

The tactical give-and-take of filibuster situations in the Senate, even today, can devolve into conflicting assertions as to which side is actually obstructing. While in the 1917 case it is clear that opponents of the bill were filibustering, the seizure of the floor by the majority provided greater credibility to the assertion by La Follette and others that they sought not to delay but to debate and explore the problems with the legislation. As time ran down, the counter-filibusters actually killed the bill. As we shall see, analogous situations are not uncommon in the present-day Senate.

The filibuster successfully, if temporarily, blocked the arming of the ships until the end of the congressional session. An angry President Wilson issued a statement from the White House:

> The termination of the last session of the Sixty-fourth Congress . . . disclosed a situation unparalleled in the history of the country, perhaps unparalleled in the history of any modern Government. In the immediate

presence of a crisis fraught with more subtle and far-reaching possibilities of national danger than any other Government has known . . . the Senate was unable to act because a little group of eleven senators had determined that it should not.

. . . The Senate of the United States is the only legislative body in the world which cannot act when its majority is ready for action. A little group of willful men, representing no opinion but their own, have rendered the great Government of the United States helpless and contemptible.[25]

President Wilson was able subsequently to order the arming of the ships by executive order. The public outrage directed at the filibusters did not subside. Exercising his constitutional powers under Article II, Section 3,[26] Wilson called a special session of the Senate. Acting swiftly, on March 8, 1917, in a compromise between those seeking to eliminate the filibuster and those favoring the status quo, the Senate agreed to Rule XXII, which established a cloture procedure while preserving the tradition of unlimited debate. The rule required a two-thirds majority to end debate and permitted each member to speak for an additional hour before voting on final passage of legislation. A few weeks later, the United States entered World War I.[27]

EFFORTS TO STRENGTHEN CLOTURE

After its creation during the special session of the 65th Congress in 1917, the cloture process was rarely used. In fact, between 1917 and 1970, cloture was invoked successfully only 8 times. Perhaps even more pertinently, cloture was only attempted 49 times over that period (58 cloture petitions were filed).[28] By contrast, the Senate invoked cloture 63 times in the 111th Congress (2009–2010) alone.[29] During the Senate's history since 1970, cloture has been invoked 421 times.[30]

The first effort to strengthen the cloture rule and reform the filibuster occurred in 1949. Although amendments weakened cloture by requiring a vote of two-thirds of senators "duly elected and sworn"—that is, two-thirds of the body no matter how many were voting—as a practical matter, this new language required a slightly larger number of senators to end debate. At the same time, however, the Senate enhanced the cloture rule in a significant way. The Senate explicitly applied Rule XXII to the motion to proceed (with the exception of proceeding to measures to change the Senate rules). This was important because in the Senate in order to begin debating and amending a piece of legislation, a motion to proceed to it must be adopted. Since that motion to proceed is a debatable matter under the Senate rules, it is subject to filibuster. This change allowed a supermajority to end debate on whether or not to begin considering a matter. It addressed a critical problem that had been created by a ruling the year before. The Senate's president pro tempore, Senator Arthur Vandenberg (R-MI), had ruled that cloture could not be applied to a motion to take up a matter. This made it clear that without a means to invoke cloture on the motion to proceed, filibusters blocking such motions would eviscerate the usefulness of Rule XXII for ending debate on important issues. Senators seeking to block legislation could act to prevent it from even coming up in the Senate without fear of Rule XXII coming into play.

In the 1948 incident, Vandenberg, one of the Senate's "Famous Seven,"[31] supported eliminating the poll tax, which was the legislative matter being blocked by a filibuster. He also made clear that, as a senator, he favored a stricter cloture rule that included the motion to proceed. But when the question arose, he believed that his oath of office as the presiding officer of the Senate required him to interpret the rules as they existed, not as he wished them to be. Vandenberg declared: "The President pro tempore is not entitled to consult his own predilections or his own convictions in the use of this authority . . . Otherwise, the preservation of any minority rights for any minority at any time would be become impossible . . . Only the Senate has the right to change the law."[32]

Vandenberg went on to say that he was "bound to recognize what he believes to be the clear mandate of the Senate rules and the Senate precedents; namely that no such authority presently exists."[33] It took only a year for the issue to crystallize. In 1949, going against Senate precedent and rules and against the advice of then Senate parliamentarian Charles Watkins, Vice President Alben W. Barkley reversed the Vandenberg precedent. Barkley ruled that despite Rule XXII as it then existed providing only that the "pending matter" was subject to cloture, it also applied to a motion to proceed to consideration of a bill. Floyd Riddick, who later became the Senate parliamentarian and who was on the floor at the time, remembers that "Barkley, having been against that line of thought while he was majority leader was consistent and refused to sustain the point of order."[34]

The ruling was appealed and Vandenberg again rose in the Senate to declare his vigorous opposition to changing the Senate rules with a ruling from the chair protected from challenge by a simple majority. He argued:

> I have heard it erroneously argued in the cloakrooms that since the Senate rules themselves authorize a change in the rules through due legislative process by a majority vote, it is within the spirit of the rules when we reach the same net result by a majority vote of the Senate upholding a parliamentary ruling of the Vice President which, in effect, changes the rules ... It is argued that the Senate itself makes the change in both instances by majority vote; and it is asked, "What is the difference?" Of course, this is really an argument that the end justifies the means ... I think there is a great and fundamental difference . . . It simply means that regardless of precedent or traditional practice, the rules, hereafter, mean whatever the Presiding Officer of the Senate, plus a simple majority of Senators voting at the time, want the rules to mean. We fit the rules to the occasion, instead of fitting the occasion to the rules.[35]

The Senate by a 46–41 vote sided with Vandenberg and restored his ruling.[36] So the Senate was returned to a circumstance in which Rule XXII was not very likely to be effective since the motion to proceed to a matter could be debated indefinitely with no possibility of cloture being invoked. A week later, on March 17, the Senate adopted a resolution formally changing the Senate rules. The change was a compromise worked out between those who wanted to strengthen the cloture rule and those desiring to further weaken it. Cloture was strengthened by applying it to end "debate upon any measure, motion, other matter pending before the Senate." But, at the same time, the change weakened cloture by requiring a two-thirds vote of the entire body, usually 64 votes (67 after the admission of Alaska and Hawaii in 1959), as opposed to two-thirds of those "present and voting" at the time.

Arthur Vandenberg's ringing admonition about the oath and obligations of the Senate's presiding officer would resonate in future debates right up to the present day, as efforts were mounted or are threatened to use the powers of the president of the Senate (limited as they may be) in concert with a simple Senate majority to overturn the existing filibuster rules. Some argue that the Constitution permits the Senate to amend its own rules on the opening day of a new Congress without following the existing rules. This would be accomplished with the assistance of a ruling from the Senate's presiding officer, probably the vice president, that a filibuster is not in order, protected from challenge by a simple majority, short-circuiting the filibuster rule itself. As Vandenburg concluded, "The rules can be safely changed only by the direct and conscious action of the Senate itself, acting in the fashion prescribed by the rules. Otherwise, no rule in the Senate is worth the paper it is written on, and this so-called 'greatest deliberative body in the world' is at the mercy of every change in parliamentary authority."[37] We will examine these arguments on both sides more closely in later chapters.

In more recent years, small changes have been made in Rule XXII. In 1975, as part of a compromise, the Senate finally did reduce the cloture threshold to three-fifths of members duly elected and sworn (sixty senators when all one hundred Senate seats are filled[38]) but left the cloture requirement on a rules change at two-thirds present and voting. In 1979, a cap of 100 hours of debate post-cloture was imposed and 7 years later that was reduced to the current 30 hours.

The historical pattern has been unmistakable. The Senate has remained firmly loyal to the principle of unlimited, or at least extended, debate. At times when this right has been systematically abused, in order to cool the passions of those enraged by the abuses and to protect the existing rules of the continuing Senate, senators have compromised and reformed the filibuster and Rule XXII. For more than 200 years, whenever the right to filibuster has come under serious fire, the Senate has found a way to protect it.

★ ★ ★

FOUR

Polarized Politics and the Use and Abuse of the Filibuster

FDR biographer Jean Edward Smith, writing in the *New York Times* in 2009, put his finger on the crux of the dilemma facing the Senate when he wrote, "a worrisome new feature in American politics [is] the trivialization of the filibuster in the Senate. A simple majority vote no longer suffices to pass major pieces of legislation. Instead, in almost every case, the Senate must muster at least 60 votes (a 'supermajority') to close off debate."[1]

THE 60-VOTE THRESHOLD

It is hard to argue with the assertion that the filibuster has been sometimes trivialized and abused by its near constant use. In fact, over the last two decades, a frustrated Senate overburdened by filibusters has succumbed to accepting a "60-vote threshold" on many controversial bills and amendments rather than endure the time-consuming cloture process. This is done by agreeing by unanimous consent to set the higher threshold, thus circumventing all of the steps required to impose cloture.[2]

In 2008, for example, during the consideration of the highly controversial Foreign Intelligence Surveillance Act (FISA), which granted
immunity for the Bush era wiretapping and permitted electronic surveillance of foreigners outside the United States without a court order,
the Senate adopted a unanimous consent agreement proposed by the
majority leader to provide for voting on amendments:

> I ask unanimous consent that when the Senate resumes S. 2248 on Tuesday
> morning, February 12, the sequence of votes on remaining amendments oc-
> cur in the following order: Whitehouse 3920, subject to a 60-vote threshold;
> Feinstein 3910, subject to a 60-vote threshold; Feingold 3979; Dodd 3907;
> Feingold 3912; Bond-Rockefeller 3938, as modified; Specter-Whitehouse
> 3927; Feinstein 3919, with a 60-vote threshold.[3]

One of the Feinstein amendments mentioned (Senate Amendment
3910), for example, was a major amendment that represented an effort
to craft a compromise between those who opposed and those who supported giving immunity to telecommunication companies for their
assistance in the Bush administration's controversial surveillance activities. It would have provided for a special court to make the determi-
nation. Because it was subject to a 60-vote threshold, the amendment
was defeated although it received more than a majority, 57 votes.[4]

EXPLODING USE AND ABUSE

One of the most widely respected authorities on the use of filibusters
and associated tactics is University of California, Los Angeles, political scientist Barbara Sinclair. Studying the use of filibusters, filibuster
threats, and holds, Sinclair has demonstrated that the number of legislative measures affected by these stratagems has increased steadily
from 8 percent in the 1960s. In the next 2 decades, it rose to 27 percent
affected and then, by the 1990s and into the middle of the first decade
of the 2000s, it jumped to 51 percent. In 2007, with the Democrats back
in the majority and President Bush still in the White House, 70 percent
of bills were impacted.[5] Asked in a *Washington Post* interview about
the acceleration of filibuster use, Sinclair replied, "It's gradual, to some
extent. But in terms of its impact on legislation, it has a big impact from

the first Clinton Congress on. If one can say there's a break point, that's where filibusters become a regularly used partisan tool."[6]

We began working on Capitol Hill in 1966 (Dove) and 1975 (Arenberg). In 1966, the year in which Dove became the second assistant parliamentarian of the Senate, cloture was never invoked in the Senate and only five cloture petitions were even filed.[7] During the entire 89th Congress (1965–1966), only seven cloture votes were attempted and the Senate cut off debate only once. In fact, in all of the history of the Senate to that time, the Senate had exercised Rule XXII to terminate debate only nine times, and only thirty-seven cloture votes had ever even been attempted.[8]

In 1979, as Arenberg came to the Senate, the Senate invoked cloture only once and held four cloture votes, all at the end of the year and all related to one issue, the Crude Oil Windfall Profit Tax bill.[9] By the next year, Jimmy Carter's last in office, the partisan polarization that has become so familiar over the past 30 years began to develop. Majority Leader Robert Byrd was able to get the Senate to invoke cloture on ten occasions. This included a successful cloture vote in August 1980 on the Alaska National Interest Lands Conservation Act.

We can vividly recall Senator Mike Gravel's (D-AK) filibuster efforts during the debate over the Alaska Lands bill. On one occasion during the consideration of the bill, Senator Gravel demanded, as he was entitled to under the rules, that a substitute amendment offered by Senator Paul Tsongas (D-MA) be read into the record in full. The bill clerk began the reading of the hundreds of pages laced with unfamiliar and difficult-to-pronounce native Alaskan place names like Alagnak, Chilikadrotna, Kantishna, Malaspina, Becharof, Selawik, Afognak, Chamisso, Shumagin, Simeonof, Tuxedni, Aniakchak, Ivishak, and Nonvianuk. The poor clerk was stumbling over the names and struggling to keep from breaking into laughter over his own travails. Down the center aisle came an obviously agitated Majority Leader Robert Byrd. In a none-too-subtle stage whisper heard, no doubt, by all in the gallery, he cried, "Will you cut that out?" The clerk, of course, was required to keep reading. He sped up and tried hard to hurry through the names he could not pronounce in an effort to keep from further annoying the majority leader.

From President Ronald Reagan's inauguration onward, the number of cloture petitions filed, the number of actual cloture votes carried out, and the incidence of cloture ending debate all began to rapidly rise. In the Congresses of the 1980s, 202 cloture petitions were filed, 139 cloture votes were conducted, and cloture was actually invoked 54 times.[10] During the next decade, there were 361 petitions and 254 cloture votes, and the Senate invoked cloture on 91 occasions.[11]

The meteoric rise in the use of Rule XXII continued over the next two decades. In the 110th Congress alone (2007–2008), with George W. Bush in the White House and Democrats in control on Capitol Hill, there were 112 cloture votes, 61 successful.[12] And during just the first 2 years of Barack Obama's presidency, the 111th Congress, with a Senate that had a large Democratic majority (60 senators, counting two independents who are members of the Democrats' caucus), cloture was invoked 63 times. Observers had thought that the near "filibuster-proof" Democratic majority would lead to a decrease in the use of filibusters and resultant cloture votes, but that didn't happen.[13]

EXPLAINING THE INCREASE: WORKLOAD

A number of political scientists have tried to explain the rapid increase in the use of the filibuster tactic. Frank Mackaman, the executive director of the Dirksen Congressional Center, has pointed out that in the wake of the 1975 reforms—which, among other things, reduced the number of votes necessary for cloture from two-thirds of those present and voting (67 votes, if all senators voted) to three-fifths of the Senate membership (60 votes)—"Filibusters seemed less Draconian. They used to be used for the most important issues, but that's changed . . . members are rewarded for blocking legislation; it's a badge of courage."[14]

Gregory Koger, in *Filibustering: A Political History of Obstruction in the House and Senate,* argues that "filibustering increases when legislators stop trying to outlast the obstructionists. In the case of the modern Senate, the motivation for this tactical shift is that the workload of the Senate has increased to the point where wasting time is more costly than accepting the outcome of a cloture vote."[15] In the past, filibusters were often defeated by attempting to simply wait out those who were blocking action, physically exhausting them, but this, of course, was time consuming.

It is clearly true that the workload of the Senate has grown over the past century. As evidence, Koger cites the work of Bruce Oppenheimer published in 1985.[16] However, based on our experience, we doubt that the workload has increased much over the past 20 years. Measures like average number of days in session, measures passed, public laws enacted, hours in session, and roll calls held are imperfect measures of workload, but all of these measures have held relatively stable over the past 20 years. For confirmation, we compared the 1990s with the 2000s. While the number of days in session rose from about 150 to 160 on average, the average number of hours of session each year actually dropped from 1,213 to 1,166. While the number of measures passed by the Senate each year rose slightly from 550 to 595, the number of public laws actually enacted dropped from 265 to 251. Seventeen fewer roll calls were conducted each year in the 2000s compared to the earlier decade, and the Senate met an average of almost 1 hour less per day (7.27 hours compared with 8.12).[17]

However, while the workload of the modern Congress has plateaued somewhat, we do believe that the time pressures created by what is, by any measure, an enormous workload continue to rise. Modern communication and transportation have actually increased the demands on members to be present in their home states as frequently as possible. As constituents' awareness of congressional actions has been expanded by the internet and 24-hour cable news outlets, members are required to increase their visibility at home. Constituents know more about members' activities and their whereabouts. Therefore, if they do not appear regularly in their states and districts, they are more easily seen as having "gone Washington." The realities of modern campaigns require an extraordinary effort by most senators to raise the necessary campaign funds, escalating with each new campaign cycle as costs such as television advertising continue to rise. In each of the last three Senate elections, the typical winning Senate candidate spent more than $7 million.[18] Even back in 2000, Jon Corzine (D-NJ) spent over $63 million on his Senate campaign and Hillary Clinton (D-NY), in the same year, spent nearly $30 million.[19] Of course, states like New York and New Jersey have huge media markets where television advertising is particularly expensive. In 2008, Republican Elizabeth Dole, wife of former senator Bob Dole (R-KS), spent $17.5 million in North Carolina in her unsuccessful reelection race. The winner, Democrat Kay Hagan, spent about $9 million. Even in the tiny (by population) state of Alaska, incumbent Republican Ted Stevens, who lost his seat, and Democrat Mark Begich, who won it in a razor-close race, spent a combined total of $8.5 million—about $26 each for the 300,000 votes. In the even much closer race in Minnesota, so close that it wasn't resolved until 8 months after the election, newly elected Democratic senator Al Franken spent more than $21 million and the defeated incumbent senator Norm Coleman spent more than $19 million. That's in excess of $40 million. These were not isolated cases. In Oregon, the candidates spent $17 million; in Georgia, it was $23 million; and in the state of Kentucky, $32 million was spent, $21 million by Republican minority leader Mitch McConnell alone.[20] Former senator Chris Dodd has described fund-raising for today's senators as "a time-eating obsession."[21] Professor Eric Redman has emphasized that "senators are increasingly distracted by the inexorable demands for constant fund-raising to cover the fast-rising costs of statewide campaigns . . . the worst part of all is the invasion of the legislator's time . . . Literal corruption is not the issue—in the Senate there is little evidence of that. The issue is distraction from the job of legislating. It has become horrendous."[22]

All of these pressures have combined to reduce the typical work week in Washington to Tuesday through Thursday. Leaders in Congress often schedule votes for 5:30 P.M. on Monday evenings to ensure that members are back in Washington in time to make Tuesday a full work day—otherwise little happens prior to the caucus lunches that both parties conduct at noontime on Tuesday. These Monday votes are referred to by Capitol Hill staffers as the "bed-check" votes.

The value of the Senate's time has increased as the workload and time pressures have increased. This has sharpened the effectiveness of delay as a tactic, particularly near the end of a session or fiscal year or before fixed holiday recesses, when Senators have other obligations or are anxious to head home. Senators (and the leadership) feel the pressure of these looming deadlines and sometimes cannot afford to wait out a filibuster or the time necessary to invoke cloture. The pressure may be heightened by a majority leader's threat to keep the Senate in session into the night or the weekend, or to cancel a recess. This sometimes becomes a high-stakes game of "chicken."

The use of time constraints to enhance the value of filibustering is an old tactic. Filibusters in the nineteenth and early twentieth century often made use of the so-called "lame duck" short sessions that began in December and ended in March of the odd-numbered years. Since the short sessions ended on a fixed date, filibusters could be effective in running out the clock. In fact, Senator George Norris (R-NE) who, in 1933, led the successful fight for the twentieth amendment to the Constitution, which abolished the short session, was convinced that it would eliminate filibusters.[23] Filibusters continued to occur, however, even in the Congress that immediately followed passage of the amendment.

EXPLAINING THE INCREASE: PARTISAN POLARIZATION

While time demands clearly play a role in the increased use of the filibuster, they are not the primary cause. In our judgment, the steady growth in partisan and ideological polarization in the Congress, reflecting a similar increasing polarization among party activists and public media, if not the general electorate, lies at the heart of increased use of tactics such as the filibuster.

As the parties have polarized in the Congress, the party caucuses have grown more homogenous, centralized their leaderships, and increasingly attempted to police the outriders—that is, the moderates most likely to vote with the other party. While all of these characteristics are more pronounced in the House than the Senate, there can be no doubt that polarization has had a profound impact on the upper chamber.

Barbara Sinclair testified before the Senate Rules Committee in July 2010:

The use of extended debate and of cloture to cope with it began to increase well before the parties became highly polarized. However, as partisan polarization increased so did the likelihood of major legislation encountering extended-debate related problems in the Senate. The Senate, at least according to the measures I have available, is more likely to produce legislation that incorporates the minority's preferences than is the House. Heightened partisan polarization has significantly affected legislative productivity in the Senate; the Senate has much more difficulty passing legislation than the House does. In the pre-1990s period, major measures were just about as likely to pass the Senate and not the House as vice versa; in the partisan period (103rd–110th Congresses, 1993–2008), this changed rather dramatically; only 1 percent of major measures pass the Senate but not the House; 20 percent pass the House but not the Senate. Partisan polarization depresses legislative productivity in the Senate mostly through the increased use by the minority party of extended debate.[24]

Gregory Koger, in his testimony before the same committee, made the point that in his analysis "this increase in partisanship has not *caused* the increase in filibustering, but it shapes the nature of the filibusters that occur."[25]

The seemingly academic question of whether the increase in use of the filibuster is caused by time constraints and shaped by partisanship or caused by increased partisanship and enhanced by time constraints becomes important in efforts to address the problem and fashion reforms. Our experience tells us that the highly polarized nature of the modern Senate plays the greater role and it is only by addressing this characteristic that the Senate will ultimately come to grips with the difficulties created by misuse of the filibuster. In fact, the filibuster, although the focus of this book and a tactic that has fundamentally shaped the Senate, is only one of a number of congressional rules, traditions, and mores that have been abused and distorted by the extreme partisan polarization of recent years. For example, prior to the impeachment of President Bill Clinton in 1998, it seemed doubtful that a modern president could be impeached on an overwhelmingly partisan vote.[26] In fact, it was thought almost axiomatic that at least some votes from the president's party would be necessary to provide the legitimacy necessary to carry out impeachment. Yet, on December 19, 1998, the House of Representatives impeached President Clinton, adopting two articles of impeachment.[27] Only five House Democrats voted to impeach the Democratic president and only five Republicans voted no.

Congressional scholars Thomas Mann and Norman Ornstein write in their book *The Broken Branch* that "over a decade of Republican control, the House went from shrill opposition to a Democratic president, culminating in his impeachment, to reflexive loyalty to a Republican president, including an unwillingness to conduct tough oversight of executive programs or assert congressional prerogatives vis-à-vis the presidency—on matters ranging from the accessibility of critical information to war-making." They conclude that "unified party government threatens to sap the institution of any will to exercise its constitutional independence."[28]

Another example is the 1995–1996 budget showdown largely between the Republican House of Representatives led by Speaker Newt Gingrich (R-GA) and the Clinton White House that led to an unprecedented shutdown of the federal government from December 16, 1995, until January 6, 1996.

Adam Clymer in the *New York Times* described the months leading up to the partisan confrontation: "Even the most ordinary tasks of Congress are subordinated to political tactics . . . Speaker Newt Gingrich explained the delay in purely tactical terms. He said he thought President Clinton would try to make headlines by vetoing them, and snapped, 'I'm not going to give his Presidential campaign new cheap-shot photo-ops.'"[29] Clymer quoted Kathleen Hall Jamieson, dean of the Annenberg School of Communications: "'The thing that the word *compromise* was designed to describe—the process by which you forge consensus—is no longer an acceptable part of the political process,' she said. That was especially true in the House . . . where 'institutional courtesies' like consideration for the minority and civility in debate have fallen into disuse."[30]

In 2003, the Republican-controlled Congress wrote the final Medicare Prescription Drug bill by abandoning the traditional formalities of a conference committee between the Senate and the House and excluding most Democrats, including Majority Leader Tom Daschle

(D-SD), a major Democratic leader on the bill. When the Medicare conference report came to the House floor for approval, the Republican leadership held the vote in the middle of the night and dragged it out for more than 3 hours, a new record, while they twisted arms and sought the necessary votes to pass it.[31] Senator Daschle said, "This is the most egregious violation of the rules of the institution that I've seen in 25 years. It's horrendous. It's reprehensible. It is very, very regrettable. I think we have seen a diminution of respect for the rule of law. And that's abhorrent."[32]

Some months later, the House Ethics Committee would formally issue a public admonishment of House Majority Leader Tom DeLay (R-TX) (who was later convicted for unrelated ethics violations) for offering Congressman Nick Smith (R-MI) financial and political support for his son's campaign to succeed him in his Michigan congressional seat in exchange for a vote in favor of the Medicare bill.[33]

THEATRE OF THE ABSURD

Sometimes in recent years the intense partisanship has encouraged both parties to descend into the theatre of the absurd. We recall a week in July 2007 when two unprecedented events occurred. On July 19, the Senate was considering a college student assistance bill under budget reconciliation instructions. Senator Ken Salazar (D-CO) (now secretary of the interior) offered a "sense of the Senate" amendment. These are amendments that have no force of law, but serve as an opportunity for the Senate, as a body, to express its point of view. Senator Salazar, in this instance, was presumably trying to politically embarrass the minority Republicans and the Bush administration. His amendment read:

> Since I. Lewis "Scooter" Libby previously served as Chief of Staff to Vice President Dick Cheney; Since Mr. Libby was convicted in federal court of perjury and obstruction of justice in connection with efforts by the Bush White House to conceal the fact that Administration officials leaked the name of a covert CIA agent in order to discredit her husband, a critic of the Iraq War; Since U.S. District Court Judge Reggie Walton sentenced Mr. Libby to 30 months in prison to reflect the seriousness of the offense, the sensitivity of the national security information involved in Libby's crime,

and the abuse of Mr. Libby's position of trust in the United States government; Since President Bush chose to commute Mr. Libby's prison sentence in its entirety, thereby entitling Libby to evade serious punishment for his criminal conduct; Since President Bush has refused to rule out the possibility that he will eventually issue a full pardon to Mr. Libby with respect to his criminal conviction; Now therefore be it determined that it is the Sense of the Senate that President Bush should not issue a pardon to I. Lewis "Scooter" Libby.[34]

A roll call vote was conducted and the amendment adopted. Minority Leader Mitch McConnell (R-KY) was then recognized to offer an amendment. He offered a retaliatory "sense of the Senate" amendment targeted at embarrassing the Democrats by

deploring the actions of former President William Jefferson Clinton regarding his granting of clemency to terrorists, to family members, donors, and individuals represented by family members, to public officials of his own political party, and to officials who violated laws protecting United States intelligence, and concluding that it is the sense of the Senate that (1) former President Clinton's granting of clemency to 16 FALN terrorists, two former members of the Weather Underground Organization, and a former member of the Symbionese Liberation Army was inappropriate; (2) former President Clinton's granting of clemency to individuals either in his family or represented by family members was inappropriate; (3) former President Clinton's granting of clemency to public figures from his own political party was inappropriate; (4) former President Clinton's pardons of individuals involved with the Whitewater investigation, a matter in which the former First Family was centrally involved, was inappropriate; and (5) former President Clinton's pardons of individuals who have jeopardized intelligence gathering and operations were inappropriate.[35]

Senator McConnell declared that "if the Senate has decided to go into debating the appropriateness of future pardons, there is plenty of material to go around on past pardons."[36] Majority Leader Reid recognized the need to steer the Senate away from the partisan "death spiral" that it was falling into. He asked for "unanimous consent that on the Salazar amendment, the vote be vitiated, stricken from the Record, and that we not have a roll-call vote on the amendment that was offered by my distinguished counterpart, Senator McConnell [regarding the Clinton pardons]."[37] Minority Leader McConnell answered: "I very much agree with the consent agreement the majority leader propounded."[38] The "crisis" ended as both "armies" stood down. The Senate, very likely for the only time in its history, wiped away a roll-call vote it had actually taken—by unanimous consent, it never happened.

The second event, which occurred 2 days earlier, on July 17, although slightly less theatrical, was nonetheless also unprecedented in the Senate. The Republicans were filibustering the Levin-Reed amendment to a defense bill that would have provided for a reduction in U.S. forces in Iraq. The majority leader decided to keep the Senate in session all night to dramatize that Republicans were blocking the amendment and denying it an up-or-down vote. (This is a tactic that we will discuss in a later chapter.) He made clear that to keep the pressure on the Republican minority to remain close to the chamber he would hold a series of procedural votes throughout the night. This particular procedure is often used by majority leaders to establish the presence of a quorum. The majority leader offers a motion "to instruct the Senate Sergeant at Arms to request the presence of absent senators."[39] This motion triggers a roll-call vote and since virtually all senators dislike having an absence recorded on their public voting record, they arrive in the chamber.

The remarkable thing on this particular night was that the partisan tensions were running so high that when Senator Reid made the first of these motions at about 8:30 P.M., all forty-seven Republicans who appeared voted "nay," and the motion was defeated by a 44–47 vote. One of the authors (Arenberg) has kept a database of these procedural votes. This was the 222nd "motion to instruct" since 1978. Never before had one been defeated. (The average number of nay votes was 7.7 over that period.) The defeat had no practical effect since the ninety-one senators who appeared in the chamber established a quorum to do business irrespective of how they voted, but in reality they were defeating a motion to request that senators meet their constitutional obligation to establish a quorum—all out of partisan pique. There could be no other reason.

A decade earlier, we witnessed an even more dramatic partisan confrontation over a motion to instruct—one of the most memorable scenes either of us ever saw on the Senate floor. On February 24, 1988, during an all-night filibuster of a campaign finance reform bill, the Republicans were initiating quorum calls and then disappearing so that a quorum could not be found. Majority Leader Robert Byrd offered a motion to instruct the Senate sergeant-at-arms to arrest absent senators in order to require them to appear in the chamber to establish a quorum. The Senate voted 45–3 to authorize the arrests. Senator Byrd dispatched sergeant-at-arms Henry Giugni to find and escort Republican senators back to the Senate floor. The sergeant-at-arms, apparently following a tip from a cleaning woman who worked in the Senate office building, discovered Senator Bob Packwood, a senior Republican, hiding in his office. The door was removed from the door frame and the sergeant-at-arms hauled Senator Packwood out of his office and carried him into the Senate chamber. The next morning the *Washington Post* reported that "angry Republicans accused Democrats of turning the Senate into a 'banana republic' yesterday after Capitol Police forced their way into the office of Senator Bob Packwood (R-OR), arrested him and carried him feet-first into the Senate chamber in a flamboyant climax to a bitter all-night filibuster fight."[40]

INCREASING PARTISAN POLARIZATION

In one way or another all these cases demonstrate how the congressional system is being stretched out of shape—even to the breaking point. The explosion of partisanship and the polarized state of both the House and the Senate is clearly intensifying. For example, Senate Majority Leader Harry Reid (D-NV) in 2010 lashed out at Minority Leader Mitch McConnell (R-KY): "Some believe that if you say something long enough, even though it's without any factual basis, people will start believing it . . . The mere fact that one says something that is without foundation a lot of times and simply is untrue does not make it truthful the more times one says it."[41] Although Senator Reid's words might have seemed a bit jarring 20 years ago given the normal courtesies of Senate debate, the tone is no longer unusual for the partisan and polarized modern Senate.

In 2004, Majority Leader Bill Frist (R-TN) violated previously unbroken Senate tradition to travel to South Dakota to personally campaign against Minority Leader Tom Daschle (D-SD). Although the current leaders, Senators McConnell and Reid, are more traditional Senate institutionalists and have not campaigned in each other's states, their parties pulled out all stops in McConnell's home state of Kentucky in 2008 and Reid's Nevada in 2010 in an effort to defeat the opposing party's leader. This is not the Senate of Mike Mansfield and Everett Dirksen or Howard Baker and Robert Byrd, or even George Mitchell and Bob Dole.

Former New York Yankees manager Yogi Berra is credited with once having said, "Right-handers go over there, left-handers go over there, the rest of you, come with me." Too often in today's Congress there is no "rest of us." It does not take a sophisticated observer to recognize that both the House and the Senate are highly polarized along party lines, so much so that there is virtually no middle ground left. Studying and attempting to explain this polarization has become a vibrant field of political science. The Congress itself wrestles with this reality on a daily basis.

In the more partisan branch, the House of Representatives, the parties are so polarized that the majority pays little real attention to minority views. Although rank partisanship has historically been more characteristic of the majoritarian House than the Senate, the body was not always polarized along strictly ideological lines. During the 1968 election, third-party presidential candidate George Wallace famously declared that looking at Democrats and Republicans, there was not a "dime's worth of difference" between the two. In 1950, political scientists were so concerned by the lack of difference between the parties that the American Political Science Association issued a report entitled "Toward a More Responsible Two-Party System." The paper stated, "It is dangerous to drift without a party system that helps the nation to set a general course of policy for the government as a whole."[42] Sixty years later, the report seems almost quaint. It proclaimed, for example, "A basis for party cohesion in Congress will be established as soon as the parties interest themselves sufficiently in their congressional candidates to set up strong and active campaign organizations in their constituencies."[43]

Congressman Joseph Martin (R-MA) spent 42 years in the House, 20 of those years as the Republican leader. Twice, when the Republicans gained the majority in 1947 and again in 1953, he was elected Speaker of the House. On both occasions, he received the gavel from the legendary Speaker Sam Rayburn (D-TX) and at the end of each returned the gavel to Speaker Rayburn. As *Time* put it, they "were synonymous with the House for two generations of Americans. Once, when Rayburn was asked to campaign against Martin in Massachusetts, the Texan responded brusquely: 'Speak against Joe? Hell, if I lived up there, I'd vote for him.'"[44]

Even as the highly charged political environment—in the wake of the civil rights battles, Watergate, and especially the Vietnam War—began to deepen the political divides (still often as much intra-party as between the parties), the folkways of civility remained on Capitol Hill. Into the 1980s, with Ronald Reagan in the White House, and Republicans in control of the Senate, Speaker Tip O'Neill (D-MA) and Minority Leader Bob Michel (R-IL) were "good friends and frequent golfing buddies; they trusted each other and could work together."[45]

When Congressman Michel was replaced by the fiery Newt Gingrich (R-GA), things began to change. As commentator Elizabeth Drew writes, "Gingrich had large goals. He was out to destroy the entire force behind the idea of an activist federal government."[46] When Republicans gained control of the House in 1994 for the first time since the 83rd Congress ending in 1955, Gingrich was elected Speaker of the House. "The unity of the Republican party was on display on opening day, when it pushed through the House a package of rules changes, some of them highly significant . . . Gingrich wanted to show right away that the House has changed."[47] Interestingly, one of the new rules adopted by the majority was a supermajority requirement making a three-fifths vote of the House necessary for any increase in taxes.

The relationship between Speaker Gingrich and Minority Leader Richard Gephardt (D-MO) was never good. In 1999, the House Rules Committee held hearings on "Civility in the House of Representatives," and the report showed that not only were the leadership of the parties not drinking and golfing together, but they barely spoke to one another—Minority Leader Gephardt and Republican Speaker Gingrich, according to the report, talked only eight times over a period of 4 years. Roger Davidson in *Congress and Its Members* reports that "the partisan rancor got so bad . . . Speaker Gingrich and Minority Leader Gephardt refused to speak to each other for a year."[48]

As Speaker Gingrich became enmeshed in ethics charges brought by the Democratic minority, the relationship deteriorated even further. Asked about the minority's motives, Gingrich lashed out: "It's about hatred and hysteria. I think they believe that I am the architect of their defeat and I think they are enraged . . . they're in tremendous agony because it's the first time in their career they've not been in the majority. I think it's driving them nuts."[49] He described the Democrats as "a bunch of bitter and vicious, mean-spirited people who capriciously lie." This was a long way from Sam Rayburn and Joe Martin. It reflected not only the personalities involved but the changes in the House itself. When Speaker Gingrich resigned his position, Minority Leader Gephardt said, "The American people sent a strong message that the Republican Congress was a failure . . . the speaker's resignation is the reaction to that message."[50]

The impeachment of President Bill Clinton along partisan lines hardened the walls between the parties in the House. In the Senate—where, of course, the Constitution requires a supermajority two-thirds vote for conviction and where the establishment of rules under which the trial would take place was subject to the filibuster—the consideration of the articles of impeachment was much more bipartisan. These events established a pattern in the House leadership—it has remained largely antagonistic, and bipartisan cooperation is rare.

Professors Kathryn Pearson and Eric Schickler point out that more than two-thirds of current House members were not in the body prior to Gingrich's election as Speaker in 1995. Many of the current representatives are unfamiliar with the era of party cooperation when the party leaders had close personal relationships and played cards and golf together. Pearson and Schickler conclude that "the bitter partisanship and strong party leadership characteristic of today's Congress are likely to persist for the foreseeable future."[51]

The Senate, too, over the past 35 years has become increasingly polarized along partisan and ideological lines. The parties and their caucuses in the Senate have become more homogenous—political values, to a far greater extent, are shared among members of each caucus and there are fewer and fewer moderates. The Republican former chairman of the Senate Appropriations Committee, a committee generally more bipartisan than most, Senator Thad Cochran (R-MS) has remarked that in the past he "had just as many close, personal friends on the Democratic side as the Republican side." He adds, "I wasn't sanctioned or looked at with suspicion by my colleagues for having friendships on the other side. Now you are viewed with suspicion for having friendships on the other side. Certainly that is true if you join with the other side in offering legislation and amendments."[52]

Senator Warren Rudman (R-NH) wrote in his 1996 memoir, "More and more Republicans were arriving who had previously served in the House, such as Trent Lott of Mississippi, Dan Coats of Indiana and Bob Smith of New Hampshire. In the House they had been part of a bitter, frustrated minority, fighting a guerilla war against the Democrats. The confrontational no-prisoners attitude they brought to the Senate was not one with which I was completely comfortable."[53]

THE ARENBERG-PARTISANSHIP MEASURE

Senate Historian Donald Ritchie points out, "We used to say a working majority was 55, because you could always get five from the other party on various issues, but that middle ground kept getting smaller and smaller."[54] One of the authors (Arenberg) has tracked the disappearance of the Senate's moderate middle and the march toward greater and greater partisan polarization in the Senate using data on the frequency with which other members of the Senate voted with Senator Carl Levin—using him, in effect, as a baseline measure of liberal votes (see the appendixes).[55] This measure, in our experience, reflects the ideological continuum in the Senate very well. (There are a number of alternative measures used by academics and other observers of the Senate, including the more scientific DW-NOMINATE statistical analysis of voting behavior to measure the "liberalness" and "conservativeness" of members of Congress developed by political scientists Keith Poole and Howard Rosenthal.)

The table in appendix A shows the scores for each senator. Included are the Arenberg-Partisanship measure; the scores calculated annually by *National Journal*; a rating created by Senator Jim DeMint's (R-SC) Senate Conservatives Fund (SCF) for 2008;[56] the annual ratings published by Americans for Democratic Action (ADA), a liberal organization; Congressional Quarterly's (CQ) annual measure of votes in support of the president;[57] and the DW-NOMINATE scores. They all show the same pattern of increased polarization.

On the Arenberg-Levin scale and all of the other rankings, virtually all Democratic senators ranked higher on the liberal scale than all Republican senators. There is almost no moderate middle at all. The table unambiguously demonstrates the highly polarized state of the Senate.

We have examined the Arenberg measure going back to 1979, focusing primarily on the moderate middle of the Senate—that is, all of the senators who fall between the most liberal Republican and the most conservative Democrat in the rankings. In 1979, there were 43 senators in that overlapping moderate grouping. From 1979 to 1984, there was an average of 31.2 senators—nearly a third of the Senate in that group. From 1985 to 1994, the average dropped precipitously to 11.1 senators. Over the past 17 years (1995–2011), there has been virtually no overlap at all, an average of *less than one senator* (.7). In each of the last 5 years (2007, 2008, 2009, 2010, and 2011), there has been no overlap at all. In fact, during the two sessions of the 111th Congress (2009–2010), the first two of President Obama's term, the gap between the most conservative Democratic senators using this measure, Senator Evan Bayh of Indiana and Senator Ben Nelson of Nebraska, and the most liberal-voting Republicans, Maine's senators Olympia Snowe and Susan Collins, was 6.3 percentage points in 2009 and 17.1 percentage points in 2010, the largest gaps since 1979.

The numbers speak volumes. Acknowledging that it is a classic mistake to get too wrapped up in vote studies, which sometimes hide as much as they reveal, these numbers do reflect realities that have helped make the Senate work—and sometimes work very well. Recall that in 1979, the Senate contained truly liberal Republicans like Senators Jacob Javits (NY), Mack Mathias (MD), and Lowell Weicker (CT). It included many moderate Republicans like Senators John Heinz (PA), Robert Stafford (VT), John Chafee (RI), Bill Cohen (ME), Mark Hatfield (OR), Bob Packwood (OR), and Chuck Percy (IL). And even among the conservative Republican senators, there were those like Senators John Danforth (MO), Henry Bellmon (OK), Bob Dole (KS), Howard Baker (TN), Nancy Kassebaum (KS), Ted Stevens (AK), Pete Domenici (NM), William Roth (DE), and John Warner (VA) prepared to work across the aisle with Democrats—and, on occasion, vote that way. In 1979, Senator Danforth voted with Senator Levin (and the Democratic liberals) 65 percent of the time, Senator Stevens 56.9 percent of the time, and Senator Bob Dole 52.8 percent of the time.

Even those among the staunchest conservatives would work with Democrats to address the nation's problems. Senator Barry Goldwater (R-AZ), for example, once told Senator Carl Hayden's (D-AZ) biographer, "I have more bipartisan political genes than you think . . . I don't want Republicans to know this . . . I always raised money for Carl Hayden's re-election to the Senate because it was so damned important!"[58] Which senator in which state today would raise campaign funds for his colleague in the other party? Majority Leader Howard Baker described trying to keep the ultra-conservative Goldwater in line with the Republicans:

> Once, when I really needed his [Senator Goldwater's] vote and leaned on him perhaps a little too hard, he said to his Majority Leader, "Howard, you have one vote, and I have one vote, and we'll just see how this thing turns out." It was at that moment that I formulated my theory that being leader of the Senate was like herding cats. It is trying to make ninety-nine independent souls act in concert under rules that encourage polite anarchy and embolden people who find majority rule a dubious proposition at best.[59]

On the Democratic side of the aisle in 1979, there were moderate and conservative senators like Sam Nunn (GA), Henry Jackson (WA), Bennett Johnston (LA), David Pryor (AR), Wendell Ford (KT), Jim Exon (NE), and David Boren (OK). Among the more liberal Democrats were a number of senators who were frequently able to cross the party aisle to craft legislation, forge compromise, and build consensus. This included Senators Ed Muskie (ME), Birch Bayh (IN), Jim Sasser (TN), Robert Byrd (WV), Warren Magnuson (WA), Lawton Chiles (FL), and Lloyd Bentsen (TX). Even among the most liberal Democrats, many like Abe Ribicoff (CT), John Glenn (OH), Daniel Patrick Moynihan (NY), Paul Tsongas (MA), and Dale Bumpers (AR) were less rigidly ideological and more ready to build legislative coalitions.

Successful major legislation of the period reflects these coalitions. The Alaska Lands Act in 1980 was offered as a Tsongas-Roth substitute amendment. There was the Magnuson-Stevens Fishery Conservation and Management Act of 1976. In 1973, Senator Jacob Javits (R-NY) was among the authors and joined conservative Senator John Stennis (D-MS) and others in leading the Senate to passage of the War Powers Act. In fact, President Richard Nixon's veto of the bill was overridden in the Senate by a 75–18 vote—twenty-five Republican senators voted to override the Republican president. In 1972, Senate passage of the Equal Rights Amendment (ERA) by an 84–8 vote was led by Senator Birch Bayh (D-IN). Congresswoman Margaret Heckler (R-MA), one of the House leaders on the ERA, was present on the Senate floor at the time of the vote.[60] Only six Republicans voted against the resolution. The ERA was not ratified by the necessary number of states before the deadline.[61] In 1983, when Senator Paul Tsongas reintroduced the ERA, nineteen Republican senators cosponsored it, including Senators Danforth, Kassebaum, Stevens, and Pete Wilson of California.

Things have changed. When Senator Ted Kennedy (D-MA) reintroduced the ERA in 2008 at the start of the 110th Congress, all 24 cosponsors were Democrats—no Republican senator endorsed it. In the House, the 204 cosponsors of the ERA included only eight Republicans.

Again using the Arenberg scale, of the 282 senators who have served between 1979 and 2010, based on their average scores for their careers over this period, only 26 fell into the moderate range between the most liberal Republican score (Senator Mathias of Maryland) and the most conservative Democratic score (Senator Zell Miller of Georgia).[62] Of those 26, only 3 were in the Senate in 2010, and one of those, Senator Arlen Specter, had changed parties and been defeated for reelection in a Democratic primary in Pennsylvania in 2010. With the exception of Senator Linc Chafee (R-RI) and his father, Senator John Chafee (R-RI), whom he succeeded, no other senators since 1996 have exhibited a moderate voting record by this measure.

Senator Olympia Snowe (R-ME), consistently among the Senate's few moderates of either party, has commented, "The whole Congress has become far more polarized and partisan so it makes it difficult to reach bipartisan agreements. The more significant the issue, the more partisan it becomes."[63]

LOSS OF CIVILITY AND THE WILL TO COMPROMISE

Another negative consequence of this increased partisan polarization has been its corrosive effect on the interpersonal relationships among senators.[64] While, because of its small size, the Senate remains a body in which there are many close relationships that cross party lines, and some committees are effectively run by chairmen and ranking members who like and respect each other, no one who has experienced the Senate over the past 30 or so years can fail to see the decline in comity and civility. Ironically, the very set of rules fueling the demand for radical change in the Senate rules has historically played a central role in encouraging good relationships in the Senate and continues to provide a safety valve for the Senate that is nearly absent in the House.

Nonetheless, the current highly polarized atmosphere in the Senate, among other effects, has greatly accelerated the use of the filibuster as a tactic of the minority party. This, of course, frustrates the majority and in turn places the Senate rules squarely in the crosshairs of many critics. As the Senate has become more intensely polarized along partisan lines, the party caucuses have become more homogenous and leadership power has become more centralized. Leaders, in turn, are expected to enforce the party line. Pressure is placed on senators to vote with their party colleagues.

However, the partisanship is not itself the core problem. The real difficulty occurs when the sharply divided parties abandon the commitment to seek legislative solutions and try, instead, to sharpen ideological issue positions with an eye on the next congressional election. To varying extents, this has been a problem with both parties. Senator Bob Corker (R-TN) put it this way: "It happens on both sides of the aisle, and I think if there's anything about this place that troubles me most—it's that. Instead of really debating the real substance of the issue, we end up in engaging in hyperbole. We end up making the unimportant important—and the most important, the least important."[65]

Even during the intense crisis in 2011 created by the battle over the lifting of the debt ceiling in order to avoid the U.S. defaulting on its debt, President Obama needed to emphasize compromise is a legitimate option. He declared that Americans were "fed up with a town where compromise has become a dirty word." He said, "They work all day long, many of them scraping by, just to put food on the table. And when these Americans come home at night, bone-tired, and turn on the news, all they see is the same partisan three-ring circus here in Washington. They see leaders who can't seem to come together and do what it takes to make life just a little bit better for ordinary Americans. They are offended by that. And they should be."[66]

Another good example is the immigration reform debate. In 2007 and again in 2010, both parties adopted highly partisan strategies aimed not so much at accomplishing immigration reform legislation and solving the nation's problem but more at maximizing their party's advantage on the issue for the next election. Republicans see the issue as a good one because they define the Democrats' position as supporting "amnesty," and polls indicate that this is highly unpopular with the electorate. Conversely, Democrats believe that the Republican position is extremely unpopular with Hispanic voters and see the opportunity to convince this rapidly growing segment of the electorate to become lifelong Democrats as a result. Consequently little gets done.

We know how to legislate on issues such as this. Everyone recognizes that the immigration system is broken. Everyone knows the rough outlines of a reform solution. It must include effective border security, work programs that meet the needs of industries like farming and tourism for workers, and a way of addressing the millions of undocumented immigrants now in the country to bring them out of the shadows. The exact details of these solutions are not easy. However, people of goodwill can get around a table and hash out the kind of compromises that make for good legislation and a broad consensus. This is what the Senate is good at when it is working well.

Barbara Sinclair told the Senate Rules Committee: "Certainly supermajority requirements have a much greater impact on the chamber's ability to legislate in a context of high partisan polarization than they did when the parties were less ideologically homogeneous and less far apart in their views of what constitutes good public policy."[67] However, the solution to the inability to legislate on highly controversial complex issues like immigration is not to abandon the rules. The House passes immigration bills, but the new House the next year may be controlled by the opposition and will quickly reverse the decision. The Democratic House had little difficulty passing President Obama's health reform legislation. The Republican House that replaced it in 2011 had even less difficulty voting to repeal it. On immigration and many other issues the Senate has great difficulty in breaking the gridlock, but it can be done and it can be done under the existing rules. It takes the commitment of the Senate's members.

Republican senator Olympia Snowe argues that the distinctive rules of the Senate are designed to build bipartisanship, making the middle ground all the more important. "It's not healthy for the country to have parties with polar opposite views without that bridge that you need to build consensus . . . It doesn't mean abandoning your principles. It means trying to solve problems that people face in their daily lives."[68] We agree.

The Founders designed the U.S. Senate to be the bastion, the guardian of mature judgment, of the "reason of the whole." At times in its history, it has served this role admirably. To do so again will require its leaders and its members to, on occasion, rise above partisanship, but more importantly to recommit, in good faith, to solving the nation's problems. This is not a problem that can be solved by rewiring the Senate's rules.

★ ★ ★

FIVE

Criticisms of the Filibuster

In an effort to understand the highly partisan polarized Senate of the current era, scholars in the academic community who have focused most directly on the filibuster have tended to view it as a form of obstructionism, undemocratic, perhaps even unconstitutional, and/or, at best, an anachronism. In *Politics or Principle? Filibustering in the United States Senate*, political scientists Sarah Binder and Steven S. Smith present what they refer to as "faulty propositions about the Senate filibuster" and evidence that "senators' political interests, not philosophical commitments, lie at the heart of the Senate's resistance to change."[1] In the end they endorse a simple majority for cloture—that is, 51 votes to end debate.[2] But such a "bottom-line" solution is unlikely to solve the problems it is meant to address. Many decisions in the real-world legislative arena are built on such pragmatic calculations. In fact, democratic theory depends on it. Senators think about getting reelected. If they did not, they would not be responding to their constituents' demands. But, more importantly, a concern with political interest cuts both ways. While senators' politics can be used to explain the Senate's apparent resistance to change, it can also be used to explain the desire on the part of some senators (usually members of the party in the majority) to eliminate the filibuster. Members of the Senate minority leadership frequently make this point. "I submit that the effort to change the rules is not about democracy," Senate Minority Leader Mitch McConnell of Kentucky said at a hearing on the filibuster question in 2010. "It is not about doing what a majority of the American people want. It is about power."[3]

Senator Lamar Alexander (R-TN), the ranking Republican member on the Senate Rules Committee in the 112th Congress, warns, "You don't want to create a freight train running through the Senate like it does in the House, because in two years it might be the 'Tea Party Express.'" He continued, "We need a change in behavior more than a change in rules."[4]

THE MAJORITARIAN HOUSE

Comparisons with the House of Representatives are instructive. The House is an efficient legislative body and one where the majority can and does work its will. The minority in the House in recent years is rarely consulted and often irrelevant to legislative outcomes. While we celebrate the "People's House," there is little doubt that the same extreme partisan polarization that has brought abuse of the rules and a tendency toward gridlock in the Senate has brought "greased lightning" to the House. The majority decides when issues will arise, when votes will occur, how long debate will last, and whether or not any amendments will be permitted.

Congressman Lee Hamilton (D-IN), who served in the House for 34 years; co-chaired the 9/11 Commission, the Iran-Contra Committee, and the 1993 Joint Committee on the Organization of Congress; and currently heads the Center on Congress at Indiana University, told us in an interview:

> I believe the way it works today is if you are in the minority, you're out of the game. You may as well not show up—to be blunt about it. It ought not to work that way.
>
> The key in the House is the Rules Committee. The old saw that if you control the procedure, you control the result is deeply embedded in the minds of the political leadership in the House.[5]

Congressman Hamilton explained:

> What has always struck me with regard to the House procedure is that a lot
> of the bitterness could come out of the relationship between the two parties
> if the majority party were just fair. Now, "fair" is a pretty subjective word—
> but, by that I mean—you bring a bill before the Rules Committee and it's a
> controversial bill—you know how the thing's going to work out before you
> testify. You know, it's all stacked . . . The majority and the minority leaders
> of the Rules Committee and of the House ought to say that the minority has
> a fair shot. That is to say, they ought to have a clean vote on their position . . .
> In almost all cases, the majority now denies that.[6]

Via the Rules Committee, the Speaker of the House has the power to
set the time of debate and vote, set the terms of debate, limit or preclude
amendments, and design all forms of "boutique rules" that might work
to the majority's benefit. For example, the Rules Committee has at times
written a "king of the hill" rule in which a number of substitute amendments are placed in a specific order and debated and voted on, and the
last one to win supersedes the others. They have also used a descendent
of the king of the hill, sometimes referred to as a "queen of the hill"
amendment. This rule permits the House to vote on a number of substitute amendments to the same bill. If more than one substitute attracts
a majority of votes, the Committee of the Whole[7] reports only the one
that receives the largest number of votes.

Another example that triggered national controversy during the 2010
health reform debate was the "deem and pass" process. These are self-
executing rules that accomplish two objectives simultaneously. When
the rule is adopted by the House, another action (the act of passing another piece of legislation) is deemed to have been taken by the House.
The result is that the second action can be accomplished without the
members of the House having to have voted on it directly.[8]

Until 2011, a similar self-executing procedure was part of the House
rules. House Rule XXVIII, the so-called "Gephardt rule," named for
the former House majority leader Dick Gephardt (D-MO), provided that
when the House passed a budget resolution, as it is required to do each
year (although it sometimes fails to do so), a bill to increase the limit
on the public debt was automatically passed.[9] The debt ceiling must be

increased from time to time to permit the Treasury to pay the debts already incurred by the federal government in order to avoid default. Both parties recognize that this is a necessary and required function of government. However, because raising the debt ceiling creates the perception of increasing government debt, whichever party is in the minority typically makes a show of opposing the legislation. This happens in both the Senate and the House. In the House, however, given majority control of the Rules Committee, the self-executing procedure under the Gephardt rule was created, relieving the members from having to cast a vote to increase the public debt ceiling.

On the first day of the 112th Congress (2011–2012), the new House Republican majority did away with the Gephardt rule. The Republicans sought to use the required debt ceiling increase as leverage in the budget battles of 2011. House Republicans were able to create an impasse with President Obama by demanding that any lifting of the debt ceiling be contingent on huge reductions in the deficit and insisting that no revenue increases be included in any deficit reduction package. The Republican majority also adopted new rules, which among other things gave the chairman of the House Budget Committee the power to establish spending ceilings for 2011 without a vote by his committee or the full House of Representatives. As *The Hill* reported, "In practice, this would give power to Representative Paul Ryan (R-WI), the incoming chairman of the panel, to impose deep spending cuts since spending bills cannot exceed the budget ceiling for the 2011 fiscal year."[10]

This remarkable new rule and the elimination of the Gephardt rule showcases the enormous power of the majority in the House. The rules can be shaped to suit and benefit the majority. To visit this condition on the Senate would do severe damage to the Founders' design for the upper chamber.

THE SENATE'S COMMITMENT TO DEBATE AND AMENDMENT

It is a mistake to assume that reason and judgment play no role in senators' unwillingness to abandon the traditions of unlimited debate and unrestrained amendment. If only hard-fought politics were the issue, why, for example, would seven Republican senators in 2005, on the brink of overthrowing the filibuster and winning the short-term hard-fought political battle over the confirmation of the Bush judges by using the "nuclear option," have chosen to join the "Gang of 14"?[11] The "nuclear option" was a Republican proposal to short-circuit the Senate rules and render filibusters against judicial nominations invalid. It was blocked when a bipartisan group of moderate senators rejected both the ongoing filibusters and the rump effort to thwart them through a summary rules coup.

In fact, at every turn in the Senate's history, when the specter of a majoritarian Senate raised its head, senators chose reasoned compromise over eliminating the filibuster. In 1917, when they created the cloture rule; in 1949, when they applied cloture to the motion to proceed and other matters; and in 1975, when they reduced the requirement from 67 votes (two-thirds present and voting) to 60 votes (three-fifths duly elected and sworn), they spurned efforts to provide for ending debate with 51 votes. Again, in January of 2011, as we will discuss in more detail, the Senate chose compromise.

Referring to the "constitutional option" or the "nuclear option," both of which proposed parliamentary maneuvers that, if successful, would result in a simple majority of senators ending debate and changing the rules, and that we discuss more fully in future chapters, Professors Gregory Wawro and Eric Schickler in their excellent work *Filibuster: Obstruction and Lawmaking in the U.S. Senate* argue: "A simple majority of the Senate with the cooperation of a sympathetic presiding officer could curb obstruction. Thus, the striking feature of Senate history is that such a committed majority had *never* been manifested."[12] They conclude that the "bottom line is that a majority of the Senate has never fully committed to going to this extreme."[13] They believe that the main reason the Senate has not opted for a simple majority vote to end debate in its 200-year history is the unwillingness of individual senators to give up the enormous power that Senate rules afford them. Protection of the historic role of each member of the Senate is clearly one of the driving reasons, but is this not a "reasoned judgment"?

Many contemporary senators who propose application of the constitutional option argue that it need not lead to such radical reform as a 51-vote Senate in which debate on all matters could be halted by a simple majority. In an interview, Senator Tom Udall (D-NM) asserted:

> I don't buy into a "slippery slope" argument on the rules. I have said and I will continue to say and it will continue to be my position that it would be very healthy for the Senate, at the beginning of the Congress, on the first legislative day, to adopt rules. It doesn't mean we need to throw out all the rules. It doesn't mean we need to throw out the traditions of the Senate. It doesn't mean we throw out the rights of the minority to be able to express their point of view. In fact, it might mean that you adopt the rules from the previous year. I didn't get into this with the idea that I was going to turn the Senate into the House. That was never my idea.[14]

In our view, however, it is a slippery slope and the outcome is inevitable over a short period of time. If a 51-vote majority is empowered to rewrite the Senate's rules, the day will come, as it did in the House of Representatives, when a majority will construct rules that give it near absolute control over amendments and debate. And there is no going back from that. No majority in the House of Representatives has or ever will voluntarily relinquish that power in order to give the minority a greater voice in crafting legislation.

FILIBUSTER NOT IN THE CONSTITUTION, BUT NOT AN ACCIDENT

Some critics of the filibuster take issue with the notion that Senate traditions demand unlimited debate because the philosophical foundation for such a principle, in their view, was not articulated or widely held in the nineteenth century. That is a little like arguing that Santa Claus is not a Christmas tradition because its roots don't go back much before the nineteenth century in the United States, or that hot dogs are not a Fourth of July tradition because hot dogs weren't invented until the turn of the twentieth century. There can be little doubt today that Santa is a central part of Christmas tradition, that hot dogs and fireworks are a key part of the Fourth of July, and that the filibuster and unlimited debate are an important part of Senate tradition whatever their historic origins.

It is sometimes suggested by critics that senators, and others who support the filibuster, do so out of a belief that the Senate filibuster was created by the Constitution. Gregory Koger insists that "no matter what you might hear from confused senators, the Constitution does not explicitly include a right to filibuster."[15] Sarah Binder and Steven Smith assert, "The conventional wisdom, in short, endows the filibuster with a constitutional basis, making it considerably more difficult to revamp Senate rules."[16] And Binder, this time in an article co-authored with Thomas Mann, writes, "Observers and members of the Senate alike generally attribute the filibuster to the designs of the Framers."[17] But it is rare for senators to make this claim, and the great majority of senators of both parties, whether they approve of the rule or not, recognize that the right grows out of the Senate rules.

THE "BROKEN" SENATE AND
THE VIEW FROM THE HOUSE

Many now argue that the Senate is dysfunctional. At times, it certainly seems so. At other times, the Senate is capable of sweeping action. And, most of the time, it is capable of deliberate action. Just recently, we have seen the Senate take such sweeping actions as the financial bailout of banks and the auto industry, a historic health reform bill, a massive stimulus bill, ratification of a new START treaty, and a huge financial reform bill. These are not the actions of a totally gridlocked institution.

Senator Daschle has rejected the charge by many critics that the Senate is "broken":[18] "I don't think [the Senate's] really broken. Look at what's happened over the course of the last Congress, the 111th Congress, it was really one of the most productive Congresses we've seen. I believe that history is going to judge it from a productivity point of view as having accomplished a great deal—even though it was messy, it was loud, it was boisterous, it was confrontational and certainly polarized."[19]

Members of the House majority party are frequently critical of the Senate's rules, particularly the filibuster. The majority's agenda can be swiftly adopted in the House. In 1995, in the wake of the "Gingrich Revolution," the Republican majority was able to pass virtually the entire "Contract with America," which included ten major bills within the first 100 days of the new Congress. The contract ran up against a solid wall of opposition in the Senate, built on the right of unlimited debate. Since a supermajority of 60 votes was necessary to end debate and the Senate Republicans lacked those votes, most of the contract never became law.

While the Obama administration actually met with somewhat greater legislative success in the Senate during the 111th Congress, Republican filibusters frustrated much of the president's and the House majority's agenda. House Majority Leader Steny Hoyer (D-MD) repeatedly attacked the filibuster. He told *Politico,* "The processes of the United States Senate, where they have one of 100 stopping legislation, shows why it is necessary to go back to the process, tried and true, of having majorities have the ability to act."[20]

Speaker Nancy Pelosi, at a July 2010 White House meeting, reportedly expressed her anger at Senate inaction on the House-passed "cap and trade" energy bill designed to address global warming and "at one point ... turned tartly to [Senate Majority Leader Harry] Reid and Senate Minority Leader Mitch McConnell (R-KY)—and announced, 'The Senate is moving at a glacial pace, slower than the glaciers are actually melting.'"[21]

Congressman David Obey (D-WI), the former chairman of the House Appropriations Committee, shocked observers in May 2010 when he announced he was leaving the House after 42 years. One of the leaders of the reforms of the 1960s and 1970s that brought stricter majority control to the House, Obey declared in his statement announcing his retirement that "there has to be more to life than explaining the ridiculous, accountability destroying rules of the Senate to confused, angry, and frustrated constituents."[22] Congressman Obey was just the latest in a long line going back in history of House members frustrated by the "inefficiency" of the Senate legislative process and particularly its rules, especially the filibuster.

Of course, House anger with the Senate can be tempered for the House minority when they need their compatriots in the Senate to use the filibuster to block legislation that they in the House cannot. Marty Paone, the former secretary of the majority who was for many years the Senate Democrats' principal rules expert, explains:

In 1993, [Senator George] Mitchell (D-ME) was [Senate Majority] Leader. We were in the majority and we would work with our House counterparts. They would always complain about [the Senate], "We're sending you all these bills and nothing's happening with them." Sound familiar? You're hearing that complaint today. And then, lo and behold, the election of '94 comes along and the first call we get that next morning is from the House Democratic leadership staff saying, "Thank God you can still filibuster, because we're not going to be able to stop anything. We're counting on you to stop all of this."[23]

Despite the House minority's secret sometime appreciation for the filibuster, the House has long resented the preeminent role that the Senate plays. In fact, writing about history's most powerful Speaker, "Czar" Joseph Cannon, the *New York Times* maintained: "His ambition for the Speakership was founded on his desire to rescue the House from its subserviency to the Senate and restore it to its old place as a co-equal branch of Congress."[24]

We asked former congressman Lee Hamilton about the roots of longstanding disdain for the filibuster by members of the House. He commented, "Part of it is the frustration of the House with the Senate, not just because of the blocking of legislation, but there's kind a tension between the two bodies on all kinds of things . . . And, so, that's kind of built into the views of members of the House."[25]

Many who now call for reform of the filibuster have been critical in the past of senators of their own party who failed to filibuster on particular issues, arguing that they were showing insufficient vigor in support of their position. For example, a piece by blogger Glenn Greenwald published in the liberal on-line magazine *Salon* criticized Democrats in 2007 for their failure to filibuster the confirmation of the nomination of Michael Mukasey to be President Bush's attorney general.[26]

Impassioned activists of both parties oftentimes see requiring a cloture vote as the litmus test of senators' commitment to their stated views. The actual confirmation vote or vote on final passage may be seen as "casting meaningless votes in opposition." In 2006, in an editorial with the headline "Senators in Need of a Spine," the *New York Times* took Democratic senators to task for their unwillingness to filibuster the nomination of Samuel Alito to the Supreme Court: "A filibuster is a radical tool. It's easy to see why Democrats are frightened of it. But from our perspective, there are some things far more frightening. One of them is Samuel Alito on the Supreme Court."[27]

FILIBUSTER: UNDEMOCRATIC OR UNCONSTITUTIONAL?

The heart of the argument against the filibuster and the supermajority requirement imposed by Rule XXII is that it undermines the Senate's constitutional powers and responsibilities to legislate. The argument is made that it is broadly undemocratic, perhaps unconstitutional, and certainly inefficient.

Many critics of the filibuster go to the extreme of arguing that the filibuster is unconstitutional. In 1951, Senator Hebert Lehman (D-NY) told the Senate Rules Committee, "In my considered judgment, Rule XXII in its present form is contrary to the spirit of the Constitution, the principles of parliamentary procedure, to the essence of democratic government, and to the best interests of the Senate and of the United States."[28] Senator Tom Harkin declared on the Senate floor in 1994, "I believe quite frankly after reading the Constitution and looking at the rules of the Senate . . . that the filibuster rules are unconstitutional."[29]

Those who criticize the filibuster in these terms suggest that since the Constitution specifies supermajority requirements in five circumstances—to ratify a treaty (two-thirds vote in the Senate), to override a presidential veto (two-thirds vote in both houses), to amend the Constitution itself (two-thirds vote in both houses, ratified by three-fourths of the States), to convict an impeached president or other federal officeholder (two-thirds vote in the Senate), and to expel a member of the House or Senate (two-thirds vote in the appropriate house)[30]—it is intended that any other vote must be by simple majority to be constitutional.[31]

However, as we have pointed out, the Constitution in Article I, Section 5 authorizes each house to write its own rules. Clearly, a rule of procedure like Senate Rule XXII setting up the three-fifths requirement to invoke cloture is well within the rights of the body, as is Senate Rule V, which states, "The rules of the Senate shall continue from one Congress to the next Congress unless they are changed as provided in these rules." Other supermajority requirements include the Senate precedent that a two-thirds vote of senators present is necessary to suspend a Senate rule and the requirement of a three-fifths vote to suspend any of a number of points of order created under the Budget Act of 1974, like the "PAYGO" rule or the famous "Byrd rule" (see chapter 9).

In a remarkable December 2010 letter circulated to members of the Senate by Senator Tom Harkin (D-IA) and signed by most of the prominent scholars who have written about the filibuster,[32] the signers assert that "many argue that senators have a constitutional right to extended debate." Having set up this straw man, they proceed to pull it down. The letter goes on to argue that "in the Constitution, the framers specified that supermajority votes would be necessary in seven extraordinary situations[33]—which they specifically listed (including overriding a presidential veto, expelling a member of the Senate, and ratifying a treaty). These, of course, are all voting requirements for passing measures, rather than rules for bringing debate to a close."[34]

This interpretation leaves one to wonder what we are to make of the fact that the Constitution specifies that a majority is required to establish a quorum, but "a smaller number may adjourn from day to day, and may be authorized to compel the attendance of absent Members"[35] and the fact that the roll-call vote requirement that the "yeas and nays of the Members of either House on any question shall, at the desire of one-fifth of those present, be entered in the Journal."[36] Why does the Constitution give no guidance on the number necessary to prevail in those yea and nay votes? The very same section of Article I states that a majority is necessary to conduct business, that a lesser number could adjourn, and one-fifth could require a roll call. Is the Senate Rule XXII provision that a motion signed by sixteen senators will bring a cloture petition to a vote 2 days later unconstitutional? If the cloture rule is unconstitutional because of some implied presumption of majority votes not specified by the Constitution, the supermajority points of order created by the

Budget Act of 1974 and the Senate precedent providing that a two-thirds majority is necessary to waive a rule would also be unconstitutional. If so, any rule could be waived by simple majority vote at any time.

The Supreme Court has never directly addressed the Senate's filibuster rule. Catherine Fisk and Erwin Chemerinsky, writing in the *Stanford Law Review,* argue that the filibuster itself is not unconstitutional. They write: "Neither the Constitution's text nor an underlying philosophy of majoratarianism impose a general rule that a majority vote must be sufficient in all instances."[37] However, they go on to argue that the aspect of Rule XXII that requires a supermajority to change the rule itself is unconstitutional because it interferes with the right of future majorities to change the rules themselves. This is known as "entrenchment."

Eric Posner and Adrian Vermeule argue the opposite. Writing in the *Yale Law Journal,* they note that "the academic literature takes the rule as given, universally assuming that legislative entrenchment is constitutionally or normatively objectionable."[38] They go on to argue that "there just is no rationale to be found; the academics have been on a fruitless quest. Entrenchment is no more objectionable in terms of constitutional, political, or economic theory than are sunset clauses, conditional legislation and delegation, the creation, modification, and abolition of administrative agencies, or any of the myriad of other policy instruments that legislatures use to shape the legal and institutional environment of future legislation."[39]

Congress has passed laws that, for example, impose expedited procedures on the Congress, like the War Powers Act of 1973, the Trade Act of 1974, the Defense Base Closure and Realignment Act of 1990, and the Congressional Accountability Act of 1995. These expedited procedures affect activities of congressional committees, the relationship between committees and their parent chambers, the prerogatives of the majority and the rights of the minority, control over the floor schedule in the House and Senate, and the ability of individual Senators to shape public policy through debate and amendments. The Defense Base Closure and Realignment Act (BRAC), for example, required Congress to pass a joint resolution of disapproval of the list of recommendations for military base closures made by an appointed commission within 45 days or the recommendations would go into effect. Under the law, this was the only action allowed to Congress: a vote, with no changes permitted.[40] The BRAC law also prohibited judicial review of the decisions to close military bases under the act. Senator Arlen Specter (R-PA) took the matter to the Supreme Court. In May 1994, the Supreme Court unanimously decided that decisions to close military bases were not subject to judicial review.[41] In a concurring opinion in that case, Justice Souter, joined by three other justices, wrote:

> If judicial review could eliminate one base from a package, the political resolution embodied in that package would be destroyed; if such review could eliminate an entire package, or leave its validity in doubt when a succeeding one had to be devised, the political resolution necessary to agree on the succeeding package would be rendered the more difficult, if not impossible. The very reasons that led Congress by this enactment *to bind its hands from untying a package,* once assembled, go far to persuade me that Congress did not mean the courts to have any such power through judicial review.[42] (emphasis added)

The Budget Act of 1974 created the reconciliation process, and the budget process has been amended to create such laws as Gramm-Rudman and, more recently, PAYGO. These have binding characteristics that Congress can only waive by supermajority votes. The cloture rule is less binding than these budget provisions because it applies only to debate, and the rules themselves can be amended by a simple majority vote.

Election of Senators by state legislatures—a design for the Senate that differentiated it from the House, which the Framers did intend—failed the test of time and was, with great effort, discarded when the Seventeenth Amendment to the Constitution was adopted in 1913. By contrast, the filibuster and the cloture rule written to restrain it, which were not a part of the original design of the Founders, have persisted for more than 200 years. Thomas Jefferson wrote: "It is not by the consolidation, or concentration of powers, but by their distribution, that good government is effected."[43] Of course, as with George Washington's cup of tea, the filibuster was not directly the subject, but the principle applies.

Former majority leader Tom Daschle (D-SD) has written:

The Senate's longstanding institutional checks on the majority make it easier for the minority to block initiatives than for the majority to pass them ... Right-wing activists have accused Democratic senators of subjecting legislation and nominees to "unconstitutional" filibusters, claiming the founders never envisioned a cloture requirement. The former allegation is both false and hypocritical ... The latter statement—that the founders never anticipated cloture—is correct, since the founders never provided any means to cut off debate ... The founders envisioned a Senate that would vigorously protect the rights of the minority against a reactionary majority.[44]

Franklin Burdette wrote more than 70 years ago, "The problem of dilatory tactics will exist to some degree so long as there are conflicts between majorities and minorities. The solution, whatever it is, will never be found to lie wholly in a set of rules. It must rest in part upon the election of legislators with a keen sense of public responsibility, men who will never allow political strife to thwart a need for action."[45] The Senate of the twenty-first century is under attack for its tendency to gridlock. Critics believe that efforts to use the filibuster to thwart the majority's efforts to enact its agenda are everything from unconstitutional to undemocratic to political expediency. Burdette was right to emphasize the accountability of senators themselves. The fault lies less with the rules and more with the consequences of the modern Senate's extreme partisanship.

The end of the infamous string of southern filibusters of civil rights legislation came in 1964, when Senate Minority Leader Everett Dirksen and twenty-seven Republicans voted with northern Democrats to invoke cloture and then to pass the 1964 Civil Rights Act. But, before the debate in the Senate began, in response to Majority Leader Mike Mansfield's plea that the minority leader help him to block a filibuster of the bill, Senator Dirksen replied, "I trust that the time will never come in my political career when the waters of partisanship will flow so swift and so deep as to obscure my estimate of the national interest ... I trust I can disenthrall myself from all bias, from all prejudice, from all irrelevancies, from all immaterial matters, and see clearly what the issue is and then render an independent judgment."[46]

We recall these words not because Senator Dirksen promised to rise above partisanship and act on his independent judgment, but because of the actions that followed months later. Senator Robert C. Byrd (D-WV) had spoken in opposition to the civil rights bill through the night, for 14 hours and 13 minutes, the longest speech of his career. The Dirksen Congressional Center quotes the *Peoria Journal Star*:

> Dirksen had the last word. In poor health, drained from working fourteen, fifteen, and sixteen-hour days, his words came quietly. Twice he gulped pills handed him by a Senate page. In his massive left hand, he held a 12-page speech he had typed the night before on Senate stationery. "I have had but one purpose," Dirksen intoned, "and that was the enactment of a good, workable, equitable, practical bill having due regard for the progress made in the civil rights field at the state and local level." He warned his colleagues that "we dare not temporize with the issue which is before us. It is essentially moral in character. It must be resolved. It will not go away. Its time has come ... The time has come for equality of opportunity in sharing of government, in education, and in employment. It must not be stayed or denied. It is here! ... I appeal to all Senators. We are confronted with a moral issue. Today let us not be found wanting in whatever it takes by way of moral and spiritual substance to face up to the issue and to vote cloture."[47]

During the historic cloture vote, one of the most stirring moments ever in the Senate occurred. California's Democratic senator Claire Engle, then dying of cancer, was wheeled into the chamber. When his name was reached in the roll call, "there was a painfully moving moment of silence. Finally ... unable to speak, [he] feebly lifted his left hand ... and pointed toward his eye. 'I guess that means aye,' murmured the clerk."[48] The Senate voted to invoke cloture (which at the time required a two-thirds vote) by an overwhelming 73–27.

Two days later, Roy Wilkins of the National Association for the Advancement of Colored People (NAACP) wrote a letter to Senator Dirksen: "Let me be the first to admit that I was in error in estimating your preliminary announcements and moves. There were certain realities which had to be taken into account in advancing this legislation to a vote. Out of your long experience you devised an approach which seemed to you to offer a chance for success."[49] Wilkins acknowledged to Senator Dirksen that the vote "tended mightily to reinforce your judgment and to vindicate your procedure."[50]

★ ★ ★

SIX

The Dangers of Overzealous Reform

It's a simple idea—majority rule. It's the answer to tyranny. A government of the people, by the people, and for the people. Democracy begins with the idea of majority rule. But the Founders understood that danger lurks among overzealous majorities. James Madison wrote, "There is no maxim, in my opinion, which is more liable to be misapplied, and which, therefore, more needs elucidation, than . . . the interest of the majority is the political standard of right and wrong."[1]

Among other checks and balances, the Founders set up a bicameral legislature. Madison wrote, "In republican government, the legislative authority necessarily predominates. The remedy for this inconveniency is to divide the legislature into different branches; and to render them, to different modes of election and different principles of action, as little connected with each other as the nature of their common functions and their common dependence on the society will admit."[2]

PROTECTION OF MINORITY RIGHTS

The "Great Compromise" adopted at the Philadelphia Constitutional Convention in 1787 created a Senate, the composition of which is based not on population but on the allocation of equal representation to each State, no matter how large or small. It follows that a simple majority of the senators may not necessarily represent a majority of the people. The Constitution granted both the Senate and the House of Representatives the right to establish their own rules. The Senate's rules, true to the Founders' hopes for a Senate where greater deliberation would serve as a bulwark against tyrannical majorities, "gave greater voice" (in the words of Senate Historian Donald Ritchie) "to the minority, whether the minority party, a faction of the majority party, or even a single senator."[3]

The Senate's first president, John Adams wrote in 1793, "Mankind will in time discover that unbridled majorities are as tyrannical and cruel as unlimited despots."[4] And many years later, Arkansas Senator J. William Fulbright (D-AR) put it, "The greatest single virtue of a strong legislature is not what it can do but what it can prevent."[5] The distinct and unique features of the Senate are central to this role of minority protection. Republican Senator John McCain (R-AZ), his party's 2008 presidential nominee, has said, "You can't say that all we're going to do around here in the United States Senate is have us govern by 51 votes—otherwise we might as well be unicameral, because then we would have the Senate and the House exactly the same."[6]

But from time to time in the Senate's history, frustration has built up, even in the Senate itself, as a minority has successfully prevented the majority from swiftly adopting its agenda. Periodically, this has led to the demand to sweep away what are perceived to be the offensive rules of the Senate, particularly the filibuster.

THE DANGER

The years 2009–2011 were just such a period of frustration. While the Obama health reform bill was in the end successfully enacted into law, the filibuster waged by the Republicans, the passage in the Senate of a bill with an all-Democratic supermajority of 60 votes, the loss of that 60th vote with the election of Scott Brown in Massachusetts (who made a virtue in his campaign of being the "41st vote" to sustain a filibuster against the healthcare legislation), and the role of the budget reconciliation process as the means to push the bill through all fueled a popular tidal wave. That wave built up strength in the media, in the House of Representatives, and among some Democratic senators, and it was further whipped up by the winds of filibusters waged against financial reform, extension of unemployment insurance, small business tax credits, and a long list of majority legislative initiatives that threatened to wash way the Senate filibuster as we have known it. The Senate's role as a counterweight against overzealous majorities, its role in oversight of the executive, and its effectiveness as an arena for reasoned deliberation, moderation, and compromise could be overwhelmed by the tide of frustration leading to hasty and ill-considered abandonment of the filibuster.

The late Senator Robert C. Byrd (D-WV), the Senate's universally respected expert on the rules, in 1995, fighting an earlier effort to eliminate the supermajority requirement to cut off debate in the Senate, made the key point that frequently gets lost in the current demand for a more "democratic" and more "efficient" Senate:

> The filibuster has become a target for rebuke in this efficiency-obsessed age in which we live . . . It does, however, take more than a little thought to understand the true purpose of the tactic known as filibustering and to appreciate its historic importance in protecting the viewpoint of the minority . . . In many ways, the filibuster is the single most important device ever employed to ensure that the Senate remains truly the unique protector of the rights of the people that it has been throughout our history.[7]

It takes a full understanding of the Senate's culture and mores to appreciate the myriad of ways that unlimited debate, virtually unlimited amendment rights, and the related pressures to build supermajorities drive the Senate in the direction of consensus building and restrain otherwise unfettered majorities. The power of small groups of senators to slow things down and to force more careful examination of even rampantly popular majority policies is invaluable, if often mostly unnoticed by many observers outside of the Senate.

IRAQ WAR RESOLUTION

In 2002, in the wake of the terrorist attacks of September 11, as President George W. Bush was preparing to go to war against Iraq, there was overwhelming popular support for an attack. The resolution that the president sent to Capitol Hill sought an unusually broad authorization to go to war anywhere in the Middle East. The resolution read: "The President is authorized to use all means that he determines to be appropriate, including force, in order to enforce the United Nations Security Council Resolutions referenced above, defend the national security interests of the United States against the threat posed by Iraq, and restore international peace and security in the region."[8]

This resolution was so broad it could, for example, arguably be used as authorization for an attack on Iran's nuclear facilities. Tom Daschle (D-SD), minority leader at the time, writes in his memoir, "Such language would have given the president—or any future president—blanket authority to put U.S. forces in harm's way at any time and anywhere in the Middle East."[9] We learned in Vietnam with the Tonkin Gulf Resolution just how dangerous a sweeping war authorization resolution could be. Senator Robert Byrd, leading a brief filibuster against the Iraq resolution, warned, "This is the Tonkin Gulf resolution all over again . . . Let us stop, look and listen. Let us not give this president or any president unchecked power. Remember the Constitution."[10]

In a magazine interview, Republican senator Chuck Hagel of Nebraska, a Vietnam War veteran, criticized the Bush administration's Iraq resolution, calling it "astounding." He complained that it was much too broad: "They could go into Greece or anywhere. I mean, is Central Asia in the region? I suppose! Sure as hell it was clear they meant the whole Middle East. It was anything they wanted. It was literally anything. No boundaries. No restrictions.[11]

In the end, the resolution adopted by the Senate deleted the most offensive language and placed new requirements to report to Congress. Those reporting requirements later played an important role in Congressional oversight of the Iraq War. Senator Daschle on the Senate floor said of the new version of the resolution: "This resolution gives the

President the authority he needs to confront the threat posed by Iraq. It is fundamentally different and a better resolution than the one the President sent to us . . . It is more respectful of our Constitution, more reflective of our understanding that we need to work with our allies in this effort, and more in keeping with our strong belief that force must be a last resort, not a first response."[12]

Even for opponents who believed that the president was rushing into an ill-advised war in Iraq, the changes were important, if insufficient. Senator Barbara Boxer (D-CA) supported the amendment offered by Senator Carl Levin (D-MI) to seek multi-national support through a UN resolution before the United States acted unilaterally. Senator Boxer declared: "[The Bush administration] wanted a resolution that gave the authority far beyond Iraq. They wanted to give the President authority to go anywhere in the world. Now that idea is gone . . . So checks and balances do work.[13]

While some of the senators who flexed their muscles and exercised leverage under the Senate rules in this instance were of the president's own party, it is not hard to imagine a strong president with majorities in both houses, in the absence of extended debate in the Senate, pushing through an overbroad, ill-thought-out war resolution.

PALM SUNDAY COMPROMISE

Another example in which a senator's right to unlimited debate was key to restraining a rash violation of the separation of powers in a way that may not have been obvious to many observers had Senator Levin at its center.[14] In March 2005, the Congress passed the so-called "Palm Sunday Compromise," which provided jurisdiction to a federal district court to review the case of Terri Schiavo. Terri Schiavo was a Florida woman in a "persistent vegetative state" whose husband, over the objection of her parents, sought to remove the feeding tube being used to keep her alive, although brain dead. The case had for some time been a cause célèbre, particularly for conservatives. It generated intense national media attention.

After a long history of litigation in the Florida state courts that had begun 7 years earlier, Florida Circuit Court Judge George W. Greer issued a final rejection of the arguments of Terri Schiavo's parents and ordered the feeding tube removed on March 18, 2005. Congress entered the situation dramatically. Legislation to shift the jurisdiction of the matter to the federal courts was circulated among senators by Florida's Republican senator Mel Martinez.

While Senator Levin considered it, as he later stated on the Senate floor, "a mistake for Congress to be moving into this area with this haste and speed, in the most difficult decision-making a family could ever face,"[15] he noted that the language of the bill made it clear that "a Federal court would have to find a violation of a constitutional right or a right under U.S. law in order to provide an order that she be maintained on life support."[16] As a result, he intended to oppose the legislation but not block it.

However, the first version of the Martinez bill contained a provision that required the federal court to issue a stay blocking the removal of the feeding tube until the court issued its ruling. Senator Levin was strongly opposed to this stay provision. As he later explained the section, it "stated that the Federal court 'shall' issue a stay . . . I was opposed to that provision because I believe Congress should not mandate that a Federal judge issue a stay. Under longstanding law and practice, the decision to issue a stay is a matter of discretion for the Federal judge based on the facts of the case."[17] Senator Levin suggested to Majority Leader Bill Frist (R-TN) and Senator Martinez that the provision be changed to read that the court "may" issue a stay, instead of "shall." This would leave the decision appropriately in the hands of the judge. This version of the bill was passed by the Senate by voice vote.

Further changes were made and Senator Martinez filed a new bill, S 686, that Majority Leader Frist was confident could be taken up and passed by unanimous consent that same day and then sent to the House. President Bush, on vacation on his ranch in Crawford, Texas, planned to return to Washington in the wee hours of the night to dramatically sign the bill into law. Since the Easter recess was scheduled to begin, most members of the Senate had already left Washington. The majority leader convened the body in an unusual Saturday session. Senator Levin, who was now in Michigan, read the new bill and noted that the section of the bill providing for a stay had been removed entirely. Being both an excellent lawyer and an experienced senior senator, he recognized a problem but also saw an opportunity.

When courts have difficulty with the language of the law as written, they often turn to the *Congressional Record* to determine "Congressional intent." That is, they study the record of the debate and actions in an effort to shed light on what Congress intended when it adopted certain language. In this case, Senator Levin feared that since the mandatory version of the stay provision had previously been changed to the discretionary version—that is, "shall" changed to "may"—the danger was that the court could misinterpret the elimination of the discretionary language from the final version. He explained that the absence of any provision in the new version "means that Congress relies on current law. Under current law, a judge may decide whether or not a stay is appropriate."[18]

Because of this concern, Senator Levin, through the Democratic leadership still in Washington, objected to the passage of the bill by placing a "hold" on it by informing the Democratic leadership that he wished them to, on his behalf, object to any proposed agreement. This meant that the bill could not be passed by unanimous consent unless and until Senator Levin's concerns were addressed. Senator Levin also knew that proponents were openly advancing the view that Congress expected the federal court to overturn the Florida court ruling and were using the media to convey that expectation. He wanted it to be explicit that the Congress, in passing this bill to allow the federal court to take the case, did not, in any way, intend to dictate to the court what action it should take—although he knew that that was exactly what many of the proponents wanted to do.

By Sunday (Palm Sunday), language was agreed to and the colloquy was placed in the *Congressional Record*. In the colloquy, Majority Leader Frist acknowledged that "Nothing in the current bill or its legislative language mandates a stay."[19] The Senate then passed the bill by voice vote (with only three senators actually on the floor).

In the House of Representatives, deliberation ran past midnight. The bill passed in the House early Monday morning at 12:41, 203–58. In a demonstration of how important he felt the bill was, President Bush returned to sign the bill into law at 1:11 that morning.

The federal district court denied the request for a temporary restraining order, and when the federal appeals court rejected the appeal, it stated, "Congress considered and specifically rejected provisions that would have mandated . . . the grant of pretrial stay. There is this *enlightening exchange* in the legislative history concerning the Senate bill that was enacted" (emphasis added).[20] The decision then repeats word for word the entire Levin-Frist colloquy.

There is little doubt, given the passions at the time, and the actions of the House of Representatives and President Bush, that a Senate in which a simple majority could act precipitously would have passed legislation instructing the court to grant a stay. We cannot say how the court would have reacted to that, but the need to get Senator Levin's consent, backed by his right to filibuster, assured a more deliberative outcome. The Schiavo case is a good example of a Congress enflamed by public passions that is pulled back from rash and ill-considered action by the need in the Senate to overcome a potential filibuster. The potential damage that could have been done had Congress interfered with the judicial process was great.

Commentator Jeffrey Toobin, in his thoughtful book about the Supreme Court, writes about the reaction to the Schiavo case. He points out the threatening words of House Majority Leader Tom DeLay (R-TX): "The time will come for the men responsible for this to answer for their behavior. We will look at an arrogant, out-of-control judiciary that thumbs its nose at Congress and the president."[21] A few days later, Senator John Cornyn (R-TX) added, "I don't know if there's a cause-and-effect connection but we have seen some recent episodes of courthouse violence in this country. I wonder whether there may be some connection between the perception in some quarters on some occasions where judges are making political decisions yet are unaccountable to the public, that it builds up and builds up to the point where people engage in violence."[22]

The threat to judicial independence was clear. Toobin describes Supreme Court Justice Sandra Day O'Connor as deeply concerned. He says, "To O'Connor, the real danger was the idea that, with this law, Congress was trying to dictate to the courts how they should rule."[23] Nonetheless, Majority Leader DeLay declared, "The Schiavo case was one of my proudest moments in Congress."[24] In this heated moment of potential constitutional crisis, the right to filibuster in the Senate did its part to cool the hot "tea."

THE HARKIN RATCHET

There have, however, always been senators anxious for a more efficient legislative process who wish to curtail or destroy the filibuster. Senator Tom Harkin (D-IA) has become the point man for an effort to essentially eliminate the Senate filibuster by amending the cloture rule to allow fifty-one senators to cut off debate. On February 11, 2010, he introduced S Res. 416, which attracted three cosponsors, Senator Barbara Mikulski (D-MD), Senator Jeanne Shaheen (D-NH), and notably the majority whip, Senator Richard Durbin (D-IL). This is not the first time that Senator Harkin has taken on this particular fight, and he is among the very few in the Senate who have stood for the elimination of the supermajority cloture rule without regard to whether he was a member of the majority or the minority. (He did, however, oppose the Republican effort to eliminate the filibuster on judicial nominations in 2005.)

When Republicans took control of the Congress in 1995, the House, led by Speaker Newt Gingrich (R-GA), rewrote its rules. In the Senate, Senator Harkin and the Democrats, newly reduced to minority status, would normally have been expected to support the filibuster, since the minority stands to benefit more than the majority. Senator Harkin, nonetheless, offered his proposal to reform the Senate's cloture rule. It was not well received. A mere eighteen other Democrats stood with Harkin, only seven of whom are still in the Senate.[25]

Helen Dewar wrote in the *Washington Post* at the time, "The winds of change that howled through the House . . . subsided into a gentle breeze . . . in the Senate, hardly rustling the cobwebs on two of its oldest traditions and practices—filibusters and freebies. A day after the Republican-controlled House ripped up many of the old Democratic rules in an unprecedented 14-hour opening day, the Senate—also under a new GOP majority—voted 76 to 19 to quash a move by two Democrats[26] to put new constraints on senators' right of virtually unlimited debate."[27]

The Harkin resolution would have amended Rule XXII by requiring that when the Senate votes on a cloture motion and fails to invoke cloture, the number of votes necessary to invoke cloture on subsequent motions with respect to the same matter be reduced step-wise by 3 votes on each succeeding motion. The proposal would have ultimately, in such cases, reduced the number of votes necessary to a majority of the Senators "duly chosen and sworn." If the Senate had its full complement of one hundred senators, fifty-one would be required to invoke cloture on the fourth try.[28] These four cloture efforts could be accomplished relatively swiftly.

Senator Harkin, testifying to the Senate Rules Committee in 2010 about essentially the same resolution, explained, "Under my proposal, a determined minority could slow down any bill for as much as 8 days. Senators would have ample time to make their arguments and attempt to persuade the public and a majority of their colleagues. This protects the rights of the minority to full and vigorous debate and deliberation, maintaining the hallmark of the United States Senate."[29]

This proposal has several weaknesses. The likely effect of this change is that the majority leader would simply wait out the required 8 days to get to the point where fifty-one senators are able to invoke cloture. There is virtually no incentive to compromise. In fact, since there is no requirement under the Harkin language that the repeated cloture motions occur consecutively, the majority could minimize the disruption of waiting out the 8 days, by creatively scheduling them.

An equally serious flaw is that the Harkin approach would undermine a senator's right to amend. Once cloture is invoked, under the rule, amendments must be germane, and since the debate is limited to 30 additional hours, the majority is able to "run out the clock." This, used in association with the majority leader's ability to tactically fill the "amendment tree"—that is, block all of the available parliamentary options for amending the pending matter—could effectively shackle the minority's amendment rights.

The Harkin approach basically boils down to a delayed "previous question" motion. A previous question motion is an effort to end debate and bring a matter to an immediate vote. Under Harkin's approach, at some point 51 votes would suffice to terminate debate and bring a matter to an up-or-down vote. Like most of the arguments surrounding the filibuster and associated tactics, this argument has very deep roots.

1873 BATTLE OVER THE MAJORITY
VOTE PREVIOUS QUESTION

More than a century ago, on March 19, 1873, Republican senator George G. Wright, one of Senator Harkin's predecessors from Iowa, offered a resolution calling for a majority vote previous question motion for the Senate. (Of course, at the time, prior to the 1917 adoption of the cloture rule, there was no limit on debate in the Senate.) Senator Wright, countering those who argued for continuity of Senate practice, argued that "it is said . . . that the policy and practice of the Senate have been, for sixty years, so and so. A great many things are quite as old . . . have been better changed. If by our practice and experience here we do not improve, we live to but little purpose. I think all experience shows that . . . we might change our rules, and every day but confirms me in that experience."[30]

The resolution was opposed by Senator Thomas F. Bayard (D-DE), who later became President Grover Cleveland's secretary of state. Senator Bayard declared:

> I look with great disfavor upon this proposition; nor do I know of any justification for the charge that the public business has been obstructed by the forms of debate in this body. I do not mean to say that members may not at times have grown impatient, especially those whose power was assured, and who were therefore eager for the victory which was sure to come to them by the force of numbers . . . Free speech is what was intended to be secured by the rules as we now have them . . . The majority have it in their power to enact measures into laws. Leave, then, at least, to those who oppose you, the privilege of protest and the privilege of giving the reasons for their protest. "Strike, but hear"; and do not hasten so to strike without hearing.[31]

Senator Bayard, defending unlimited debate, continued:

> I shall at all stages oppose any proposition that undertakes to limit debate beyond the just discretion of members here. There is a personal responsibility of men to their country and their constituency on this subject which ought to be sufficient, which, in the past, has proved sufficient, to protect the country . . . I look with great disfavor upon the proposition of introducing any gag-law into the rule of debate in this body.[32]

Ohio's Democratic Senator Allen Thurman, who, in 1888, would be his party's nominee for vice president[33] also rose in opposition, first issuing what sounds a bit like a filibuster threat, "I hope that the resolution will not be taken up now . . . It must necessarily give rise to a long discussion; it cannot be otherwise. It cannot be that the whole practice of the Senate, from the foundation of the Government to this day, is to be overturned without due consideration."[34]

A short while later, Senator Thurman elaborated: "The moment you adopt a previous question in the Senate—the moment you confine and limit debate . . . from that moment the weight and power and influence of the Senate in this country will begin to decline."[35]

This point was true in the 43rd Congress and rings true in 2011, 138 years later. If the Senate were to render itself a majoritarian body, it would soon recede into the shadows of the House of Representatives. Most of the advantages of bicameralism would be gone, and the Senate would suffer the fate of most upper chambers around the world. Senator Thurman, perhaps overstating the relative obscurity of the House, went on:

> There was a time when the House of Representatives was the great power in this Government. Then, the Senate sat with closed doors, and no word of its debates went to the country; but for the moment the Senate opened its doors and debated in public, the influence of the Senate began to increase, until its relative influence in the country became greater than that of the House of Representatives, even with open debate, had it not been for the hour-rule which was adopted in the House of Representatives, and its previous question. That is the truth about it, and long-sighted men in that House saw it and predicted, when the hour-rule was adopted, that that was signing the death-warrant of the influence of the House of Representatives in this country; and it has proven to be true.[36]

Senators Thurman, Bayard, and their colleagues were arguing against limiting debate based on 60 years of Senate experience. Today the same argument in defense of the filibuster is based on more than 200 years of Senate experience. Admittedly, the senators of 1888 argued that they saw no abuse of unlimited debate, and as is clear, abuse of the rules is a problem in recent Congresses. The question remains, should the desire for expedience, the impatience and frustration at obstruction, drive senators to a radical change of 2 centuries of practice in hope of remedying a problem that has its roots outside of the body? We have had periods of extreme partisan polarization before, and the Senate and its rules have survived intact. The problem rests not with the rules of the Senate but with the senators themselves.

FRIST VERSION OF THE HARKIN PROPOSAL

The Senate had another brush with a Harkin-like resolution during the 2003 conflict between the Republican majority and the Democratic minority over a number of President George W. Bush's nominations to the circuit courts. Democrats were filibustering seven of President Bush's nominees. Majority Leader Bill Frist (R-TN) proposed a rule, S Res. 138, that was very similar to the Harkin proposal of 8 years earlier, except that the reductions in the number of votes required to invoke cloture would have applied only to confirmation of judicial nominations. On June 26, 2003, S Res. 138 was reported by the Senate Rules Committee. The Frist language, endorsed by the Rules Committee, however, had another significant deviation from the Harkin proposal that made it an even more virulent attack on the right of unlimited debate and the protection of minorities. Senator Frist's language failed even to protect a Senate majority.

The Frist language that was approved by the Republican-controlled Rules Committee stated "that the affirmative vote required to bring to a close debate upon that nomination shall be reduced by 3 votes on the second such motion, and by 3 additional votes on each succeeding motion, until the affirmative vote is reduced to a number equal to or less than an affirmative vote of a majority of the Senators duly chosen and sworn. The required vote shall then be a simple majority." This would arguably permit a majority of senators voting at the time to invoke cloture. Since a quorum would be fifty-one senators, in theory as few as twenty-six senators could actually constitute a simple majority and invoke cloture, ending debate under the Frist formulation. While this would be a highly unlikely outcome, cloture invoked by something less than fifty-one senators would seem not that unlikely under this language.

Although reported by the Rules Committee, the Frist version was never raised on the floor of the Senate. The moderate Democrats and Republicans who joined forces—the so-called "Gang of 14"—imposed a compromise on the chamber that eliminated the "nuclear option" threat to the filibuster.

During the 2010 buildup to the rules reform debate that would occur at the outset of the 112th Congress, Senator Harkin began expressing support for the view that the Senate can change its rules by majority vote at the start of a new Congress, the view being advanced by Senator Tom Udall (D-NM) and others. However, once the precedent has been established of using a simple majority at the start of the Congress to change the rules, why would a future majority in a future Congress want to stop there? Why put up with a built-in 8 days of "obstruction" under the Harkin format? Why not control the time of debate and the number of amendments?

In a meeting with the Democratic freshmen of the Senate in August 2010, many of whom have expressed great frustration with the filibuster and support for the Udall and/or Harkin positions, Senator Chris Dodd (D-CT), a former chairman of the Senate Rules Committee, told them that he opposed these changes. He later commented, "These are people who have never been in the minority."[37] Senator Dodd further explained to the *Washington Post*'s E. J. Dionne, a severe critic of the Senate filibuster, "Those ideas are normally being promoted by people who haven't been here in the minority and don't understand how the rules, if intelligently used, can help protect against the tyranny of the majority."[38]

THE EFFICIENCY PITFALL

It is a mistake to think that simply overrunning the intransigence of the minority, whether with a step-by-step ratchet like Harkin's or by sweeping away the filibuster entirely, will lead to solutions of our nation's problems. Montana University professor Robert Saldin, writing with Andrew Rotherham, Fellow of the Democratic Leadership Council, observed that "tossing the filibuster out altogether conflates cause and effect and would lead to even more partisanship and even less cooperation."[39]

The authors of the 1974 Budget Act, by providing expedited procedures that prohibited filibusters on budget resolution and reconciliations bills, and guaranteed an up-or-down vote, thought they were building a budget process that would foster bipartisan cooperation. It had the opposite result. With the exception of a consensus budget resolution passed in 1997, when President Clinton worked with congressional leadership to balance the federal budget, most budget votes have followed nearly straight party lines. Since 1994, on average, only 3.5 senators from the minority have voted with the majority on budget resolutions. Without the exceptional 1997 vote, the average is less than 1 senator.[40] Table 6.1 shows each of the votes from FY1992 through FY2011.

The danger of sweeping away the defining characteristics of the Senate is that the body will be left a pale shadow of the House of Representatives. If the majority party is able to control the Senate and rewrite the rules, it is almost certain to establish a body like the House Rules Committee, controlled by the majority leadership. The Rules Committee decides when and if certain bills reach the floor; what amendments, if any, will be permitted; even the rules for how amendments will be adopted. Time limits on debate are controlled by the House Rules Committee as well.

Former Congressman Lee Hamilton (D-IN) has written: "Especially in the House, [partisan] polarization tends to force the exclusion of the minority party from deliberations—the majority has the votes, and so controls procedures to keep the minority from participating. Republicans did this when they were in power, and Democrats did it after they

TABLE 6.1. MINORITY PARTY VOTES IN SUPPORT OF
SENATE BUDGET RESOLUTIONS, FY1992–FY2011

Fiscal Year	Date	Senate Vote	Minority Votes	Majority Party
1992	5/22/1991	57–41	8	D
1993	5/21/1992	52–41	15	D
1994	4/1/1993	55–45	0	D
1995	5/12/1994	53–46	1	D
1996	6/29/1995	54–46	0	R
1997	6/13/1996	53–46	0	R
1998	6/5/1997	76–22	36	R
1999	None	None	None	R
2000	4/15/1999	54–44	0	R
2001	4/13/2000	50–48	0	R
2002	5/10/2001	53–47	5	R
2003	None	None	None	D
2004	4/11/2003	51–50	1	R
2005	None	None	None	R
2006	4/28/2005	52–47	0	R
2007	None	None	None	R
2008	5/17/2007	52–40	2	D
2009	6/4/2008	48–45	2	D
2010	4/29/2009	53–43	0	D
2011	None	None	None	D

took over. The result was the same in both instances: the minority got so incensed that it spent its time searching for ways to obstruct and frustrate majority rule."[41] In fact, even current Speaker John Boehner (R-OH), when still in the minority, bitterly complained that the 111th Congress (2009–2010) was "the first in our history that has not allowed one bill to be considered under an open amendment process[42]—not one."[43]

Why would a majority, able to control the rules of the Senate, not establish such powers? As in the House, the majority party would quickly move to tighten its control over all the Senate committees. For example, both the House and the Senate establish the party ratios in their committees. Whereas the ratios of party membership on Senate committees have historically closely reflected the overall ratio in the Senate, in the House, where the minority party has many fewer tools with which to protect itself, the majority makes sure that its control of key committees is unchallengeable. For example, in the 111th Congress, the Democratic majority outnumbered the Republicans by a 257–178 margin, which gave the Democrats 59.1 percent of the seats. However, the Democratic majority allocated 69.2 percent of the seats on the powerful House Rules Committee to itself. On the tax-writing Ways and Means Committee, which also has jurisdiction over entitlement programs like Social Security and Medicare, Democrats had 63.4 percent of the seats, an 11-vote majority. In fact, this was the pattern for powerful committees like the Appropriations Committee (61.7%), the Budget Committee (61.5%), and the Energy and Commerce Committee (61.0%).

In the Senate, the committee ratios reflect the overall ratio between the parties in the Senate as a whole. The Congressional Research Service recently examined the ratios over a 34-year period and concluded, "Data from this study indicate that the majority party ratios on committees roughly approximate the majority party strength in the Senate chamber, regardless of which party is in control."[44]

The equitable distribution of committee seats in the Senate doesn't happen by accident. The majority must negotiate with the minority in order to establish fair committee ratios and the staff funding levels for majority and minority committee staffs. The majority would be unable to pass the necessary resolutions without the votes to overcome a minority filibuster. In fact, unlike in the House where the election of a new majority gives it very effective control over most of the decisions regarding organization of the body and rule making, in the Senate the filibuster dictates that the majority must consult the minority.

It is instructive to remember the razor-thin 2000 election. Republicans were awarded the White House by virtue of a Supreme Court decision in *Bush v. Gore* and the mechanics of the Electoral College. George W. Bush became president although Al Gore received half a million more votes in the election. In the House of Representatives 222 Republicans were elected and 212 Democrats, giving the Republicans a very small majority, 51.2 percent of the seats. In the Senate, after the 2000 election, there were 50 Republicans and 50 Democrats. With the newly elected Republican vice president, Dick Cheney, casting the deciding vote in the case of a tie, the Republicans became the majority party.

Speaker Dennis Hastert (R-IL) and the Republican leadership in the majoritarian House, controlling only 51.2 percent of the votes, were able to establish comfortable committee margins, including 69.2 percent of the votes in the House Rules Committee and 58.5 percent in Ways and Means. In the Senate—because of the potential for a filibuster by the minority—it was a different story. Then–Minority Leader Daschle describes the circumstance at the outset of the 107th Congress: "The fifty-fifty split created an intriguing institutional challenge—determining who would control the chamber and set its agenda in this evenly divided Senate . . . Both the majority and minority parties have their own weapons of parliamentary procedure, developed over the course of the Senate's history, to advance or defend their particular positions."[45] Democrats in the Senate demanded shared power. As Senator Daschle describes it, "[Democrats] were pretty clear about what we wanted. We wanted equal committee membership, to replace the one-member advantage the Republicans had enjoyed as the majority party [in the previous Congress]. We wanted the budgets for each committee . . . to be divided evenly between both parties . . . If the money and memberships were evenly divided, the chairmanships would be hardly more than cosmetic."[46]

In his memoir, then–Majority Leader Trent Lott (R-MS) acknowledges how difficult the Democrats' demands were for his party's caucus to swallow: "I had difficulty selling the deal to my fellow Republicans . . . They thought we should have insisted on having a one-seat margin in the committees because of the vice-president's vote. But I told them, the Democrats would never in hell have agreed. Daschle had made that crystal clear."[47]

Senator Lott had to overcome the bitter opposition of Senator Phil Gramm (R-TX) and others who believed the Republicans should take a much harder line. Senator Lott explains: "The agreement may have involved a few compromises, but it helped the White House avoid what might have been a long, contentious, perhaps paralyzing battle on the floor over the organization of the Senate—a battle Daschle had vowed repeatedly to undertake."[48]

Without the filibuster, in a majoritarian Senate, Minority Leader Daschle would have been in the same posture as Minority Leader Richard Gephardt (D-MO) had been in the House that year—run over by the "bulldozer," the victorious majority party. Another likely impact for senators in a Senate controlled by a simple majority would be a weakening of their power on the Senate floor. The leverage each senator would have in a Senate without a filibuster would be severely limited. As political scientists Chris Deering and Steven Smith write, "The defining institutional arrangements of that chamber [the Senate]—unlimited speech and lack of a germaneness rule—force committees, parties, and leaders to accommodate wider participation."[49]

Professor Dick Fenno points out that because of the individualism that the Senate rules foster, Senate committee chairs have less control within their committees than House chairs. He quotes a Senate staffer: "No committee chairman in the Senate, no matter how strong he is, can keep the kind of tight rein on his members that a strong House chairman can . . . House members aren't treated as individuals. That's why nine out of ten of them want to come over to the Senate . . . They look over here and see every Senator wheeling and dealing and doing what he wants to do and it's like the rich man looking across the river into heaven."[50]

In short, the dangers to the Senate and the Congress as a whole that would be posed by drastically curbing the right to filibuster in the Senate far outweigh any benefits. In fact, allowing a simple majority to control the Senate, as a response to the abusive overuse of the filibuster, would be counterproductive. Conservative former senators Jim McClure (R-ID) and Malcolm Wallop (R-WY) put it more aptly and colorfully than we are able to: "When you find a bear in your cabin, it's not smart to try to burn him out."[51]

★ ★ ★

SEVEN

Related Tactics
Holds

The Senate can tie itself in knots without resorting to a filibuster. Filibusters represent only one of the ways that the right to unlimited debate can impact the functioning of the Senate. Because debate can be difficult to bring to a close, other related tactics such as the "hold" can have the effect of delaying and sometimes defeating legislation and nominations. A hold occurs when a senator notifies leadership that he or she is unwilling to agree to unanimous consent to allow some action to take place in the Senate. In effect, it signifies an implied threat to filibuster if necessary. To outside observers the functioning of holds can be mystifying.

UNANIMOUS CONSENT AGREEMENTS

The Senate's rules are difficult to navigate and complicated by the potential for unlimited debate and numerous amendments, some of which have nothing to do with the main legislation. As a result, most business is conducted by circumventing its formal procedures. This is typically done through unanimous consent agreements, known on Capitol Hill as "UCS" or "consent agreements."[1] UCS are an integral part of the Senate's operations and many will be consummated during any given day when the Senate is in session.

It is typically through such agreements that the Senate is able to proceed on many routine matters. Most are negotiated among the leadership, but individual senators routinely propose consent agreements. They are proposed on the Senate floor, and if no objection is heard the chair declares, "So ordered." UCS cover a multitude of matters from a simple request to be the senator recognized next to, for example, complex and lengthy UCS on such matters as scheduling and structuring the debate on a given bill.

On major issues, UCS are often used to establish a fixed time to begin consideration of a measure, to regulate the number of amendments, to set the time for debating each amendment, and, on occasion, to list the specific amendments that will be in order. When time is limited, it is usually equally divided between the parties or, on occasion, allocated to specific senators. When the number of amendments is limited, either an equal number is allotted to each party or specific amendments may be listed. When the Senate proceeds under a UC, it typically imposes a germaneness or "relevancy" requirement.[2] Once agreed upon, a UC can only be changed by a subsequent UC.

A legislative body that relies on the unanimous agreement of all of its members yields great power to each. If all must agree, it takes only one to delay or even block action. The majority can still proceed, but at the mercy of the filibuster, and a supermajority may be required. On many routine matters, just the time required to invoke cloture and run out the post-cloture debate time makes this an unattractive option that majority leaders tend to avoid.

THE HOLD

Legislative action is further complicated by a Senate custom known as the "hold." The precise origins of holds are not known.[3] The Senate historian traces the hold back at least to Majority Leader Lyndon Johnson (D-TX),[4] and political scientist Gregory Koger says that the earliest written reference to a hold in the Senate was in 1958.[5] But we suspect that as a form of senatorial courtesy the practice likely has older roots. Holds probably evolved from the early traditions of comity, courtesy, reciprocity, and accommodation that characterized the Senate's work.

The 1993 Joint Committee on the Organization of Congress, chaired by Senator David Boren (D-OK) and Congressman Lee Hamilton (D-IN), in its final report described the problem:

> They [holds] are understood to have been an established practice as far back as the 1950s, if not much earlier. As commonly understood, a "hold" is a request from an individual Senator that floor action be delayed to allow a concerned Senator sufficient time to prepare his arguments, amendments, or other tactics. Holds are premised on the recognition that any Senator could object to a unanimous consent request to proceed to the consideration of a measure on the calendar. Rather than to precipitate avoidable debate on a motion to proceed . . . or to escalate controversy by encouraging the leadership to use a non-debatable motion in the morning hour, holds evolved as a reasonable accommodation to the conflicting needs of Senators. However, the hold process now allows Senators of both parties to attempt to delay floor action for relatively inconsequential reasons. The resultant "powder-puff" filibuster allows opponents to delay a bill without imposing any of the pressures or costs associated with a formal, public process of extended debate under the formal rules of the Senate.[6]

Holds do not appear anywhere in the Senate's rules. A senator (or sometimes a member of the senator's staff) notifies the leadership that he or she needs a delay in the consideration of a legislative matter or a nomination. Holds are supposed to be in the form of a letter to the leader, but in practice they are often communicated orally. They can be devastatingly effective. As the Congressional Research Service (CRS) puts it, "They are a potential blocking device because they are linked to the Senate's tradition of extended debate and unanimous consent agreements. Party leaders understand that to ignore holds could precipitate objections to unanimous consent requests and filibusters. Unlike filibusters, which may be partly educational in their purpose and which are televised nationally over C-SPAN, holds require no public utterance. Not surprisingly, holds are sometimes referred to as a 'silent filibuster.'"[7]

They can be public or secret depending on the strategic intent. Most holds are not anonymous. For example, if a senator's purpose for holding a bill is to get its authors to negotiate and compromise, the hold needs to be public so that the authors know with whom to negotiate. Such holds are sometimes referred to amusingly as "Mae West holds," the idea being that the senator imposing the hold is saying to the author of the bill or amendment, "Come up and see me sometime."

Some holds are intended to kill a bill or amendment or to permanently block a nominee. These are sometimes referred to as "choke holds." If the intent is to kill or delay, it is sometimes more advantageous to keep one's role hidden. The unspoken rule is that the leadership will not divulge the identity of the anonymous senator who has put the hold on the bill or the nomination.

The full meaning of holds is somewhat elusive even to senators themselves. The meaning can be in the "eye of the beholder." Some senators see a hold not so much as a threat to filibuster but as a request to be consulted before a bill moves forward in the legislative process, particularly before it is brought up on the floor. This can be a legitimate and important reason for a hold—that is, to slow a bill or nomination down to provide time to work out minor issues, even large ones on occasion, or to prepare amendments. "Holds are good government," says Senator Jeff Sessions (R-AL).[8] Former senator John Sununu (R-NH) has argued that "reformers fall back on clichés by throwing around scary phrases like 'secret hold.' The facts are more mundane ... Objecting on someone's behalf is simply an extension of professional courtesy."[9]

However, the difference between the "request for consultation" and "the threat of a filibuster" is often merely rhetorical. Intent becomes the controlling factor. Political scientist Larry Evans points out that "holds often are bargaining tactics and the content of a hold request will vary depending on the bargaining context."[10] The range of intents can vary all the way from attempting to kill the bill or nomination to simply wanting to be kept in the loop.

HOLDS ON NOMINATIONS

On occasion, holds, particularly on executive branch nominees, are used to take "hostages" in order to cause another action to take place. For example, a senator who wants to pressure the State Department to take a particular action may place a hold on all State Department nominations until that senator is satisfied on the matter. Sometimes it is a matter of documents being sought, sometimes a particular action by the department. Barbara Sinclair cites the interesting example of President Clinton's 1999 nomination of Richard Holbrooke to be the U.S. ambassador to the UN.[11] While Senator Chuck Grassley (R-IA) was not hiding the fact that he had no problem with Holbrooke's nomination, he was trying to pressure Secretary of State Madeline Albright to rescind the disciplining of a State Department "whistle-blower" whom Grassley wanted to protect.[12] Weeks later, Walter Pincus, writing in the *Washington Post*, revealed that two other senators had an "anonymous hold" on the Holbrooke nomination and quoted a source who identified the senators as Trent Lott (R-MS) and Mitch McConnell (R-KY). The two were apparently holding the nomination hostage for a different purpose: they were trying to pressure President Clinton to name their preferred candidate to the Federal Election Commission.[13]

INCREASING USE OF HOLDS

In the era of hyper-partisan polarization in the Senate, the use of holds as a tactic to block action, like other filibuster-related maneuvers, has exploded. The Brookings Institution's Senate expert Thomas Mann has noted that "not that long ago it was rare that nominees would linger . . . On Memorial Day 2002, during George W. Bush's administration, 13 nominations were pending on the Executive Calendar. Eight years later, under Obama, the number was 108."[14] A report by the Center for American Progress concludes that "the gap between the number of nominations and number of confirmations was larger for the Obama administration than any previous administration after one year. President Obama had . . . 64 pending. There were 46 nominations pending at the end of President George W. Bush's first year and 29 pending at the end of President Clinton's."[15]

The current levels of use and the purposes to which holds are being put, much like the filibuster from which it gains its leverage, can only be described as abusive. Even a leader like Senator Tom Daschle complained, "There are holds on holds on holds. There are so many holds, it looks like a mud wrestling match."[16] On the other side of the aisle, Republican leader Lott agreed: "The Senate in my judgment [has] become increasingly dysfunctional . . . The hold was originally created to signal a senator's special interest in being completely involved in discussions about the individual or piece of legislation. Now, the hold sends a different message. It says: 'Look, I'm blocking this nominee or this bill, and if you try to call my bluff, I'm going to filibuster.'"[17]

WHO'S BLOCKING WHOM?

As the Senate's party caucuses have become increasingly polarized over the past 30 years, they have become more homogenous and ideological. As a result, party message often trumps a genuine effort to legislate. As Larry Evans and CRS's Walter Oleszek have pointed out, the increasing use of modern message strategies means that senators are often seeking "to structure floor action to dramatize proposals that reflect their own party messages, and to restrict the ability of the opposition party to advance its own message via roll calls and amendments."[18]

It can be difficult for outside observers to be certain whether progress is being obstructed by minority tactics or the majority's efforts to prevent the minority from even offering amendments and getting votes on their issues. During the closing weeks of the 110th Congress, Republicans were first holding and then filibustering the Defense authorization bill containing the repeal of the "Don't Ask, Don't Tell" (DADT) policy regarding the service of gays in the military.

Democrats accused the minority of blocking the overall bill from even being taken up and discussed because they lacked the votes to strip the DADT language that they opposed from the bill. But a crucial swing vote on bringing the bill up in the Senate, Republican moderate senator Susan Collins (R-ME), declared, "Society has changed so much since 1993 and we need to change this policy as well. But I cannot vote to proceed to this bill under a situation that is going to shut down the debate and preclude Republican amendments. That too is not fair."[19] The implication was that she feared that Majority Leader Reid would employ the parliamentary maneuver of "filling the amendment tree" (see chapter 8) to preclude Republican issue amendments that Democrats did not want to deal with just weeks before the election.

Left unclear in the DADT maneuvering was whether this important national decision profoundly affecting the nation's gay community and its military forces was blocked by minority holds and filibuster tactics or by plans (which he denied) by the majority leader to fill the amendment tree and thus preclude Republican amendments. But blocked it was. A cloture vote on the motion to proceed to the bill failed 56–43.[20] In the end, the majority was able to cap a very productive 111th Congress with a very successful lame-duck session, including a cloture vote on the repeal of DADT, decoupled from the Defense bill, invoked by a 63–33 vote with the support of six Republican senators.[21]

SECRET HOLDS

Much of the criticism and controversy surrounding the filibuster has focused on the practice of allowing holds on nominations and legislation to be placed anonymously. Leaders of both parties protect members of their caucus from criticism for delaying tactics by permitting so-called "secret holds." This informal practice has over the years hardened into a firm expectation that a senator may place a hold anonymously.

Senator Ron Wyden (D-OR), who along with Senator Charles Grassley (R-IA) has fought anonymous holds since 1997, says, "A secret hold is a thorough violation of the public's right to know . . . There isn't any accountability."[22] Senator Grassley adds, "I don't believe there is any legitimate reason why a single senator should be able to anonymously block a bill or nomination. If a senator has the guts to place a hold, they ought to have the guts to say who they are and why they have a hold."[23] In one instance in 2001, an anonymous hold on a bill he wrote so enraged the late senator Paul Wellstone that he retaliated by placing holds on any legislation filed by a Republican. He declared, "I would like to know which brave Senator has put an anonymous hold on this bill . . . These anonymous holds drive me up a wall. I have never put an anonymous hold on a bill—never."[24]

Senators Grassley and Wyden are apparently not opposed to holds if they are not secret. They have argued for transparency and accountability. With no intent to keep them secret, they have each, in the past, used a senator's prerogative to place holds. We mentioned Senator Grassley's hold on Richard Holbrooke's nomination. Barbara Sinclair cites a 1997 hold placed by Senator Wyden against a nomination by a president of his own party. Senator Wyden placed a hold on the Clinton nomination of General Henry Shelton to be chairman of the Joint Chiefs. The hold was successful in convincing the Department of Defense to reopen an investigation into a military plane crash involving the death of a constituent of the Oregon senator.[25]

In 2007, Congress passed and President Bush signed an ethics law, the Honest Leadership and Open Government Act, that contained a section intended to regulate anonymous holds in the Senate. The provision created a new section of the Senate calendar to identify those senators who had filed "an intent to object"—in other words, placed a hold against the consideration of a matter. If, and only if, a unanimous consent request to proceed to the matter was raised and objected to would the provision be triggered. At that point, a 6-day clock begins ticking. After 6 days have elapsed, the senator who objected to the UC is obligated to have his or her name listed in the special section of the calendar, in effect notifying the public of the hold. In this way, the hold would obviously no longer be anonymous.

The provision never had a realistic chance of success. After all, it was always within the power of the majority leader, if he chose, to force the issue by going to the floor and offering a UC or a motion to proceed. This would require the senator with the hold to come to the floor to object or to, in effect, stand aside. Moreover, the intended impact of the new provision was easily avoided. Senators interested in placing a secret hold on a nominee or a piece of legislation could exercise "rolling holds."

Several senators acting in tandem could place anonymous holds, each taking care to remove the hold before the 6-day clock expired. Another senator's hold would then take its place.[26]

Despite the well-publicized abuses of the hold, as with the filibuster, the Senate tradition of recognizing and honoring holds has its appropriate role. Holds are valuable to majority leaders. They provide information. The process of "clearing" unanimous consent agreements provides the leadership with an early warning system. Larry Evans has made the point that "with a hold, a Senator is signaling to the leadership that he or she may object to a unanimous consent request, enabling the leadership to orchestrate the discussions and adjustments necessary to facilitate the legislative process. Sometimes it may be in the interest of the holder and the leadership not to share this information with other Senators."[27]

ADDRESSING ABUSE

The large number of nominations that have been subject to Senate holds in recent years has created frustration among legislators and the public. It is undeniable that they hamper the president's ability to staff the executive branch properly and have created difficulties in filling the federal bench. Perhaps least defensible have been the sweeping "blanket" holds applied to nominations (and sometimes to legislation). For example, in 2010, Senator Richard Shelby (R-AL) placed a blanket hold on all executive nominations on the Senate calendar. More than seventy nominations were said to be affected. Senator Shelby who was seeking to have an air force tanker built by a contractor located in Mobile, Alabama, was unhappy with the Defense Department's handling of the matter.[28]

As with the cloture rule, it is important to resist the easy conclusion that the problem can be simply addressed by sweeping away the practice. Of course, it is not a healthy development that the president's ability to staff his government is retarded by holds in the Senate often unrelated to the nominees themselves. In most circumstances secret holds are unwarranted. As a general rule, transparency and accountability would address much of the abuse. Sunlight is the best disinfectant.

While the Senate has attempted to legislate an end to anonymous holds, the most straightforward reform, as Evans writes, would be for both parties' leadership to "refuse to keep the information private. And the best way to ensure that holds placed by individual senators do not derail legislation or nominations supported by a wide majority is for the leadership simply to call these bluffs and bring such matters to the floor."[29]

The Senate at the start of the 112th Congress also addressed this problem with an agreement between the majority and the minority to reduce the number of nominations that will be subject to Senate confirmation. Senator Jack Reed (D-RI), a thoughtful and practical member of the Senate, strongly advocates changing the rules to reduce the number of nominations subject to unlimited debate. While supporting allowing filibusters on major cabinet positions and ambassadors, for example, he argues, "You can reduce the range of executive appointments that are subject to cloture rules significantly . . . Elections have consequences. The president won. The president should have his team."[30]

Requiring that holds be transparent, making the motion to proceed non-debatable, and reducing the number of positions in the executive branch subject to filibuster would eliminate some holds and lessen the frustration caused by holds. On the other hand, such steps are not complete solutions. The majority leader, even now, has the right, under the rules, to proceed to any nomination on the Senate's Executive Calendar. This means that no one can filibuster the step necessary to bring up a nomination for debate. Nonetheless, because so many confirmations are necessary, most must be accomplished by unanimous consent, and in these cases, the time required to get cloture on the confirmation vote keeps majority leaders from "calling the bluff" of senators holding nominations. The same would be true of routine legislative matters, even if the motion to proceed to them were no longer debatable.

In the end, the solution is much more straightforward. Holds cannot be abused if the leaders will not cooperate. There is no Senate rule enforcing a hold. For it to have effect, the majority leader must be willing to accept and honor that privilege. Senators can and should insist that holds be public and that their leaders impose limits on how long they will be honored. Unless the Senate leadership is willing to crack down on the practice of holds, and unless senators return to greater self-restraint in the exercise of their power to insist on holds (as naïve as that may sound), rules changes in this area are unlikely to help. There will be a way around the rule. A hold can be, and sometimes is, but a wink and a nod.

★ ★ ★

EIGHT

Related Tactics

Filling the Amendment Tree

"Filling the amendment tree" is the colloquial way of describing the situation in which all amendments to a piece of legislation that are possible at a given time under the Senate rules have been offered and are pending. The name comes from the diagrams[1] that Senate Parliamentarian Floyd Riddick drew to depict the possible amendments that could be pending simultaneously, depending on the parliamentary circumstance, and the sequence in which votes upon them would be held. Since the diagram showed multiple "branches" representing amendments, the overall appearance was that of an "amendment tree." Filling all of the branches of the tree blocks any additional amendments until one of the amendments has been disposed of or unanimous consent is granted to lay one aside. In the Senate, depending on the details of the particular parliamentary situation at the time, as many as eleven amendments can be simultaneously pending before any are disposed of.

In theory, any senator could accomplish the feat of filling the tree. However, as a practical matter, the majority leader, by virtue of one of his few formal powers—the "right of first recognition"—is the only senator who can offer a series of amendments until the tree is filled. This is because senators lose their right to the floor after offering an amendment. The majority leader alone, because he has the right to be recognized by the presiding officer before any other senator, can be assured of regaining the floor to offer additional amendments.

MAJORITY LEADERS ADOPT THE
TACTIC OF FILLING THE TREE

Beginning in the mid-1980s, as the parties in the Senate became increasingly polarized and ideologically homogenous, majority leaders of both parties, at least partially in response to the growth of politically motivated non-germane amendments, began using the tactic of filling the amendment tree. By doing this, they could control the flow of amendments on a bill on the floor and prevent votes on politically difficult amendments offered by the minority. When combined with the filing of a cloture petition, the majority leader could both attempt to cut off debate and ascertain that no non-germane amendments would be voted upon prior to cloture being invoked. Cloture, under Rule XXII, if invoked, would then preclude non-germane amendments on the bill.

On occasion, a majority leader will fill the tree as a way of completely controlling the flow and timing of amendments, allowing only those that the leader approves for consideration. By asking unanimous consent to lay aside the amendment on the outmost "branch" of the tree, the leader can then allow that amendment to be replaced with whichever amendment is to be considered. At any point, by denying unanimous consent, further amendments can be blocked. In this way, the majority leader becomes the gatekeeper of the amendment process.

Of course, the minority is frequently upset by this tactic and refuses to cooperate by denying unanimous consent for amendments and by launching a filibuster on the bill. It is important to note, however, that filling the amendment tree does not amount to a majority trump card. The majority leader can, using this tactic, potentially seize control and deny any opportunity for the minority to offer amendments to legislation under consideration. But unless the majority leader can muster 60 votes and invoke cloture, he cannot reach final passage on the bill or even reach a vote on any of the pending amendments without the co-operation of the minority. This is why such circumstances often result in off-the-floor negotiations or stalemate. Triggering such negotiations can be the objective of one or both parties. In most cases, presumably, the minority wants to offer its amendments and the majority wants to limit amendments and complete action on the bill.

Walter Oleszek points to a classic case of tree filling during consideration of the 1997 campaign finance reform bill. Republican Majority Leader Trent Lott, locked in a battle with the Clinton administration over a bill he and most Republicans vehemently opposed, filled the tree with virtually identical amendments[2] that were anathema to Democrats' labor allies. Democrats were left in the politically difficult position of being forced to filibuster on a bill that they supported in order to avoid allowing the majority to vote on the anti-labor legislation blocking the amendment tree.[3]

At times the tactic of filling the tree leads to a successful outcome for the leader. Political scientist Barbara Sinclair cites an instance in which Majority Leader Bill Frist employed the filling of the amendment tree "on a gunmaker liability bill in 2005. The bill had the support of more than sixty senators, but in the previous Congress Democratic opponents had blocked it by offering 'killer' amendments—ones that passed but were anathema to the bill's strongest supporters. By filling the amendment tree, Frist rendered that tactic impossible."[4]

Sinclair also describes another successful use, when "in early 2007 [Majority Leader Harry] Reid filled the amendment tree on the continuing resolution (CR) necessary because Republicans had not passed most of the appropriations bills for fiscal year 2007. He then filed for cloture, a vote which Democrats won. The result was that the continuing resolution passed the Senate quickly and in a form identical to the House measure. Reid was able to succeed with such aggressive tactics because the resolution was must-pass legislation, the deadline was imminent, and Republicans were leery about calling attention to their own dereliction."[5]

UNDERSTANDING THE TANGLED TACTICS

Tree-filling tactics often arise in highly ambiguous parliamentary circumstances in which the minority is objecting to any unanimous consent agreement limiting amendments and may or may not be negotiating in good faith to accomplish such a UC. The situation can be unclear because this may be an undeclared filibuster, or the minority may simply be delaying progress on a bill or angling for a favorable UC that permits a large number of minority amendments. While in the eyes of the majority this may be perceived as a filibuster or an effort to obstruct, the minority may be simply responding to the majority leader filling the tree and blocking their ability to offer the amendments that they want to propose. In response, they may oppose cloture on the grounds that they are simply protecting their right to amend.

To the outside observer, whether media analyst, political scientist, or voter, this might well be a "chicken or egg" situation, difficult or impossible to unravel. Senate Historian Don Ritchie tells the story of one senator seeking to interest the media in the issue of abusive tree filling: "reporters in the press gallery had to advise him that no story was likely to appear because 'it couldn't be explained to anybody beyond the Beltway.'"[6]

In May of 1996, an extended exchange on the Senate floor highlighted the lack of media understanding of or interest in such complex but important procedural issues. Democrats complained bitterly about the practice of tree filling by Republican Majority Leader Bob Dole. Senator Byron Dorgan (D-ND) opened the attack on the Senate floor: "Is it not the case that in a couple of recent occasions, just in recent weeks, we have seen legislation . . . in the Senate and a cloture motion filed on the bill . . . before the Senate before debate began on the legislation? In other words, a motion to shut off debate before debate began on two pieces of legislation in the last several weeks; is that not the case?"[7] Minority Leader Tom Daschle (D-SD), entering the colloquy with Senator Dorgan, replied: "The Senator is absolutely correct. A bill . . . is proposed; the amendment tree is completely filled; and cloture is filed. It is a pattern now that has been the practice here for the last several weeks."[8] Senator

Dorgan added: "It is hardly stalling to suggest there ought to be some debate on legislation. Filing a cloture motion to cut off debate before debate begins is apparently a new way to legislate but not, in my judgment, a very thoughtful way to legislate."[9]

Later, Majority Leader Dole defended himself: "We will have a cloture vote . . . on Friday, if not before. If there are amendments, we always try to accommodate our colleagues. I learned about how you introduce and file cloture by . . . the former majority leader, Senator Mitchell. I thought it was very effective. I made notes at that time."[10] Majority Leader Dole continued his defense: "We do not have it down to the art he had it down to, but we want to tell the press how to spell 'gridlock,' [a word] they used extensively when we were in the minority. You never see the word . . . This is Democratic gridlock, because the labor bosses do not want this to happen."[11]

Minority Leader Daschle replied: "This is unnecessary gridlock. This has nothing to do with the Democratic minority. This has everything to do with Republicans simply not allowing the Senate to be the Senate. I do not recall a time—and we can go back and check—when my predecessor, Senator Mitchell, filled the tree every single time a bill was presented on the floor. I would like to go back and find that time in the last Congress when that happened . . . We have different views about what happened in the last Congress."[12] Senator Daschle then issued a threat that has been apparently carried out by successive majority leaders, resulting in an escalation in the use of filling the tree: "I will tell my colleagues on the other side, we are taking notes, and should we have the opportunity again—and I know we will—to be in the majority, what goes around comes around."[13]

Senator Dorgan reentered the debate: "Having listened . . . to the presentation by [Senator Dole] . . . that complained that there was stalling and gridlock in the Senate, first, and then a second presentation that concluded with a cloture motion being filed to shut off debate on something where debate has not yet started, I guess the presumption is that we are pieces of furniture on this side of the aisle, we are not living, contributing Senators that are interested in legislation. But we are more than furniture. We have a passionate agenda that we care deeply about

... I am confused by someone who alleges that there is stalling and then files a cloture motion to shut off debate before debate begins. What on Earth kind of process is this? It does not make any sense."[14] Once again addressing Senator Daschle, Senator Dorgan asks rhetorically whether the circumstance is unusual: "The majority leader ... offer[s] a proposition to fill up the tree so that no one else can intervene with amendments and then claim somehow that somebody else is causing their problems. Is it not true they are causing their own problems? ... We have these parliamentary games and then ... pointing across the aisle to say, 'By the way, you're the cause of this.' Apparently, it is a new way to run the Senate."[15]

A more recent case with the Democrats now in charge occurred in September 2010. As we mentioned in the last chapter, Senator Susan Collins (R-ME), the necessary swing vote, refused to vote to permit the Defense authorization bill to come to the Senate floor for consideration even though she maintained that she supported it. She declared: "What concerns me ... is the practice of filling the amendment tree to prevent Republican amendments. If that is done on this bill, it would be the 40th time [in the 111th Congress (2009–2010)]."[16]

Armed Services Committee Chairman Carl Levin (D-MI) replied to Senator Collins: "The Senator from Maine, as far as I am concerned, has raised a very legitimate question about whether amendments will be offerable to this bill, and the majority leader has spoken on that on the Record. This is what he ... said: '... in addition to issues I have talked about in the last couple days, there are many other important matters that both sides of the aisle wish to address. I am willing to work with Republicans on a process that will permit the Senate to consider these matters and complete the bill as soon as possible.'"[17]

The majority leader was promising to allow Republican amendments. With the partisan heat turned up high, Senator Levin pointed out that Republicans needn't take Senator Reid at his word since once they ended their filibuster on the motion to proceed to the defense bill, if the majority leader didn't keep his word, the Republicans could simply filibuster the bill itself. Emphasizing that the majority leader was promising not to immediately fill the amendment tree, Senator Levin continued: "I think many Senators have amendments they want to offer. It is not unusual on a Defense authorization bill. We usually have hundreds of amendments that are offered. Last year, I believe we adopted something like 60 amendments. That process will again occur but only if we can get to the bill. To insist in advance there be an agreement, let me tell you, as manager of the bill, I love unanimous consent agreements. I love time limits. I love time agreements. I love agreements to limit amendments. That is fine. But until you get to the bill, you are not in a position to work out such agreements."[18]

Republicans, led by Senator John McCain of Arizona, the ranking Republican on the Armed Services Committee, which had reported the bill, did not back off of their filibuster, continuing to assert that they were being denied the opportunity to offer amendments: "This majority leader has filled up the tree and has not allowed debate 40 times—40 times—more than all the other majority leaders preceding him . . . Last year, the hate crimes bill was arranged in such a way that there were not amendments that could be proposed by my side of the aisle. So let's vote against cloture."[19]

The cloture vote on the motion to proceed failed, 56–43. Observers are left to puzzle out whether Republicans were raising a smoke screen to justify their filibuster and an unwillingness to vote on the "Don't Ask, Don't Tell" repeal or whether it was Democrats trying to maneuver Republicans, just weeks before an election, into voting on a bill with provisions they did not support but which by virtue of a filled amendment tree they would not have the opportunity to change.

INCREASED USE OF THE TACTIC

As with filibusters and holds, the practice of filling the tree has been increasing in recent years. Beginning with the 99th Congress in 1985–1986, when Majority Leader Bob Dole (R-KS) filled the tree on five occasions, Majority Leader Robert Byrd followed suit three times in the 100th Congress. Majority Leader George Mitchell, during his three Congresses leading the Democratic majority in the Senate, filled the tree ten times. The Republicans, led by Majority Leader Trent Lott, answered by using the ploy seventeen times over the next 6 years. Republican Bill Frist used it another twelve times in the 108th and 109th Congresses. Then Senate Majority Leader Harry Reid blew the top off the record with sixteen uses of the tactic in the 110th Congress in 2007–2008.[20] According to the Congressional Research Service, Senator Reid filled the tree a total of forty-four times through the end of the 111th Congress.[21]

In most circumstances when the tree-filling maneuver is used by a majority leader, the minority objects and, on occasion, is enraged. Senator Chuck Grassley (R-IA), on September 15, 2010, bitterly complained about Majority Leader Reid having filled the tree on the Small Business Jobs and Credit Act, which had been enmeshed in both parties' messaging efforts leading up to the 2010 congressional elections only weeks away:

> The tax provisions included in the Senate small business package provide real relief to small businesses. They generally have the support from Members on both sides of the aisle. In fact, you would have thought this small business bill would have been a slam dunk. However, the Democratic leadership has used the small business bill as a political football, scoring political points. The majority leader refused to allow the small business bill to be considered under regular order. The majority leader filled the amendment tree, thereby limiting amendments that could be offered. The Democratic leadership and the administration then proceeded to blame Republicans for blocking relief for small business.[22]

Senator John Thune (R-SD), in the previous Congress, on November 15, 2007, similarly objected to Majority Leader Reid's tactics, this time on the farm bill:

> In many cases a farm bill reflects regional priorities. Different people around the country look at these issues very differently . . . a number of amendments were filed, some 200-plus, almost 300 amendments. But what happened very early on in that process was the leader, the majority leader [filled the amendment tree] . . . The leader . . . now has precluded the opportunity for other Members of the Senate . . . to be able to come down and offer amendments they think would ultimately improve the bill.[23]

Senator Thune continued:

What is significant about that is it is not unprecedented. It has been done. They said it was done when the Republicans controlled the Senate. I am sure it was—I do not believe very successfully because I do not think it is a tactic or a procedure that lends itself to the nature of this institution or how it works. The Senate is unique in all the world. It is the world's greatest deliberative body. We really value the opportunity to come and amend the bill that is brought to the floor of the Senate, which is generally open to amendment. So when the tree gets filled and amendments are blocked from consideration, it essentially shuts down the process that the Senate normally uses to consider and amend bills and ultimately vote on bills . . . We have not had one vote on an amendment to the farm bill after now having it on the floor for almost two weeks . . . on a piece of legislation that is 1,600 pages long and spends 280 billion tax dollars over the next five years. Not one amendment has been voted on.[24]

As with other filibuster-related parliamentary maneuvers in the Senate, the role of plaintiff and defendant shifts back and forth depending on which party wields the gavel. We have quoted Republican Senators Thune and Grassley as the "injured parties" in the Democratic 110th and 111th Congress, respectively. Majority Leader Reid was framed as the culprit. In the 109th Congress, with a Republican Senate majority, the roles were reversed. Senator Chris Dodd (D-CT) objected to the strong-arm tactics of Majority Leader Bill Frist (D-TN) on legislation to build a fence on the U.S.-Mexico border:

This Senate has had no opportunity to debate and amend the bill before us today. There are some very important amendments that our colleagues would have liked to offer which now they cannot. Those who do not understand Senate procedure might ask, how could that be possible? . . . Let me explain. The Senate majority leader has, as is his right, used Senate procedures to block Senators from offering or voting on amendments. He has done what is called filling the amendment tree. Until the Senate voted last night to limit debate on this legislation, no vote was taken on any amendment to this bill. Now that cloture has been invoked, many otherwise pertinent and important amendments are no longer in order to this bill.[25]

Senator Dodd concluded: "Unfortunately, that has been the pattern of conduct with respect to this legislation and others in this Congress

... That is not the way this Senate ordinarily does business, and it is certainly not the best way to address legislation that is supposed to be improving our Nation's security."[26]

One senator proposed a change in the rules to strip majority leaders of the ability to fill the amendment tree. Pennsylvania Senator Arlen Specter,[27] during the Senate debate on February 7, 2007, on the motion to proceed to a bill to disagree with President Bush's then-pending proposal to send more than 21,000 additional U.S. troops to fight in the Iraq War, objected to Democratic tactics to thwart Republican amendments:

> What is happening is largely misunderstood . . . before debate even began, the majority leader[28] filed a motion for cloture, which means to cut off debate. Now, a cloture motion would be in order, but why before the debate has even started? The cloture motion is designed to cut off debate after debate has gone on too long. But what lies behind the current procedural status is an effort by the majority leader to do what is called filling the tree, which is a largely misunderstood concept, not understood fully by many Members of this body. But the Senate is unique from the House, and the Senate has been billed as the world's greatest deliberative body, because Senators have the right to offer amendments.[29]

Contrasting the Senate with the majoritarian House, Senator Specter continued:

> In the House of Representatives they established what is called a rule, and they preclude Members from offering amendments unless it satisfied the Rules Committee. In the Senate, generally a Senator doesn't have to satisfy anybody except his or her own conscience in offering an amendment. But if the majority leader, who has the right of recognition . . . is on the floor and seeks recognition, he gets it ahead of everybody else. And if the majority leader offers what is called a first-degree amendment to the bill, which is substantively identical to the bill but only a technical change, and then again seeks recognition and gets it and offers a second-degree amendment to the bill, which is substantively the same but only a technical change, then no other Senator may offer any additional amendment. That is a practice

which has been engaged in consistently by both parties for decades, under-cutting the basic approach of the Senate, which enables Senators to offer amendments and get votes.[30]

Continuing, Senator Specter said:

> Now, what is happening today is that charges are being leveled on all sides. There has been a lot of finger-pointing with most of the Democrats saying the Republicans are obstructing a vote—a debate and a vote on the Iraqi resolutions. And Republicans are saying: Well, we are insisting on our right to debate the motion to proceed. We don't think you should file cloture before the debate even starts, to cut off debate before you have debate, but the reason we are doing it is so this procedural device may not be used on what is called in common parlance to "fill the tree."[31]

He pointed to the opposition to cloture by Senator John Warner (R-VA), co-author of the Warner-Levin resolution and opponent of President Bush's plan, as evidence that the Republican filibuster was not aimed at defeating the legislation but at thwarting the majority leader's tactic. Senator Specter concluded:

> It would be my hope there would be a truce. Let me say candidly that I think there is very little chance there is going to be a truce in the Senate on using this procedural rule. It has been used on both sides. It has been used by Democrats and Republicans when it suits the partisan advantage of one party or another, and suiting the partisan party advantage of one party or another is not consistent with sound public policy and the public interest.[32]

The next day, Senator Specter returned to the Senate floor to intro-duce a proposed rules change to reform the practice of filling the amend-ment tree, S Res. 83, which simply stated: "Notwithstanding action on a first degree amendment, it shall not be in order for a Senator to offer a second degree amendment to his or her own first degree amendment."[33] Senator Specter declared, "It is not understood in America what is hap-pening because it is arcane, it is esoteric, it is unintelligible—they can't figure it out . . . But this procedure of allowing the majority leader to stop alternative considerations is inappropriate and unfair."[34]

Most senators' views of the appropriateness of given procedural tac-tics are colored by the situation in which they find themselves. For most, the rules and precedents are a means to an end and the shift from the minority to the majority or vice versa can profoundly change the perception of those means. In this instance, Senator Specter aptly made the point by using Majority Leader Reid's own words against him, quoting him from a year earlier when Democrats were in the minority and seeking to amend the Patriot Act reauthorization. On that occasion, Senator Reid, the minority leader in the 108th Congress, declared:

> I will vote against cloture to register my objection to the procedural maneuver under which Senators have been blocked from offering any amendments to this bill. While I will vote against cloture, I nonetheless support the underlying bill . . . which improves the Patriot Act. . . . I support the Patriot Act. I voted for it in 2001 . . . Of course even a good bill can be improved. That is why we have an amendment process in the Senate . . . [Senator Feingold] has tried to offer a small number of relevant amendments that I believe would make this bill even better. I am disappointed that he has been denied that opportunity by a procedural maneuver known as "filling the amendment tree."[35]

Senator Reid concluded:

> This is a very bad practice. It runs against the basic nature of the Senate. The hallmark of the Senate is free speech and open debate. Rule XXII establishes a process for cutting off debate and amendments, but Rule XXII should rarely be invoked before any amendments have been offered. There is no reason to truncate Senate debate on this important bill in this unusual fashion. I will vote against cloture to register my objection to this flawed process.[36]

Senator Specter's proposal to eliminate the majority leader's tree-filling tool failed to attract much support in the Senate. Senate rules expert Norman Ornstein, testifying before the Senate Rules Committee, suggested a more moderate approach than Specter's, one that we think has merit. He acknowledged the "justifiable frustration" that minorities feel when confronted with a loaded amendment tree, but noted: "There is no simple answer here, but I do want to note that while some of the filibusters in recent months have clearly been in response to the premature use of the amendment tree by the majority leader, there are way too many instances of delay tactics used on measures or nominees that achieved unanimous or near unanimous support, with the multiple filibusters and full exercise of the thirty hours post-cloture that had nothing to do with real minority grievances and everything to do with using up more of the Senate's precious time."[37]

As in many of the cases we have cited, it can be difficult even for the participants to sort out who is doing what to whom. With partisan passions frequently ramped up and, in recent years, with mutual mistrust oftentimes supplanting "senatorial courtesy," these collisions are increasingly common and marked by both sides believing that they are in the right and the aggrieved party. But, as Ornstein told the Rules Committee, there is "no excuse for avoiding the real issue about overuse and misuse of the amendment tree."[38] Ornstein went on to suggest to the committee: "One approach is to have a new, nondebatable motion to set aside a filled amendment tree and allow, by a simple majority vote, a single amendment from the minority to be called up and debated. The majority could of course still offer a motion to table; ideally, the rules would allow some debate on the amendment before the motion to table."[39]

This is a rational approach that stops short of robbing the majority leader of the means to protect the majority. To work, it would likely have to be limited to germane amendments, which in the Senate are defined very narrowly. Rampant minority abuse of the amendment process can threaten the majority leader's already limited ability to control the agenda. When a torrent of amendments, germane and non-germane, is aimed solely at obstruction and delay, we believe the majority leader needs recourse. At the same time, it is reasonable to seek a way to protect the right of the minority not to be shut out of the amendment process by abusive majority tactics.

★ ★ ★

NINE

Circumventing the Filibuster
Reconciliation

Senator Lindsey Graham (R-SC) made a brief effort in March 2010 to resurrect the "Gang of 14" senators.[1] This time the tactic to be averted was the use of the budget reconciliation process to enact President Obama's health reform bill with a simple majority vote of fifty-one senators rather than the 60 votes needed to invoke cloture and block a filibuster. Graham noted, "Many Republicans who were ready to pull the trigger on the nuclear option on judges are now glad they didn't. This place would have ceased to function as we know it. If they do health care through reconciliation, it will be the same consequence. So if you are a moderate Democrat out there looking for a way to deliver health care reforms and not pull the nuclear trigger, there is a model to look at."[2]

Of course, no "Gang of 14" rode to the rescue and Democrats did use the reconciliation process to facilitate their passage of a broad health reform bill. Unlike the early proposals that some Democrats were making in 2009 to resort to reconciliation to circumvent any filibuster and pass the whole massive health reform bill, reconciliation was used in a more modest manner. It was deployed largely to make budgetary adjustments to the massive bill that had been passed in the previous December with 60 votes in the Senate. Nonetheless Republicans were outraged.

But Republican outrage over the tactic was short-lived. After the passage of health reform was completed, by February 2011, the "brain" of the Bush White House, Republican strategist Karl Rove, writing in the *Wall Street Journal,* argued that reconciliation could be used to repeal what he called "ObamaCare": "Democrats harp on the 60-vote threshold and ignore the reconciliation option because they want Americans to accept the inevitability of ObamaCare. But its roots are clearly in shallow soil."[3]

THE GROWTH IN THE USE OF RECONCILIATION
BEYOND ITS ORIGINAL PURPOSE

The health reform bill was the twenty-fourth time reconciliation had been used since 1980, the eighth with Democrats in control of the Senate. Where did this process come from? Why was it used? And what was the source of the outrage?

In 1974, in response to the combination of growing deficits, President Nixon's refusal to spend money appropriated by Congress, and the Watergate scandal, Congress enacted the Congressional Budget and Impoundment Control Act. This imposed on Congress the requirement that it pass an annual concurrent budget resolution to serve as the blueprint for shaping that year's budget policy. The president does not sign the resolution and it does not become law. It is strictly a congressional blueprint and binds only Congress.

In order to facilitate the yearly passage of the budget resolution, it was established with a fast-track process, referred to as "expedited procedures." These procedures have some significant impact on the House of Representatives, but their real effect is on the Senate. Since the expedited procedures limit debate to 50 hours, there is no need for the Rule XXII provisions to end debate. The budget resolutions come reliably to a vote and can be passed with a simple majority. No filibuster is possible.

At the time, Senators Edmund Muskie (D-ME), Henry Bellmon (R-OK), Robert Byrd (D-WV), and others actively involved in the writing and passage of the 1974 Budget Act[4] fully expected that they were creating an ultimately bipartisan process that would bring rational debate and decision making to the annual enactment of a federal budget. For better or for worse, over the past 30 years or so, as the Senate became increasingly more polarized along partisan lines, and with only a simple majority required under the expedited procedures to fashion the budget blueprint, the budget process became only more partisan with, of course, the majority party controlling the budget resolution.

The 1974 law also set up a second optional procedure known as "budget reconciliation." Budget reconciliation was meant to be used as a minor mechanism at the end of the fiscal year to bring spending legislation passed in the interim into line with the budget resolution that had been passed the previous spring. Since changes would be made to provisions that had been signed into the law, the adjustments contained in the reconciliation bill would also require a presidential signature in order to have the force of law. The reconciliation process was given expedited procedures much like the budget resolution. Debate in the Senate was limited to 20 hours and amendments were limited to those germane in substance to the bill. This book's co-author Dove participated in writing the reconciliation provision and now wistfully admits that if there were anything he could undo in his career, it would be helping to create the reconciliation process in the budget act. The reconciliation provision was included in the act with virtually no discussion or debate. It seems clear that no one anticipated what was to come.

For example, Senator Muskie, one of the principal architects of the budget act and later the first chairman of the Senate Budget Committee, explained on the floor: "The second budget resolution[5] . . . provides Congress with the opportunity to reassess its initial budget and priority decisions . . . If . . . the individual spending measures previously enacted differ from the appropriate levels established in that second budget resolution, the resolution will also direct committees of jurisdiction to recommend the legislative action necessary to reconcile those differences."[6]

Senator Muskie was referring to the inclusion of a reconciliation process in the new budget law. Senator Lee Metcalf (D-MT), another major proponent, added:

[The second budget resolution] would be a "second look" at the economy, at the Nation's needs; and at what Congress had done with respect to spending and revenues since the first budget resolution. If the spending and revenue estimates were within limits set out in the first budget resolution, and there is no need to raise the appropriate deficit or surplus figures, the second budget resolution could merely reaffirm the first budget, and the spending and revenue bills would be enacted as implemented. Chances are that this would be unlikely, since political, economic, and social factors change rapidly and require budgetary adjustments. Thus, in revising the budget . . . Congress would have a range of options . . . The budget committees would assemble the various reported legislation into separate titles of a "reconciliation bill."[7]

What Senators Muskie and Metcalf and the other authors of reconciliation failed to fully consider was the fact that the inclusion of expedited procedures foreclosed the possibility of filibuster and therefore circumvented the normal circumstance in the Senate that 60 votes could be required to end debate. This made use of reconciliation an almost irresistible temptation for the majority party for any number of legislative purposes.

Beginning in 1980, the Congress began to expand the use of reconciliation. Initially it was used to instruct committees to make major policy changes in line with the budget resolution that had been adopted, often by a party-line vote. Over the years that followed, it was increasingly used to avoid the normal slow and deliberate Senate process. The use (and abuse) of reconciliation now made it possible for a partisan majority, acting alone without the minority, to pass sweeping legislation quickly. To make matters worse, the reconciliation process tightly restricted floor amendments with a strict germaneness rule. While the committees were free to pack reconciliation with all sorts of unrelated matters, senators' amendments were constrained during consideration on the floor.

In June 1981, Republican Majority Leader Howard Baker said on the Senate floor that "including such extraneous provisions in a reconciliation bill would be harmful to the character of the Senate. It would cause such material to be considered under time and germaneness provisions that impede the full exercise of minority rights."[8] Majority Leader Baker continued: "It would evade the letter and spirit of Rule XXII [cloture rule]. It would create an unacceptable degree of tension between the budget act and the remainder of Senate procedures and practices. Reconciliation was never meant to be a vehicle for an omnibus authorization bill. To permit it to be treated as such is to break faith with the Senate's historical uniqueness as a forum for the exercise of minority and individual rights."[9]

BIRTH OF THE BYRD RULE

Alarmed by the growing reconciliation loophole in the Senate rules, in 1985, the Senate adopted the Byrd rule to limit extraneous matters in a reconciliation bill, basically prohibiting provisions that do not have a budgetary impact. Unlike other Senate points of order, which act on a measure as a whole, the Byrd rule can be applied to individual provisions within the measure. For most points of order when a bill is found to be in violation, the entire bill falls. In the case of the Byrd rule only the specific provision is dropped from the bill, unless the Senate votes to waive it. Waiving the Byrd rule requires a supermajority of 60 votes. This obviously undermines the use of the expedited procedures to circumvent the supermajority requirement of cloture. Therefore, there is a high premium placed by the majority on avoiding Byrd rule violations.

Beginning with the Clinton administration and even more so during the George W. Bush administration, Congress enacted most major tax bills (and even a major welfare reform bill) using reconciliation, including the $1.7 trillion tax cut in 2001. That was the first time that the deficit was *increased* through reconciliation.

Senator Robert Byrd in February 2001 warned, "Reconciliation is a nonfilibusterable 'bear trap' that should be used very sparingly and, I believe, only for the purposes of fiscal restraint. That was the intention in the beginning. It was not intended to be used as a fast track in order to ram through authorization measures that otherwise might entail long and vigorous debate. In other words, reconciliation should be used only for reducing deficits or for increasing surpluses."[10] Senator Byrd continued: "I believe the [then Republican] majority fully intends to bring the budget to the Senate floor with the President's tax proposal shrouded in this protective armor of reconciliation, virtually shutting out debate and precluding amendments by the full membership of this body."[11] And that's ultimately what occurred both in 2001 and 2003.

The complexities of the rules applying to reconciliation, particularly as affected by the Byrd rule, have placed a heavy burden on the Senate's parliamentarian. Given the increased stakes created by using reconciliation as an end-run around the filibuster for sweeping political agendas of the majority party, the parliamentarian, always the Senate's "umpire," is now called on repeatedly to make the call on repeated collisions at "home plate."

The Byrd rule is also resented by the House of Representatives because it is a Senate procedure that can be used against provisions in the bill that the House favors. In 1993, the chairman of the House Budget Committee, Congressman Martin Sabo (D-MN), complained that "widespread use [of the Byrd rule] this year was extremely destructive and bodes ill for the reconciliation process in the future . . . [T]he use of mechanisms like the Byrd rule greatly distorts the balance of power between the two bodies," and strict enforcement of the Byrd rule "requires that too much power be delegated to unelected employees of the Congress."[12]

VOTE-A-RAMA

Another egregious aspect of the reconciliation process is that while it constrains the amendment process, making it difficult to actually change the bill, it ensures that a vote be provided to every amendment that is filed and called up. When all of the debate time permitted is used up, the Senate then must proceed to vote on any amendments not previously disposed of. This has led repeatedly to the unseemly scene of the Senate voting on large numbers of amendments back to back in what Capitol Hill staffers call the "vote-a-ramas." This entails vote after vote on amendments, some added to the list even as the voting proceeds, without any further debate (the Senate usually allows 1 minute per side by unanimous consent). In 2008, for example, the Senate voted a record forty-four times in a single day. This can hardly be seen as serious legislating.

AVOIDING THE BEAR TRAP

Fast forward to early 2009 and some Democrats were proposing that the massive health reform proposal that was then on the table be passed as a reconciliation bill in order to reduce from 60 to 51 the number of votes needed for passage in the Senate. Senator Robert Byrd, one of the architects of reconciliation in 1974, and the father of the Byrd rule in 1985, consistent with his long-held views about abusing the process to avoid extended debate, said:

> I cannot, and will not, vote to authorize the use of the reconciliation process to expedite passage of health care reform legislation or any other legislative proposal that ought to be debated at length by this body. Using reconciliation to ram through complicated, far-reaching legislation is an abuse of the budget process. The writers of the Budget Act, and I am one, never intended for its reconciliation's expedited procedures to be used this way. These procedures were narrowly tailored for deficit reduction. They were never intended to be used to pass tax cuts or to create new Federal regimes.

Senator Byrd continued:

> Whatever abuses of the budget reconciliation process which have occurred in the past, or however many times the process has been twisted to achieve partisan ends does not justify the egregious violation done to the Senate's Constitutional purpose. The Senate has a unique institutional role. It is the one place in all of government where the rights of the numerical minority are protected. As long as the Senate preserves the right to debate and the right to amend we hold true to our role as the Framers envisioned. We were to be the cooling off place where proposals could be examined carefully and debated extensively, so that flaws might be discovered and changes might be made.

Senator Byrd reminded his own caucus that reconciliation, like many of the tactics we have discussed, including the filibuster and filling the amendment tree, could be wielded against them by the Republicans in a future Congress when the shoe was on the other foot:

Remember, Democrats will not always control this chamber, the House of Representatives or the White House. The worm will turn. Some day the other party will again be in the majority, and we will want minority rights to be shielded from the bear trap of the reconciliation process. Under reconciliation's gag rule there are twenty hours of debate . . . and little or no opportunity to amend. Those restrictions mean that whatever is nailed into reconciliation by the majority will likely emerge as the final product . . . We must not run roughshod over minority views. A minority can be right. An amendment can vastly improve legislation. Debate can expose serious flaws. Ramrodding and railroading have no place when it comes to such matters as our people's healthcare.[13]

Senator Byrd, always first among senators in defense of the traditions of the Senate, was right. Bill Dauster, a longtime Senate staffer, in a wonderful speech referred to reconciliation as "the monster that ate the United States Senate."[14] It has shown its monstrous qualities repeatedly as used by both parties. The result is to damage the glory of the Senate, the ability to debate and amend.

★ ★ ★

TEN

Reforming the Filibuster
The Constitutional Option

The U.S. Senate is a continuing body, meaning that from the seating of the first Senate to the present, and despite election turnover and annual recesses, it has been a single, continuous legislative body. The Constitution establishes a rotation of Senate terms that ensures that in most normal circumstances no more than one-third of the Senate seats are at stake in any given biennial congressional election, while roughly two-thirds of incumbents carry over from one session to the next.[1]

As Richard Beth, a respected authority on Senate rules formerly at the Congressional Research Service, has written, "Even at the beginning of a new Congress . . . before newly elected Senators are sworn in for new terms of office, a quorum of the Senate remains in being, and the body remains capable of functioning and acting. By this criterion, a Senate, with membership sufficient to do business, has been in continuous existence ever since the body first achieved a quorum on April 6, 1789. That the Senate is a 'continuing body' in this sense was explicitly enunciated at least as early as 1841."[2] Beth refers to this as "not a doctrine, but merely a fact."[3] In the view of Beth and others who share, as we do, this perspective, Senate rules continue from Congress to Congress and the Senate cannot end debate and change its rules by majority vote at the beginning of each new session of Congress.

New Mexico's freshman Democratic senator Tom Udall sees it differently. Senator Udall has adopted the view that the Senate has the constitutional right to change its rules at the outset of each session. He bases that assertion on Article I, Section 5 of the Constitution.[4] During the 111th Congress, he offered a resolution stating:

> To enable each newly constituted Senate to carry out its responsibility to determine the Rules of its Proceedings at the beginning of each Congress. Whereas article I, section 5 of the United States Constitution provides that "Each House may determine the Rules of its Proceedings"; Whereas it is a longstanding common law principle, upheld in Supreme Court decisions, that one legislature cannot bind subsequent legislatures; Whereas rule V of the Standing Rules of the Senate states that "the Rules of the Senate shall continue from one Congress to the next unless they are changed as provided in these rules"; Whereas rule XXII of the Standing Rules of the Senate requires an affirmative vote of two-thirds of Senators present and voting to limit debate on a measure or motion to amend the Senate Rules; and Whereas rule V and rule XXII of the Standing Rules of the Senate, taken together, can effectively deny the Senate the opportunity to exercise its constitutional right to determine the Rules of its Proceedings under article I, section 5, thus allowing one Congress to bind its successors: Now, therefore, be it *Resolved,* That upon the expiration of the Standing Rules of the Senate at the Sine Die Adjournment of the 111th Congress, the Senate shall proceed in accordance with article I, section 5 of the Constitution to determine the Rules of its Proceedings by a simple majority vote.[5]

THE CONSTITUTIONAL OPTION HAS A LONG HISTORY

Senator Udall states that his proposal is the "constitutional option." (This is also the name that proponents of the "nuclear option" favored for their approach in 2005, although it was not necessarily tied to the start of a new Congress.) Udall notes in addition to the Article 1, Section 5 language, the Constitution states that a "Majority of each [House] shall constitute a Quorum to do Business." He concludes that "the

Framers provided a means for the Senate, and the House, to consider, by a majority vote, the adoption of rules as the need arose."[6]

This argument is hardly new. In 1951, Walter Reuther, then the president of the United Auto Workers, in a legal brief supporting reform of Rule XXII, suggested that the Senate was not a continuing body and that the tradition was merely "folklore."[7]

A predecessor to Senator Udall in the New Mexico Senate seat, Democratic former senator Clinton P. Anderson, was a longtime proponent of the idea that the Senate's rules could be changed by a simple majority vote at the outset of a new Congress. At the beginning of each Congress in 1953, 1957, and 1959, Senator Anderson attempted to do so. At the outset of the 83rd Congress in 1953, Anderson offered a resolution on the Senate floor that stated, "In accordance with Article I, Section 5 of the Constitution which declares that 'Each House may determine the rules of its proceedings . . . ,' I now move that this body take up for immediate consideration the adoption of rules of the Senate of the Eighty-Third Congress."[8]

As the Senate's parliamentarian from 1964 to 1974, Dr. Floyd Riddick, one of the foremost experts on the Senate's rules, explains:

> The first thing that the proponents for change tried to do, was to establish a basis for change. I don't think there's any question but what most people have always conceded that the Senate was a continuing body, certainly in certain respects. There's always, unless they've died or a catastrophe should occur, two-thirds of the Senate membership duly elected and sworn, because only one-third of the senators go up every two years for reelection. So, for certain purposes, there's never been any question, I don't believe, in anybody's mind, but what the Senate was a continuing body. The proponents for change began to try to differentiate between the Senate as a continuing body in some respects and with regard to changes in the rules. It was argued pro and con that since the bills all die at the end of a Congress you begin a new Congress *de novo,* and therefore it should be in order to change the rules at the beginning of each new Congress, because the Constitution specifically specifies that each house shall make its own rules.[9]

Opening the floor debate, Senate Majority Leader Robert Taft (R-OH), referring back to the Senate's very first filibuster in 1841, which had raised the issue of the Senate as a continuing body, quoted one of his Ohio predecessors, Senator William Allen (D-OH), who had argued: "To the assertion that this was a new Senate . . . There was no such thing as a new Senate known to the Constitution of this Republic. They might as well speak of a new Supreme Court."[10]

In the end, the Anderson resolution was tabled by the Senate on a 70–21 vote.[11] The issue, however, was to rise again and again right up to the present-day Senate. Anderson tried again 4 years later at the beginning of the 85th Congress. This time his motion was tabled by a 55–38 vote in the Senate on January 4, 1957.[12] Yet again, as the 86th Congress began, Senator Anderson tried to convince the Senate that a simple majority could rewrite its rules at the start of a "new" Senate. Once again the Senate rejected Anderson's motion, this time 60–36.[13] This effort, however, led in 1959 to a compromise put forward by Senate Majority Leader Lyndon Johnson. The Senate returned the cloture rule to two-thirds present and voting, thus making it easier to attain. In 1949, 10 years earlier, the Senate had applied Rule XXII to the motion to proceed, thus making it possible to close off debate on the motion to proceed to a bill. But at that time, the Senate had changed the cloture requirement to a two-thirds vote of all senators. Previously, ever since the enactment of Rule XXII in 1917, cloture had required two-thirds of those voting, an easier threshold to attain. Majority Leader Johnson's 1959 compromise returned the cloture rule to two-thirds present and voting. Cloture would henceforth be easier to invoke. Senator Johnson was able to convince the defenders of Rule XXII that they faced a change in that rule designed by liberals if they failed to agree to his compromise.[14]

Senator Tom Udall emphasizes that although these motions were tabled, Senator Anderson gained more support each year. Proponents of the "constitutional option" like to characterize the 1959 compromise as a successful instance of pressure being brought to bear by the credible threat that the idea that rules can be changed by majority vote would be adopted by the Senate. However, the Senate in 1959, as a part of this compromise, addressed the question of itself as a continuing body by adopting a new rule stating that "the rules of the Senate shall continue from one Congress to the next unless they are changed as provided in these rules."[15] This is an explicit declaration that the rules of the Senate continue from one Congress to another and that a two-thirds vote, not just a simple majority, is necessary to change them.

A particularly extensive battle led by Senator George McGovern (D-SD) took place in 1967 at the outset of the 90th Congress. Senator McGovern offered a resolution that stated, "Under Article I, section 5, of the Constitution, which provides that a majority of each House shall constitute a quorum to do business, and each House may determine the rules of its proceedings, I move that debate upon the pending motion to proceed to the consideration of S. Res. 6 be brought to a close."[16] S Res. 6 was a proposal to change the rules to provide for cloture by a vote of three-fifths of senators duly elected and sworn. The Senate sustained a point of order raised by Senator Everett Dirksen, the minority leader, against the McGovern resolution and then by a large margin refused to end debate on the rules change.

Senate Majority Leader Mike Mansfield declared, "We decided by an overwhelming vote that the uniqueness of this body should be maintained; that reflection and deliberation should be assured of all proposals from whatever quarter."[17] Lindsay Rogers, in the introduction to the reprint of his classic *The American Senate,* concluded that "the attempt in the first session of the 90th Congress to amend Rule XXII was a dismal failure."[18]

Senator Tom Udall correctly observes that the cloture rule was further amended in 1975 when Senators Walter Mondale (D-MN) and James Pearson (R-KS) also used an attempt to amend the rules by simple majority at the beginning of a Congress to leverage a compromise rules change. The issue was brought to a head after more than two decades of attempts by the Senate's liberals. In the end, again, the Senate chose to compromise. A compromise resolution offered by then–Majority Whip Senator Robert Byrd (D-WV), supported by the leadership of both parties, reduced the threshold for cloture from two-thirds of senators voting to three-fifths of the whole Senate. As part of the compromise, the requirement for cloture on a change in the rules was kept at two-thirds. Senator Byrd maintained that this change with adjustments made in 1979 and 1985 to curb post-cloture filibusters "has provided a more effective tool in overcoming all but the most determined filibusters carried on by a sizeable minority."[19]

Udall adds the observation that "only three sitting senators—Byrd,[20] Daniel Inouye (D-HI) and Patrick Leahy (D-VT)—were in Congress then. This means that 97 of us have never voted on the rule that has effectively prevented the Senate from acting on hundreds of bills already passed by the House, as well as on scores of presidential appointments."[21]

The issue of the continuity of the Senate and its rules is older than the cloture rule (adopted in 1917) itself. During the 1891 filibuster of the so-called "Force Bill" introduced by Judiciary Committee Chairman Senator George Hoar (R-MA), Senator Nelson Aldrich (R-RI) proposed a cloture rule "permitting any senator, after a matter has been considered 'for a reasonable time,' to demand that debate be closed, after which, only motions to adjourn or recess would be in order."[22]

Senator Francis Cockrell (D-MO), seeking to embarrass Senator Hoar for his support of the cloture proposal, read into the *Congressional Record* an article authored by Hoar published just weeks earlier in *The Youth's Companion*:[23] "The men who framed the Constitution had studied thoroughly all former attempts at republican government. History was strewn with the wrecks of unsuccessful democracies. Sometimes usurpation of the executive power, sometimes the fickleness and unbridled license of the people, had brought popular governments to destruction. To guard against these two dangers they placed their chief hope in the Senate."

Senator Cockrell continued reading, emphasizing that the Senate rules continue from Congress to Congress: "In the first place, they made it a perpetual body . . . [T]he Senate is indestructible. The Senate which was organized in 1789 at the inauguration of the Government abides and will continue to abide, one and the same body, until the Republic itself shall be overthrown or until time shall be no more . . . The Senate . . . alone of all the departments of Government is unchangeable and indestructible by any constitutional process."[24]

The president at the time, Benjamin Harrison, who had previously served in the Senate, later wrote in his book, *This Country of Ours*, published in 1897, "The Senate is always an organized body . . . The rules of the Senate remain in force from one Congress to another, save as they may from time to time be modified."[25]

In 1917, Senator Thomas Walsh (D-MT) argued that the question of whether the rules of the Senate continued from one Congress to another had never been specifically considered by the Senate.[26] Vice President Thomas Marshall, who was presiding at the time, replied: "I do not want any misconceptions about this matter. One thing particularly is clear, and I think everyone will agree upon it. The Vice President of the United States as the Presiding Officer of this body has absolutely nothing to do with making the rules. It is not any of his business what they are. The question whether there are or are not rules . . . [is a question] for the Senate and it makes no difference what opinion I express, the Senate will settle it, and will settle it without any regard whatever to what my views are."[27]

Senator Walsh offered a resolution to adopt the rules of the Senate as they existed with the exception of Rule XXII governing motions and pending questions. Walsh proposed that a committee be appointed to write a cloture rule and that the debate on that rule be conducted under "general parliamentary law," including the provision that it would be "in order to move to fix a time when the Senate shall take a vote on the pending question or to move the previous question with a view to closing debate."[28]

In their treatise on the subject, Martin Gold and Dimple Gupta conclude that

> although the Senate was not forced to act on Walsh's constitutional option, there is strong reason to believe that the proposal was the impetus for cloture reform. Looking back on the 1917 rule change, Senator Clinton Anderson concluded that Walsh's proposal carried the day: "[Walsh] made a very powerful argument [in favor of adding a cloture rule] . . . When he finished, someone surrendered. Senator Walsh won without firing another shot. A cloture rule was brought forth . . . and, with the exception of three, every one of [the opposing Senators] . . . fell into line." Senator Paul H. Douglas (D-IL) concurred that the 1917 rules change would not have been made had not Senator Walsh presented his original resolution: "[W]hile there was no formal rule or decision dealing with the Walsh motion, it was not overruled, and the result he was seeking to accomplish was attained,

because the objectors had hanging over their heads general parliamentary law, under which the previous question could be moved to shut off debate."[29]

However, it seems clear that Walsh's argument provided only part of the impetus for the change. The popular uproar against the Senate fueled by President Woodrow Wilson's criticisms had left little doubt that the Senate would amend its rules and create a cloture provision. This would have happened, we believe, without Senator Walsh's maneuverings. The debate throughout and the overwhelming 76–3 vote at the end to adopt the rule support this view.

Congressional Quarterly points out that "as a political scientist in 1882, Wilson had celebrated 'the Senate's opportunities for open and unrestricted discussion.'"[30] But after the 1917 bill to arm merchant ships was blocked by filibuster in the Senate, Wilson fumed, "The Senate of the United States is the only legislative body in the world which cannot act when the majority is ready for action. A little group of willful men . . . have rendered the great government of the United States helpless and contemptible."[31] CQ concludes, "Public outrage finally forced the Senate to accept debate limitations."[32]

At the same time, as many of the eighty-six senators who voted to adopt a cloture rule made clear, these senators supported a conservative rule that would not interfere with extended debate in the Senate, and that they did not support Senator Walsh's contention that the rules could be changed by a simple majority at the start of a Congress. As Senator Warren Harding (R-OH), the man who would succeed Woodrow Wilson as president, declared on the floor during the 1917 debate: "I am quite content to say that I favor some modified form of cloture rule; but the point I want to make is, that where the sentiment of this body is favorable to a change of the rules, no dilatory tactics can long obtain in opposing that change of the rules . . . I am not ready to accept the soundness of the Senator [Walsh]'s argument, that this is not a continuing body; and I cannot accept the contention that we must first enter into a state of chaos in order to bring about the reform which the Senator seeks."[33] He later added: "I have the abiding faith that a conservative cloture rule can be made a rule of this body along the lines of regular procedure for the amendment of the rules, without adopting a chaotic condition here wherein a majority of the Senate can fix the rules."[34]

And Senator Francis Warren (R-WY), who when he died in 1929 was the longest-serving senator in Senate history and another supporter of the proposed cloture rule, rejected the argument that the Senate could use general parliamentary rules at the outset of each Congress: "I do not object to some manner of procedure that may terminate what sometimes becomes intolerable: but I am not willing yet to take the ground that every two years we are at sea without rudder or compass regarding rules."[35]

WHETHER OR NOT THE SENATE IS A CONTINUING BODY IS A CRITICAL QUESTION

The debate about continuity of the Senate is crucial. It is likely that any future effort to change the cloture rule, if controversial, will include a battle over this issue. Senate rules require only a majority vote to amend the Senate rules. This can be deceptive, however, because, under Rule XXII, it takes a two-thirds vote of senators present and voting to end debate on the rules change. Therefore a supermajority, even larger than the normal 60-vote cloture, is required to get to the vote on changing the rules (unless, of course, fewer than ninety senators happen to be present and voting or there is sufficient consensus so that there is no filibuster). This makes it unlikely that major controversial changes will occur unless the Senate decides that it was not a continuing body after all.

As we have noted, the Senate rules themselves state: "The rules of the Senate shall continue from one Congress to the next Congress unless they are changed as provided in these rules."[36] So, without a grand compromise, it will take a very cooperative vice president, willing to join with the Senate's majority and ignore the Senate's rules and/or precedents to get the Senate to the point where it can or will change the rules in the absence of a two-thirds cloture vote.

Norman Ornstein, one of the most authoritative scholars on Congress and a proponent of filibuster reform, pointed out prior to the Senate's 2011 consideration of rules reform:

Reform ideas are fine—but they are academic exercises unless 67 Senators can agree to change their rules, a near impossibility . . . Since its origins, the Senate has been considered a continuing body . . . Thus, the rules in the body remain in effect—and those rules require two-thirds to invoke cloture for a rules change. [Vice President] Mondale [in 1978–1979] considered taking the chair as President of the Senate and making a parliamentary ruling that the Senate is not a continuing body; rather, like the House, it has to adopt rules at the beginning of each Congress, and that can be done by majority action. That might work—but like the nuclear option, it would be radioactive, with collateral damage that would reverberate for a long time, in a Senate where business is mostly conducted by unanimous consent.[37]

It is not clear that so much unanimous consent would be necessary any longer in a new majoritarian Senate, since the majority would be free to operate the legislative agenda as it saw fit.

Senator Udall's proposal to change the rules by simple majority is at the same time more radical than Senator Harkin's proposal to weaken the filibuster by allowing the reduction in the number of votes needed for cloture over time culminating in majority cloture, and less so. More radical because, if embraced by the Senate, it would open the door to a complete rewriting of the Senate's rules, perhaps to the Harkin proposal, but maybe an even more sweeping change leaving the Senate a shadow of the more impetuous House. Less radical, at least for the short term, if the Senate were to follow Senator Udall's expressed intent.

Senator Udall has said: "We don't have to make drastic changes. We can modify the filibuster in a way that still respects minority rights but prevents our current state of minority rule. We have [time] to discuss reasonable changes that would help restore the collegiality and comity of the 'world's greatest deliberative body.'"[38] In our interview with him, Senator Udall insisted that "it doesn't mean we need to throw out the traditions of the Senate. It doesn't mean we throw out the rights of the minority to be able to express their point of view."[39]

However, once the keys to the bulldozer are available to each new majority at the start of a Congress, particularly in light of the extreme partisan behavior, the abandonment of civility, and the lack of will to compromise that we have seen in recent years, who can have any faith that tearing down 200 years of Senate practice will result in a restoration of "collegiality and comity of the world's greatest deliberative body"?

The Udall effort put before the Senate one of the most critical questions about its own nature, one that has been debated repeatedly over the years, at least since the middle of the nineteenth century. A quorum of senators (at least fifty-one under the Constitution) is, at all times, duly elected and seated. Since the Senate has been a continuous body from the outset, its original rules have survived in a straight line to the present. The Senate under Article I, Section 5 has the power to write its own rules. The Senate has done so. And, again, the Senate in its Rule V has clearly declared, "The rules of the Senate shall continue from one Congress to the next Congress unless they are changed as provided in these rules."[40] There is nothing in Article I, Section 5 that directly supports Senator Udall's contention that the Constitution empowers the Senate to change its rules in contradiction to its existing rules and the provisions for changing those rules under those rules.

The 1953 battle, led by Senate liberals frustrated by repeated filibusters conducted by Southern Democrats against civil rights legislation, sought to reduce the necessary number of votes for cloture from two-thirds of the whole body, which was the case in the wake of the 1949 compromise that made possible cloture against the motion to proceed. Their strategy was to argue that, under the Constitution, the Senate could vote at the beginning of a session with a simple majority to change its rules. The issue was not resolved and the Senate voted to table a motion by Senator Clinton Anderson to consider a change in the rules, as discussed earlier in this chapter.[41]

Senate Historian Donald Ritchie asked rules expert Martin Gold in his Senate oral history interview about this era of attempted changes in Rule XXII using the "constitutional option":

RITCHIE: At the beginning of every Congress from the Truman and Eisenhower administrations right on through to Nelson Rockefeller, when he was still vice president, they were still hoping to do that. It's interesting that the ideologies and parties have changed, but the talk of the tactics has stayed the same. What really did change things in the past was whenever you had an election that gave one party or the other a large majority, instead of having things as evenly balanced as they are now, or at least that's the way it's seemed to me.

GOLD: ... [T]hat's right ... I have looked at a lot of that history and can trace some interesting people. You talk about how people have changed after they got accustomed to the Senate. When Mike Mansfield was elected to the Senate in 1952, and when he arrived in 1953, the first issue before the Senate was reform of the filibuster rule by the so-called constitutional method. There were twenty-one senators who supported that change that year, almost all of whom were Democrats. Mansfield was one of them. He was part of that intrepid group that tried to change the rules by such a means. By the time he got into the leadership and the same efforts were being made by others, he spoke out vigorously against it. Part of that was a change in role from being a freshman member pursuing a particular ideology without regard to Senate traditions to being the majority leader and being the defender of those traditions; also lots of years of experience in the Senate and an evolving sense of what the Senate was supposed to be about.[42]

The late Senator Robert Byrd, the Senate's leading expert on its rules and their history, at the Senate Rules Committee's May 19, 2010, hearing just a month before his death, declared, "Our Founding Fathers intended the Senate to be a continuing body that allows for open and unlimited debate and the protection of minority rights. Senators have understood this since the Senate first convened."[43]

THE VICE PRESIDENT AND THE MAJORITY CAN DECIDE

For the "constitutional option" to succeed, it will rely upon a vice president ignoring the Senate rules and almost certainly the advice of the Senate parliamentarian[44] and ruling that a simple majority, under the Constitution, can invoke cloture. During the 2005 debate on the "nuclear option" that was based on much the same reasoning, the current vice president, then-senator Joe Biden, rejected the argument in the strongest terms. His statement makes the case strongly and is significant because Biden himself, as the president of the Senate, may be at the center of just such a historic decision-making moment. In 2005, he declared:

We should make no mistake. This nuclear option is ultimately an example of the arrogance of power. It is a fundamental power grab by the majority party . . . to eliminate one of the procedural mechanisms designed for the express purpose of guaranteeing individual rights, and they . . . would undermine the protections of a minority point of view in the heat of majority excess . . . Quite frankly, it is the ultimate act of unfairness to alter the unique responsibility of the Senate and to do so by breaking the very rules of the Senate . . . Put simply, the nuclear option would transform the Senate from the so-called cooling saucer our Founding Fathers talked about to cool the passions of the day to a pure majoritarian body like a Parliament. We have heard a lot in recent weeks about the rights of the majority and obstructionism. But the Senate is not meant to be a place of pure majoritarianism . . . At its core, the filibuster is not about stopping a nominee or a bill, it is about compromise and moderation . . . It does not mean I get my way. It means you may have to compromise. You may have to see my side of the argument. That is what it is about, engendering compromise and moderation.[45]

At this point in his statement, one might imagine that the 2005 Senator Biden is providing advice to now Vice President Biden:

If there is one thing I have learned in my years here, once you change the rules and surrender the Senate's institutional power, you never get it back. And we are about to break the rules to change the rules. I do not want to hear about "fair play" from my friends. Under our rules, you are required to get ⅔ of the votes to change the rules. Watch what happens when the majority leader stands up and says to the Vice President . . . he calls the question. One of us . . . will stand up and say: Parliamentary inquiry, Mr. President. Is this parliamentarily appropriate? In every other case since I have been here, for 32 years, the Presiding Officer leans down to the Parliamentarian and says: What is the rule, Mr. Parliamentarian? The Parliamentarian turns and tells them. Hold your breath, Parliamentarian. He is not going to look to you because he knows what you would say. He would say: . . . You cannot change the Senate rules by a pure majority vote . . . He will not look down and say: What is the ruling? He will make the ruling, which is a lie, a lie about the rule . . . We are the only in the Senate as temporary custodians of the Senate. The Senate will go on. Mark my words; history will judge this Republican majority harshly, if it makes this catastrophic move.[46]

There are two instances that some proponents of eliminating the filibuster claim as precedent. The first occurred in 1969 when Senator

Frank Church (D-ID) offered a cloture motion on his proposal to change Rule XXII, which at the time required a two-thirds vote to a proposed three-fifths requirement. He asserted that under the Constitution cloture on his proposal would only require a simple majority. Vice President Hubert Humphrey ruled that at the beginning of a Congress a simple majority could invoke cloture and if the Senate did vote to invoke cloture with less than a two-thirds vote but more than a majority, he would rule that cloture was invoked. The Senate voted 51–47 to invoke cloture. The vice president's ruling was appealed, and the Senate voted not to sustain the opinion. This does not create a precedent because the vice president's judgment was not sustained by the Senate and cloture was not invoked.

The second occasion was 1975. Senators James Pearson (R-KS) and Walter Mondale (D-MN) attempted to use the "constitutional option." Senator Pearson offered a motion providing for majority cloture on a change in the rules to reduce the supermajority required for cloture to three-fifths vote. The motion included the proposition that cloture on his proposal could be invoked by a simple majority. Majority Leader Mike Mansfield (D-MT) raised a point of order against the motion. Vice President Rockefeller ruled that if the Senate were to reject the Mansfield appeal, it would be the judgment of the Senate that the Pearson motion was constitutional and he would enforce cloture by a simple majority under the constitutional option. The Senate tabled the point of order, but Senator James Allen (D-AL) was able to divide the question because the Pearson motion had two parts. Under Senate rules, any senator can demand that the parts be voted separately. Rockefeller allowed the division and ruled that the first part was debatable, nullifying the Pearson-Mondale victory in effect. Mondale offered another motion for an immediate simple majority cloture vote and again Mansfield raised a point of order that was tabled by the Senate.

Senator Robert Byrd, backed by Senator Mansfield and the Republican leadership, offered a compromise three-fifths cloture (duly elected and sworn, rather than present and voting as in the Mondale proposal and retaining two-thirds for rules changes). The compromise was adopted and the Senate reconsidered and adopted the Mansfield point of order.

Some view this action as reversing the precedent. Some believe that it did not reverse the initial point of order and that the precedent stands. In our view, the Senate has been consistent for its more than 200-year history. The Senate, through this point of order, backed away from the consequences of allowing a simple majority to invoke cloture on a rules change. The Senate did what it does well; it arrived at a viable and stable compromise. Senator Byrd, in his excellent history of the Senate, points out that "by this action, as the Rules Committee's published history stated, the Senate 'erased the precedent of majority cloture established two weeks before, and reaffirmed the continuous nature of the Senate rules.'"[47]

The argument over a precedent may be a side issue because, in reality, the vice president or presiding officer can do whatever a majority will permit as long as he or she and the Senate's majority are willing to ignore the Senate rules. In 1967, Senator Sam Ervin (D-NC), who had served as a justice on the North Carolina Supreme Court and who later became famous for his chairmanship of the Senate Watergate Committee, pointed out:

> If a majority can act as proposed . . . at the beginning of the session, it can so act on any day of the session . . . [T]he only rule the Senate could have under this theory would be that the majority of Senators present on any given occasion could do anything they wish to do at any time regardless of what the rules of the Senate might be. If the Constitution does not permit the Senate to adopt rules which can bind a majority of the Senate at the beginning of the session, it does not permit the Senate to adopt rules which can bind a majority at any time in the session. This conclusion is inescapable because the provisions of the Constitution applicable to the Senate are exactly the same on every day of the session, however long it may last.[48]

BINDING FUTURE CONGRESSES

The question of majorities binding future majorities and legislatures binding future legislatures is central to the "constitutional option" argument. This is particularly true because the Senate acted in 1959 to adopt Senate Rule V, making clear its view that the rules continue. The question arises whether that rule binds future Senates.

There are many circumstances in which the Congress "binds" future Congresses in much the same way. These provisions like Rule V, however, do not truly bind the future bodies because the Congress is able, under the rules, to change or reverse the actions. Examples include laws that Congress has passed that impose expedited procedures affecting activities of both houses, their committees, and the role of senators in shaping public policy through debate and amendments.

In addition, the Budget Act of 1974 created the reconciliation process, and the budget process itself has been amended. In addition, the Senate has imposed the Byrd rule on itself to limit amendments under reconciliation. These have binding characteristics on the Congress that can only be waived by supermajority votes. Actually, Rule XXII is less binding because it applies only to debate and the rules themselves can be amended by a simple majority vote.

As mentioned earlier, the compromise in the 1980 Alaska Lands Act requires that any oil and gas drilling in the pristine Arctic National Wildlife Refuge be approved by future law. Senator Ted Stevens (R-AK), seeking to permit drilling, argued 22 years later for just such a law: "One Congress cannot bind another Congress. But one Congress can enact a law that it takes another Congress to enact and have a President sign it. This is one of the things that was required, and it was a great error of my career in agreeing that the area would be open only if a subsequent law was passed by Congress."[49]

Senator Stevens's regrets at having agreed to the compromise notwithstanding, no one argues, not even the late Senator Stevens, that it does not require the Congress to take a future action in order to overcome the prohibition put in place by the 107th Congress.

Also, in the Constitution, the Founders bound all future Congresses, the states, constitutional conventions, and potentially huge majorities of the American people when they wrote in Article V "that no State, without its Consent, shall be deprived of its equal Suffrage in the Senate."[50]

Finally, James Madison in a letter to Thomas Jefferson written on February 4, 1790, refers to three categories: (1) constitutions; (2) *laws irrevocable at the will of the legislature;* and (3) laws involving no such irrevocable quality." Clearly, he saw the second as a legitimate category of laws. Madison writes:

> On what principle does the voice of the majority bind the minority? It does not result I conceive from the law of nature, but from compact founded on conveniency. A greater proportion might be required by the fundamental constitution of a Society, if it were judged eligible. Prior then to the establishment of this principle, *unanimity* was necessary; and strict Theory at all times presupposes the assent of every member to the establishment of the rule itself. If this assent cannot be given tacitly, or be not implied where no positive evidence forbids, persons born in Society would not on attaining ripe age be bound by acts of the Majority; and either a *unanimous* repetition of every law would be necessary on the accession of new members, or an express assent must be obtained from these to the rule by which the voice of the Majority is made the voice of the whole.[51]

The Senate exercised its right, under the Constitution, to establish a rule (Rule V) that sets out the procedures for future Senates to amend its rules. This is far less binding than "laws irrevocable at the will of the legislature" since Senate rules are revocable.

THE DANGERS OF THE USING THE CONSTITUTIONAL OPTION

Conservative icon Senator Barry Goldwater (R-AZ), who actually opposed the filibuster, wrote in his journal in February 1963: "Some senators want to do away with Rule XXII ... Now I am, basically against the filibuster and I so stated in my campaign. I said that if the opportunity arose where I could vote against the filibuster, I would do so ... I feel that the filibuster should be changed through the normal channels ... as the debate developed, it was obvious that this was a constitutional question involving the continuity of the Senate. Or, in other words, the question is whether the Senate is a continuing body or not? After listening to the debate and studying the constitution, I became convinced that it is a continuing body."[52]

Senator Mike Mansfield, even though he strongly supported changing Rule XXII from the two-thirds requirement to the three-fifths rule, opposed the "constitutional option" approach. During the 1967 debate on the motion by Senator McGovern that would have invoked cloture by a majority vote, Senator Mansfield warned: "The urgency or even wisdom of adopting the three-fifths resolution does not justify a path of destruction of the Senate as an institution and its vital importance to our scheme of government. And this, in my opinion, is what the present motion would do. The proponents would disregard the rules which have governed the Senate over the years simply by stating the rules do not exist."

He continued:

> This biennial dispute for a change in the rules has brought to issue the question of the Senate as a continuing body. The concept is really symbolic of the notion of the Senate in our scheme of government...What should be considered is whether the motion at hand—the motion for simple majority cloture—would destroy the character of the Senate as a parliamentary body...If a simple majority votes to sustain...this motion at this time, it necessarily means that henceforth on any issue, at any time, and during any future session of any Congress a simple majority, with a cooperative presiding officer, can accomplish any end they desire without regard to the existing rules of process and without consideration or regard to the viewpoint of any minority position...The issue of limiting debate in this body is one of such monumental importance that it reaches, in my opinion, to the very essence of the Senate as an institution.[53]

★ ★ ★

ELEVEN

Reforming the Filibuster
The Nuclear Option

In 2005, the Senate faced and narrowly avoided a major crisis over the use of the filibuster. The Senate Democratic minority was blocking final votes on the confirmation of seven of President George W. Bush's nominees to the federal circuit court of appeals. In response, Majority Leader Bill Frist (R-TN) threatened a parliamentary maneuver to sweep away any possibility of the use of filibusters to block judicial nominations.

The idea was essentially a variant of the "constitutional option." The difference is that this parliamentary maneuver would be applied in the middle of a congressional session. This plan dropped even the pretense that a rules change could properly be carried out by simple majority if it occurs at the outset of a new Congress when, in the view of its proponents, no ongoing Senate rules exist.

Then–Senate Rules Committee chairman and former Republican majority leader Trent Lott explained the genesis of the idea:

> A group of Republicans—led by me . . . settled on a tactic to ensure that judicial nominees in the future wouldn't get the Pickering treatment [filibuster of a judicial nomination by the Democrats[1]]. It was simplicity itself:

> We would ask the presiding officer, as a point of order, what vote was required to approve a judicial nominee. The answer, of course, would be a simple majority. The Democrats would appeal that ruling by the presiding officer of the Senate. After that, however, the motion could be tabled by a majority vote. Bam! We'd have a new precedent that would defeat filibusters and give nominees what they deserve—a clean vote, with victory or defeat determined by a simple majority.[2]

There is no controversy over the statement that only a simple majority is required to confirm a nomination. Everyone agrees on that. The contested issue would have arisen when the majority leader raised, as planned, a point of order against the continuation of the Democratic filibuster, arguing that debate could be ended by majority vote. Vice President Dick Cheney, president of the Senate, would then be expected to ignore the rules and precedents of the Senate as well as the near-certain recommendation of the parliamentarian against the point of order. He was expected to rule by fiat in favor of the point of order that would cut off debate. When the expected appeal by the Democrats was tabled by the Republican majority, the Cheney ruling on the point of order would be left standing and a precedent would be created, sweeping away the ability of Senate minorities to filibuster on judicial nominations.

Although this was framed as a variation of the "constitutional option," it came to be known, almost universally, as the "nuclear option." Senator Lott recalled the origins of the name:

> This was famously known as the "nuclear option," a phrase that first came from my lips—at least according to some reporters and pundits. What happened, as I recall, is that a reporter told me the Democrats would go nuclear if we tried this ploy. Well, fine, I responded, let 'em go nuclear. In any event, political journalists embraced the term, predicting that the Democrats would pull down the Senate walls and bring the body to a standstill rather than submit to what we were doing. I prefer to call it the "constitutional plan" since it's inspired by prose about appointing judges found in both the Constitution and the Federalist Papers.[3]

Charles Babington wrote in the *Washington Post*, "Both parties call the proposed option 'nuclear' because it would inevitably prove explosive. If Republicans carry out their threat, Democrats vow to use parliamentary tactics to grind the Senate to a standstill. Republicans who oppose the [nuclear option] plan say long-standing rules that protect the minority party and encourage bipartisan compromises should be preserved, no matter who holds the majority at a given time."[4] During the debate, judicial nominations were singled out by filibuster opponents as a particularly egregious misuse of the tactic. They argued that the Constitution intends an up-or-down vote to confirm nominees.

But the Constitution gives the Senate the right to write its own rules, and we believe that the supermajority requirement, which arises as a consequence of filibuster, makes even more sense as a feature of the Senate's advice and consent than its role in the legislative process. Federal judges serve for life. Once appointed and confirmed, they may be removed only by impeachment and conviction. It is not a bad thing when considering a lifetime appointment to these powerful positions on the federal bench to require that at least some members of the minority agree that the nominee is a mainstream appointment, capable of fairness and impartiality, even if in the end they do not wish to support him or her. It's a good thing that presidents are required to weigh the ability of potential judges to be confirmed by the Senate under a requirement that includes at least part of the minority party. It is clear that in many instances, they do. With the exception of Samuel Alito, who was confirmed 58–42, no Supreme Court nominee since Clarence Thomas in 1991 has failed to receive at least 60 votes in the Senate for confirmation.

Republican Senator Robert Griffin of Michigan, a leader of the 1968 filibuster against the confirmation of Abe Fortas, nominated as chief justice of the Supreme Court by President Lyndon Johnson, said at the time, "Whatever one's view may be concerning the practical effect of Senate rules with respect to the enactment of legislation, there are strong reasons for commending them in the case of a nomination to the Supreme Court."[5] Senator Griffin argued, "If ever there is a time when all Senators should be extremely reluctant to shut off debate, it is when the Senate debates a Supreme Court nomination. If Congress makes a mistake in the enactment of legislation, it can always return to the subject matter and correct the error at a later date. But when a lifetime appointment to the Supreme Court is confirmed by the Senate, the nominee is not answerable thereafter to the Senate or to the people, and an error cannot be easily remedied."[6]

The *New York Times*, like other newspapers and many political figures, has been less than fully consistent on the filibuster, but their argument against the nuclear option was clear: "The Bush administration likes to call itself 'conservative,' but there is nothing conservative about endangering one of the great institutions of American democracy, the United States Senate, for the sake of an ideological crusade."[7] The *Times* was not alone. One website listed more than 275 newspaper editorials in forty-two states in favor of maintaining the Senate rules permitting filibusters on judicial nominations.[8]

Colbert King, writing in the *Washington Times*, made the point that the filibuster is a legislative device used to "achieve victory or at least stave off defeat—no more, no less." He quoted then-chairman of the Congressional Black Caucus, Congressman Melvin Watt (D-NC): "Segregationists used the filibuster to defeat laws 'on which the rights of millions of people of color depend.' Today it is being used to protect those same rights against the foes of judicial enforcement."[9]

THE "GANG OF 14"

The crisis over the "nuclear option" was ended when a group of seven Democrats and seven Republicans came together, in a classic Senate maneuver, to forge a compromise and avert the showdown over the fundamental Senate rules. The group, which became known as the "Gang of 14," arrived at a brilliant—if somewhat unfavorable for the Democrats—pact. The seven Republicans would agree to withdraw support for their leadership's nuclear option. In exchange, the seven Democrats would withdraw their support for their leadership's filibuster. They would further agree not to support future filibusters against judicial nominees, except under "extraordinary circumstances." It was never clear what "extraordinary circumstances" might mean, but the phrase seemed sufficient to convince the Republicans involved to trust the word of the Democrats involved. "I'll know it when I see it," commented Senator Joe Lieberman (D-CT) a member of the "Gang of 14."[10]

Given the 55–45 margin at the time, seven Republicans was a sufficient number to defeat the nuclear option, if pursued. Seven Democrats, joined with the Republicans, was a sufficient number to invoke cloture should the filibusters continue. The compromise included majority votes on the confirmation of five of the seven blocked nominees. This never seemed a particularly good deal for the Democrats. However, at least the crisis that might have been created by the hijacking of the Senate rules by a sweeping edict from Vice President Cheney was averted.

DANGERS OF THE NUCLEAR OPTION

In an op-ed piece in the *New York Times,* former Senate majority leader George Mitchell (D-ME) put his finger on the threat represented by the flimsy rationale on which the "nuclear option" rested:

> Senate rules can be changed, and they often have been. But Senate Republicans don't have the votes for a change within the rules. So they propose to go around them, to act unilaterally to get their way. It's what they call the "nuclear option." Most Americans may not be aware of the complexities of the Senate's rules, but they do know and understand two fundamental principles: playing by the rules and dealing fairly with others. The nuclear option violates both. If it's exercised, I hope that enough modern-day Senator Smiths, guided by what is best for the nation and the Senate, will vote to stop it.[11]

Many of the nation's newspapers and magazines, some of which more recently have endorsed drastic filibuster reform, agreed that the nuclear option lacked validity. Raising once again that story about Washington and Jefferson, the *Chicago Tribune* argued:

> When Thomas Jefferson asked George Washington why he favored creating a Senate, Washington replied, "Why did you pour that coffee into your saucer?" Jefferson said he wanted to cool it. "Even so," answered Washington, "we pour legislation into the saucer to cool it." The filibuster fits perfectly with that conception of the Senate. This device has never been popular among those who favor speed, efficiency and pure democracy in legislative matters. But it has been one of many useful restraints that help to prevent

hasty government action based on a consensus that may prove transient. Republicans should be the last people to suggest we need fewer of those.[12]

The *Nation* magazine, often referred to as the "flagship of the left," wrote in an editorial: "Republican leaders in the Senate . . . are so determined to satisfy the Administration and their party's social conservative base that they have signaled their willingness to invoke the 'nuclear option' of radically rewriting the Senate's rules to make filibusters of judicial nominees virtually impossible. So the fight is on, not just to save a Senate rule but to maintain this country's already compromised system of checks and balances on executive and legislative overreach."[13]

The *Nation*, 5 years later in another editorial, would offer advice to Majority Leader Harry Reid about how to eliminate the filibuster, arguing, "before we can end supermajority rule, the groundwork has to be laid. First we must demonstrate the irresponsibility of the filibuster."[14] On the earlier occasion, with the "nuclear option" on the table, they wrote:

> As with most tools, the filibuster can be used for good or ill. For every Paul Wellstone filibustering to block a corrupt bankruptcy "reform," there was a Strom Thurmond filibustering to slow the civil rights movement . . . But there has rarely been serious discussion about eliminating the filibuster until now. If the nuclear option is invoked, Congress will become an altered branch of government. In the absence of rules that require the consideration of minority views and values, the Senate will become little different from the House, where the party out of power is reduced almost to observer status. That's why Robert Byrd, dean of the Senate and the most ardent champion of the chamber's rules, called the nuclear option "a legislative bomb that threatens the rights to dissent, to unlimited debate and to freedom of speech."[15]

The forceful editorial defense of the filibuster concluded: "This is a moment when we decide whether this country will remain a democracy in which those who govern must play by the rules, or will become a winner-take-all system where the gravest fear of the founders—tyranny of the majority—will be the lasting legacy of George W. Bush, [Republican House Majority Leader] Tom DeLay and [Republican Senate Majority Leader] Bill Frist."[16]

Current minority leader Mitch McConnell (R-KY), as the Republican's majority whip in 2005, supported the "nuclear option" and worked to eliminate filibusters for judicial nominations. Much more recently, he summed up his view of the "nuclear option" effort: "God, that was a dumb idea."[17] Senator McConnell added, "All majorities flirt with rules changes." Expressing skepticism that the current Democratic majority would use a nuclear option–like approach, he commented, "My guess is most of the current majority aren't suffering from amnesia."[18]

★ ★ ★

TWELVE

Bring in the Cots

Many critics of the Senate majority leadership decry their unwillingness to break the backs of the filibusterers as was done with the "old-fashioned" filibusters. Such wars of attrition on the Senate floor with senators reading from the phonebook and sleeping on cots in the cloakrooms are now rare. The image of Jimmy Stewart as Senator Jefferson Smith comes to mind, heroically holding the Senate floor hour after hour.

DEMAND FOR OLD-FASHIONED FILIBUSTERS

There is a widespread conviction that simply requiring the obstructing minority to talk long enough to drive them to exhaustion would defeat them in the end. In the media and among other commentators the call for requiring those engaged in filibustering to practice "old-fashioned" filibusters is common. Most accept it at face value. In fact, Majority Leader Harry Reid (D-NV) has been criticized for not employing this strategy. Historian Doris Kearns Goodwin, speaking of Republicans filibustering health reform legislation, told Jon Stewart on *The Daily Show,* "Let them filibuster. You realize how great they're going to look, these Republicans, trying not to go to the bathroom?"[1]

The majority has been criticized for allowing "painless" and "gentlemen" filibusters. Even sophisticated voices in the House of Representatives and the Senate itself have called on the leadership to require the filibusterers to publicly declare and exhaust themselves by talking through the night and for as long as it takes to defeat the filibuster. During the battle for the Obama administration's stimulus package, House Majority Leader Steny Hoyer (D-MD) "called on Senate Majority Leader Harry Reid (D-NV) to force Senate Republicans to mount actual filibusters if they want to stand in the way of bills 'so that the American people can see who's undermining action.'"[2]

Early in 2010, Naftali Bendavid wrote in the *Wall Street Journal* that "it has been a long time since there was a filibuster worthy of the name, with cots rolled out of storage rooms, bleary-eyed senators speechifying at 3 A.M. and the Capitol held in thrall to round-the-clock debates."[3] He reported that some Senate Democrats want to change majority practices, arguing that "filibusters, holds and other roadblocks shouldn't be bloodless affairs . . . if Republicans want to hold up action, they should stay on the Senate floor and make their case."[4] Senator Sheldon Whitehouse (D-RI) declared, "It would achieve greater visibility . . . as to why things are jammed up in Washington."[5] And Senator Ben Cardin (D-MD) added, "We are determined, even if it means . . . staying throughout the night, that we want to demonstrate to the American people that there is a filibuster going on and a Republican, or Republicans, are trying to block an up-or-down vote on issues."[6]

And when the shoe was on the other foot, when Democrats, in 2003, were filibustering to block the Bush judicial nominees, Kate O'Beirne wrote in the *National Review*: "A threatened filibuster alone should not allow 41 senators to block the confirmation of federal judges. Rather than surrender preemptively to the need for 60 votes to confirm a judge, Senate majority leader Bill Frist should call the Democrats' bluff, and bring back the traditional filibuster. Let Kate Michelman, leader of the abortion lobby, man the cots and wipe the brows of weary Democrats forced to talk 'round the clock."[7] She went on to invoke the familiar image from *Mr. Smith Goes to Washington*: "The notion of the drama-laden, longwinded Senate filibuster is an outdated one arising from

Hollywood movies . . . The 'modern,' 'silent,' or 'gentleman's' filibuster might more accurately be called the 'lazy man's' filibuster. It has become so trivialized that there is no longer any need to silence an objecting senator . . . [Majority Leader] Bill Frist must be prepared to make the Dems stay there, for as long as it takes. By calling their bluff, Frist will have set a good precedent: that under his management, 51 votes represents a Senate majority."[8]

In the same vein, Senator Frank Lautenberg (D-NJ) even introduced the "Mr. Smith Act," an effort to reform Senate rules by requiring that those who are attempting to block legislation by filibuster actually hold the floor and speak. In his testimony to the Senate Rules Committee in July 2010, Senator Lautenberg recalled: "In the iconic movie, *Mr. Smith Goes to Washington,* to maintain his filibuster, Mr. Smith stood on his feet on the Senate floor and spoke continuously for 23 hours. Eventually his passion, fortitude and arguments win the day . . . [T]he 'Mr. Smith Act'—is a modest measure that will bring Mr. Smith back to Washington by bringing the Senate back to its roots . . . It simply requires Senators who want to filibuster to actually filibuster."[9]

LONE WOLVES AND SMALL GROUPS CAN BE WORN DOWN

In truth, a lone-wolf filibuster pressed by one senator or a small group of senators can be defeated in this way. In such cases, the votes exist for cloture, and unless the calendar is somehow on the obstructer's side, like an impending Christmas recess or sine die adjournment,[10] it is, in fact, up to a determined majority to wear the filibusterers down by attrition. Even then, it can be difficult, but like Senator Strom Thurmond (D-SC) filibustering the 1957 Civil Rights Act for 24 hours, 18 minutes[11] with a Foley catheter strapped to his leg so he wouldn't need bathroom breaks, attrition will finally do the lone filibusterer in.

Filibusters conducted by a very small group are susceptible to the "wear them down" style of filibuster busting. This was true even prior to the adoption of Rule XXII, the cloture rule, in 1917. For example, in 1908, famed Senator Robert La Follette (R-WI), Senator Thomas Gore (D-OK), and Senator William Stone (R-MO) filibustered the Emergency

Currency Act. The Senate website describes the circumstance: "A filibuster in the early twentieth century could be particularly unpleasant.
In the summer, an extremely hot Senate chamber customarily drove
senators to the cloakrooms for relief."[12]

A 1915 *New York Times* story headlined "The Art of Filibustering"
explained what then occurred:

> The majority is merciless and is willing to let filibusters take the most des-
> perate chances with their health. Nor . . . has it ever shown any disposition
> to be chivalrous or "play fair"; not that there is any reason why it should,
> when the filibuster is itself a stratagem . . . The majority was waiting silently
> to pounce the moment the three senators had to yield to nature and give
> in. The filibuster had hardly started. La Follette had talked for about a day,
> and then sought the cloakroom for rest, turning the floor over to Gore. That
> senator talked a few hours and then decided to give the floor to Stone and
> take a short nap for refreshment.

Pointing out that Senator Gore was blind and therefore could not see
that his compatriots had left the floor, the *Times* continues:

> Real chivalry would have suggested to some majority senator to pull Gore's
> coat-tails and inform him that he had better hold the floor a minute longer.
> Instead the enemy took full military advantage of Gore's affliction. As he
> sat down, expecting the absent Stone to take his place, the gavel fell, the
> Senator in charge of the bill moved its passage, and La Follette came dash-
> ing into the chamber only to find that his filibuster had died a-borning.[13]

The planning for such a filibuster some 7 decades later in April 1983
led to a meeting involving both of this book's authors. Senator Paul
Tsongas (D-MA), for whom (co-author) Rich Arenberg was working at
the time, was leading a small group of senators who were planning to
filibuster President Reagan's nomination of Kenneth Adelman to head
the Arms Control and Disarmament Agency. *People* magazine featured a
two-page article about the young senator's use of the "ultimate weapon"
in the fight: "'It's not an issue where you run out of things to talk about,'
Tsongas chuckles. He means to stay on the arms control topic even if he
has to read aloud from written texts. 'Reading the phone book discredits
your activity dramatically,' he notes. Aide Rich Arenberg . . . is to be his

parliamentary counselor-of-war, ready to head off antifilibuster maneuvers. Tsongas has warned him, 'You're going to be with me every minute, so you better know what you're doing.'"[14]

Panicked by Tsongas's public disclosure of his responsibility, Arenberg sought the calming advice of Parliamentarian (and co-author) Bob Dove. In the end, the filibuster was averted and the nation never got to see if Arenberg was a competent "parliamentary counselor-of-war."

FOR MOST FILIBUSTERS, ATTRITION WILL NOT WORK

Those who call for forcing the filibusters to talk either ignore or are unaware of the fact that for a sizeable organized minority, and certainly for a minority of forty-one senators or more (who cannot be beaten by a cloture vote), lengthy sessions are little more than exercises in scheduling. The filibusterers are able to take turns holding the floor, and since they can demand the presence of a quorum at virtually any moment, it is the majority that carries the heavier burden because they need to keep fifty-one senators (a quorum) nearby. If the filibusterers call for a quorum and it is not produced, under the rules the Senate must adjourn.

Princeton political scientist Franklin Burdette, in his classic *Filibustering in the Senate,* identified three types of filibusters, "one-man, cooperative and organized."[15] Writing in 1940, he observed that "examples of filibustering by a single Senator are not so common as the casual observer of the Senate might suppose."[16] He pointed out: "The purpose of the prolonged session, as it is used by opponents of a filibuster, is patently to inconvenience and if possible exhaust the obstructionists and to increase the burden of their responsibility for delay. Unless the number of filibusterers be very small the prolonged session is actually more spectacular than effective . . . [A]ny experienced maneuverer in the Senate knows that a determined group of filibusterers, before they are themselves exhausted, can usually manage to wear out the patience and endurance of the majority."[17]

Commentator Elizabeth Drew made the point more recently:

Many people now insist that those who use filibusters should actually be made to stand up and talk through the night, but there's a reason that doesn't happen anymore. In the 1970s, Majority Leader Mike Mansfield realized that the real punishment was not to the small band of all-night speakers but to the majority party, which had to keep a quorum (51 members) on hand, sleeping on the famous cots near the Senate floor, lest the person conducting the filibuster suddenly make a motion to adjourn the Senate, thus defeating the purpose of keeping them talking. Historian Ritchie says, "The all-night filibuster wore down the majority much faster than it did the minority." Majority leaders haven't used the tactic since.[18]

Breaking such an organized filibuster has been tried, and it has almost always failed. Majority Leader Lyndon Johnson (D-TX) tried breaking the back of a 1960 civil rights filibuster by keeping the Senate in session non-stop for 9 days—the longest session in Senate history. Senator Johnson's effort did not work. According to *Congressional Quarterly*, the "eighteen southerners formed into teams of two and talked nonstop in relays."[19]

Civil rights supporter Senator William Proxmire (D-WI) described the scene: "We slept on cots in the Old Supreme Court chamber [near the Senate floor] and came out to answer quorum calls. It was an absolutely exhausting experience. The southerners who were doing the talking were in great shape, because they would talk for two hours and leave the floor for a couple of days."[20]

FORCING ALL-NIGHT SESSIONS HAS ITS TACTICAL USES

While the tactic of all-night sessions has been used by majority leaders several times in more recent years, it has been for different objectives. In 1988, Majority Leader Robert Byrd forced 3 days of non-stop sessions to counter a Republican filibuster against a campaign finance reform bill. Senator Alan Simpson (R-WY) frustrated this effort for much of the time, simply by repeatedly requesting quorum calls. Senator Simpson basically guarded the floor and the other Republicans simply went home. The filibusterers, at one point, attempted to deny a quorum to the majority by failing to appear on the Senate floor. We earlier described

Senator Byrd's response. He asked the Senate to instruct the sergeant-at-arms to arrest those senators who were not responding to the quorum call. Senator Bob Packwood (R-OR) was tracked down and carried to the Senate floor. We, the authors, both observed the resulting farce.

Senator Byrd recalled, "Having drawn the lines in the sand, we . . . decided that we [would] just go around the clock . . . there [was] no point in continuing the casual, gentlemanly, good-guy filibuster because it will just turn out . . . [the Senate will] have a few cloture votes, everybody just takes it easy . . . everybody goes home and gets a good night's sleep, and everybody protects everybody else. The American people will understand this is a filibuster. They will understand who is not willing to let the Senate vote on the bill."[21]

The focus was not breaking the back of the filibuster, it was an effort to marshal public support against the filibuster by drawing dramatic attention to it. Senator Simpson's reply was, "We are ready to go all night, we are ready to go all day . . . we are prepared and will have our sturdy SWAT teams and people on vitamin pills and colostomy bags and Lord knows what else we will have to have to improve our ability to stay here."[22]

The bottom line is the bill never passed. The minority that was blocking the bill was able to sustain their filibuster through a record eight cloture votes. In the end, Majority Leader Byrd had to back down.

Majority Leader Bill Frist in November 2003 forced a 39-hour session through the night. An AP story at the time was typical, breathlessly reporting, "The Senate readied cots and coffee for a talkathon set to last all Wednesday night on who's to blame for some of President Bush's nominees not making it to the federal appeals bench."[23] Senator Rick Santorum (R-PA), a member of the majority leadership, explained: "Filibusters are put forward by the minority to try and block action from occurring. We're trying to move to the floor to try to force action on judicial nominations. We're going to do everything we can to get a vote on judges, and they're going to do everything they can to block a vote on judges." The Democratic minority leader Tom Daschle (D-SD) fired back, "If they need help filibustering themselves, we'll be glad to pitch in."[24]

According to the *New York Times,* "The event featured some but not all of the features of marathon debates of bygone days—cots outside the chamber for weary orators, for example, but no senators claiming they were equipped with personal plumbing devices to allow them to hold the floor at length without pause. While the procedures may have been civilized, the feelings were bitter; Republicans called the exercise an important and needed display of 'justice for judges' while Democrats said it was a stunt and a preposterous waste of time."[25]

The Republican majority had no illusion that they were breaking the back of the Democrats' filibuster by staging an all-night session. They would not be forcing the Democrats to the point of exhaustion by requiring them to hold the floor and talk. In fact, they knew full well that *they* would be doing most of the talking. As the *New York Times* reported, the Republicans were "candid about their interest in the dramatic and their hopes in getting attention for the session."[26] As part of the theatre of the moment, they "had cots brought in . . . and invited the news media to witness the event. Whether any Republican senators actually plunk themselves down in the cots in the remote hours but for a brief photo opportunity is uncertain; they also have nice offices in which to spend the time."[27]

Majority Leader Frist himself admitted, "If we stay in overnight or two nights or three nights, that doesn't change a thing . . . Maybe it would help you educate the American people that it's no longer the days of Jimmy Stewart."[28] Senator Dick Durbin (D-IL) recognized the intent: "This is all about grinding red meat for their conservative wing."[29] The ranking Democrat on the Senate Judiciary Committee, Senator Patrick Leahy (D-VT), summed it up: "This is 'Alice in Wonderland' stuff."[30]

A few years later, in 2007, the Democrats had regained control of the Senate. Senator Harry Reid (D-NV) was now the majority leader. The Republicans had been successfully blocking consideration of the Levin-Reed amendment to the FY 2008 Defense Department authorization bill that would set a timetable for withdrawal of U.S. combat troops from Iraq. Senate Majority Leader Reid stood on the Senate floor and declared, "My worst fears . . . have been realized. We have just seen the Republican leadership again resort to this technical maneuver to block progress on this crucial amendment . . . that could bring the war to a responsible end. They are protecting the president rather than protecting our troops. They are denying us an up or down—yes or no—vote on the most important issue our country faces."[31]

Vowing not to back down, Senator Reid then issued the dramatic threat to keep the Senate in session night and day: "We have no choice but to stay in session to continue speaking out on behalf of our troops and all Americans, to continue requesting consent for an up-or-down vote on our amendment to end the war."[32] Reid forced an all-night debate that featured 24 hours of Iraq speeches on the Senate floor, stretching from 11 A.M. on July 17 until a cloture vote was held at 11 A.M. on the next day. The *Washington Post* commented, "Cots that had been brought in for the overnight session were wheeled back out to a congressional storage facility, after being used by just six senators."[33] Senator Reid was even compared to a character in *The Godfather,* "Looking at the cots, one couldn't help but think of the scene in . . . which . . . the Corleone family's consigliore . . . and Sonny Corleone argue over how to respond to an attempt to kill Sonny's father, Don Corleone. 'Sonny,' [the consigliore] says, 'let's talk about this and get a meeting up.' 'No!' Sonny shouts back. 'No more meetings . . . we go to the mattresses.'"[34]

But Senator Reid and the Democrats knew that the filibuster would not be broken by forcing debate and trying to wear out the filibusterers. Their intentions were different. They were attempting to dramatize for the American people that the Senate's Republican minority was using the Senate's rules to obstruct the majority of senators who wanted to place further restrictions on President Bush's Iraq war policy. The rare all-night Senate session attracted media attention, although the rally held in the park outside the Capitol building at which senator after senator was addressing large crowds was probably creating more news.

As the 24 hours of speeches wore down, the cloture vote revealed that a majority of the Senate did indeed support the Levin-Reed amendment. The vote was 52–47. Of course, the 52 votes were 8 too few to end the filibuster and Majority Leader Reid was forced to back down. A strategist for one of the groups lobbying most strongly for the Democrats to force the all-night confrontation over the filibuster (MoveOn.org) argued, "I think Senator Reid took an important step toward confronting Republican obstructionism and ending the war . . . Ultimately, we end the war by creating a toxic political environment for war supporters like the Republicans in the Senate."[35]

Senator Lamar Alexander (R-TN), a Republican somewhat critical of the president's handling of the war, disagreed. He argued that the political theatre of creating an old-fashioned filibuster confrontation on the floor was counterproductive to the majority's objectives. According to the *Washington Post*, Senator Alexander said that "the all-night debate had discouraged GOP senators who oppose the current Iraq strategy from joining Democrats on alternatives. The result, he said, is a solid majority of the Senate opposed to Bush's handling of the war but unable to reach a compromise."[36]

More recently, a new tactic to generate drama entered the filibuster arena when Majority Leader Harry Reid sought to bring up the 2011 Defense authorization bill that contained the repeal of the controversial "Don't Ask, Don't Tell" (DADT) policy. Pop music star Lady Gaga used her Twitter account to send a tweet to her 6.3 million "followers." The tweet created the kind of attention sought and the star followed it up with a trip to Maine for a rally intended to put pressure on Maine's two moderate Republican senators, Susan Collins and Olympia Snowe, to vote for cloture. Majority Leader Reid even tweeted to Lady Gaga on his Twitter account, "There is a vote on DADT next week. Anyone qualified to serve this country should be allowed to do so."[37] *The Hill* commented, "Celebrities have emerged as an unexpected force in the push to repeal the military's longstanding "Don't ask, don't tell" (DADT) policy toward gays serving openly in the military . . . No one has drawn more attention to the debate than the edgy entertainer Lady Gaga."[38]

Like the cots, the tweets can benefit either side. While Senator Reid and the Democrats clearly welcomed the heightened attention to their efforts, so did the filibusterers. They welcomed the support generated for their efforts to block the repeal of DADT. Senator John McCain (R-AZ), leading the filibuster, asserted in a radio interview on KYFI in Phoenix, "I'm glad she's [Lady Gaga] paying attention. I hope she'll continue to pay attention, and to watch the debates on the Senate floor, and understand that this is a pure political ploy on the part of [Senate Majority Leader] Harry Reid and Democrats."[39]

No Republican voted for cloture. Majority Leader Reid was forced to abandon his effort to bring the bill up. However, because public opinion so solidly supported an end to the DADT policy (a December 2010 poll showed 77% favoring repeal[40]), the pressure continued, and by December a bipartisan majority of sixty-five senators enacted the repeal.

Cots, tweets, and battles of attrition may help to call attention to the use of filibuster strategies, building support for one side or the other, but they do not and will not, as many seem to believe, serve to reduce the incidence of filibusters in the Senate.

★ ★ ★

THIRTEEN

Defending the Filibuster

At important moments in the Senate's history majorities have complained about the filibuster. In the 111th Congress (2009–2010), great frustration was generated by the inability of the large Democratic majorities in the Congress and the newly elected Democratic president in the White House to enact their ambitious political agenda as quickly and efficiently as they would like. This was further fueled by abuse of the Senate rules by the Senate's minority, seemingly at times for the sole purpose of obstruction for its own sake, and exacerbated by lone-wolf filibusters like that of Senator Jim Bunning (R-KY) when he used the rules to block the broadly supported extension of unemployment benefits.[1] The eventual use of the budget reconciliation process to assure the enactment of health reform and avoid a filibuster may, in the end, have defused some of the anger among Democrats, while sparking anger among many in the minority.

Some Democrats have begun to press for wholesale changes in Rule XXII, much as liberal Democrats did in reaction to the almost yearly filibusters of the 1950s and 1960s against civil rights legislation.[2]

When majorities have the strong support of public opinion, they may be overzealous in their demand for rash action. The Founders feared majorities that moved too quickly. The supermajority requirements imposed by the Senate rules for the most controversial issues provide a useful test of when a majority may be overzealous. Perhaps an even greater concern is that legislative majorities might not even reflect public opinion and, without sufficient examination, might be able to force action.

THE CHARACTER OF THE SENATE

The Senate, true to its own nature, has sought moderation and compromise. The filibuster itself has played a central role in fostering this character of the Senate and it has come to the fore each time the Senate has addressed changes to Rule XXII. The Senate has for more than 200 years protected unlimited or extended debate. It is clear that the Founders feared overzealous majority rule and wanted the passage of legislation to be difficult. The House was designed to reflect the majority will, but the Senate in our bicameral legislative branch was formed to, in those words attributed to George Washington, "cool the hot tea" coming to it from the House. The Senate has served the role intended by the Founders well. While those Founders never contemplated the debate rules within the Senate, in the Constitution they provided the Senate with the right and obligation to write its own rules. Those rules, informed by the design of the Framers of the Constitution, after more than 200 years of molding, are no accident. Again and again, over its history, whenever the principle of supermajority requirements to end debate in the Senate has been assaulted, the Senate has backed away from adopting simple majority cloture. In fact, even in 1917, a number of the senators in both parties who supported the original adoption of the cloture rule in the Senate, Rule XXII, expressed their fears of rampant reform taken too far.[3]

WHERE YOU SIT IS WHERE YOU STAND

For many, perhaps most, senators, their position is situational. Senators in the majority are perplexed by the delay and by the difficulty of carrying out their agenda in pursuit of what they may view as their mandate from the voters. Senators in the minority see the Senate's rules as the last protection against imprudent action—an essential part of the checks and balances built into our system of government. These views, on both sides, are enhanced when government is "unified"—that is, both the Congress and the White House are controlled by the same party. When the majority shifts from one party to the other, the views about the filibuster tend to be exchanged along with the gavel.

In the early 1990s, with President Bill Clinton in the White House and Democrats controlling both houses of Congress, many Democrats railed against the supermajority requirements of Rule XXII, while Republicans defended it. When Republican majorities swept in on the wave of the 1994 "Gingrich revolution" election, the roles were reversed. Democrats embraced the filibuster as a defense against what they viewed as the extreme elements of the "Contract with America," an ambitious and aggressive legislative agenda on which Republicans across the country had run. And in the 2003–2005 battle over President Bush's judicial nominations, Republicans, as mentioned earlier, contemplated sweeping the filibuster away as a tactic to end the Democratic filibusters. The showdown was averted by a group of seven centrist senators from each party—the "Gang of 14."

As the debate over health reform heated up in the 111th Congress, with Democrats back in the majority once more, many in both caucuses swapped sides. For example, Senator Richard Durbin (D-IL), a Democratic leader, the Senate minority whip during the 2005 battle over judicial nominations, said in response to the "Gang of 14" compromise that saved the filibuster but led to confirmation of several of the Bush nominees, "These judges were bitter medicine, but I believe the Senate and our caucus is better for it. We preserved the right of extended debate and filibuster, and when and if a Supreme Court vacancy occurs, we have preserved our rights, if a controversial person is named, to exercise our traditional authorities in the Senate."[4] But in 2010, now in the majority, Senator Durbin launched an on-line petition titled "Fed Up with the Filibuster" and declared, "The American people are sick of process blocking progress. They're fed up with an arbitrary tradition that allows a minority of Senators to prevent popular, much-needed legislation from even coming to a vote. Frankly, so am I."[5]

On the other side, former Senate Majority Leader Bill Frist (R-TN), who led the charge toward the "nuclear option" in 2003–2005, at the very outset of the 109th Congress warned, "If my Democratic colleagues continue to filibuster judicial nominees, the Senate will face this choice: Fail to do its constitutional duty or reform itself and restore its traditions, and do what the Framers intended. Right now, we cannot be certain judicial filibusters will cease. So I reserve the right to propose changes to Senate Rule XXII, and do not acquiesce to carrying over all the rules from the last Congress."[6] But, much more recently, in 2010, former Senator Frist appeared on a cable television show defending the filibuster against attacks by TV personalities Bill Maher and Rachel Maddow. He declared, "In defense of our Congress, over 200 years ago we set up a House of Representatives which is majoritarian rule, which is 50% or more and that is one branch of government [*sic*]. The balancing branch of government was set up with what is called primacy of the minority, to empower the minority so the minority has voice. It is not just a majority vote overall. That balance of power has been in the United States Congress for over 200 years."[7]

This is not to say that the positions that senators across the whole history of the Senate have taken on the filibuster are never deeply rooted in principle. Obviously, the tactical concerns of daily battle in the Senate arena place different pressures on the majority and the minority in the effort to shape public policy outcomes. Although some in each party have sought radical reform, most senators seek to protect the Senate's traditional filibuster and its historical role, while minimizing dilatory obstructionism.

A MINORITY OF SENATORS MAY REPRESENT
A MAJORITY OF THE NATION

While the public and media debate about the filibuster is almost entirely framed as a partisan confrontation, in the Senate itself it is often about the burdens of representation of their states that the Constitution places uniquely on senators.

The on-line magazine *Slate* published an analysis showing that when Democrats successfully filibustered against the Republican majority during the nearly two decades between 1991 and 2008, they represented a majority of Americans 64 percent of the time.[8] Overall, "senators who successfully filibustered something represented about 46 percent of Americans on average."[9]

The argument against "government by adding machine," as George Will called it, goes back to the earliest roots of Rule XXII. In a 1918 debate, Senator Lawrence Sherman (R-IL) raised an analysis of the earlier successful filibuster against the Ship Purchase Bill. He pointed out that the states represented by the thirty senators who blocked the measure had forty-one million inhabitants. By contrast the states of the bill's supporters had thirty-seven million citizens.[10] Sherman concluded, "If . . . a majority means voters, then the majority by senatorial votes in this body, applying a limitation upon the right of debate, does not promote the rule of a majority of votes; it promotes the denial of the right of a majority of votes even to be heard, much less to vote."[11]

PROTECTION OF SMALLER STATES

Senator Byrd in his 1995 speech went on to underline the importance to the smaller states of the guarantee of debate in the Senate: "[The Senate] is the forum of the States. We are here to represent States. And the State of West Virginia, the State of Iowa, the State of Kentucky, the State of Mississippi, each of these States is equal to the great State of California with its 30-odd million—equal. We speak for the States, and it is the only forum in the Government in which the States are equally represented . . . Now, if we do not have the right for unlimited debate, these poor little old States like West Virginia, they will be trampled underfoot. We have three votes in the House."[12]

In a letter to Senators Lott and Dodd, historian Robert Caro wrote: "What if a Senator—let us say a senator from a small-population state without any other means of defense—votes to support a new limitation on debate today? What will he do in some future year when he is trying to stop a bill or a nomination that a bare majority of the Senate supports, but that he and 40 colleagues believe will be terribly detrimental to their states or to the nation—an action that he feels a few members of the Senate may change their view about if only he has enough time to explain the full consequences to them and to the public?"[13]

Critics such as historian Jean Edward Smith dispute the argument that the unique role of the Senate as defender of the states, and of minorities, is still valid. He asserts:

> The routine use of the filibuster as a matter of everyday politics has transformed the Senate's legislative process from majority rule into minority tyranny. Leaving party affiliation aside, it is now possible for the senators representing the 34 million people who live in the 21 least populous states—a little more than 11 percent of the nation's population—to nullify the wishes of the representatives of the remaining 88 percent of Americans. It will be argued that the Senate, with two senators per state, has never been based on majoritarian principles. But look at the record. Congress, like the British Houses of Parliament, was designed to reflect two distinct bases of representation. In Britain, with rigid social and economic stratification, representation hewed to class lines . . . In the United States the House represented the interests of the people, and the Senate reflected the will of the states. Until the adoption of the Constitution's 17th Amendment in 1913, United States senators were elected by state legislatures. Indeed, senators were considered representatives of state governments, not the people. Equality among the states had been the basis of union in 1787, and for that reason it may have been justifiable to afford a significant number of states a veto over national policy. But with the direct popular election of senators, all of that changed. Senators no longer represented state governments, they represented the people. The rationale for providing states a veto through the use of the filibuster no longer obtained.[14]

While the Seventeenth Amendment changed the election of senators from the more indirect method of election by the people's elected representatives in the state legislature to direct election by the people of each state, this hardly means that senators no longer represent their states just as the Founders intended. In fact, in drafting the Constitution, the equal representation of the states was viewed as so critical that it was the only provision in all of the Constitution shielded from the normal means of constitutional amendment. The Constitution states that no state, "without its consent, shall be deprived of its equal suffrage in the Senate."[15] In other words, two-thirds of both houses of Congress and three-fourths of the states, or a new constitutional convention, in this one case, will not suffice. Such a change requires the acquiescence of any state in the union that would be losing its equal representation.

STRONG PUBLIC OPINION OVERCOMES THE FILIBUSTER

Many analysts believe that filibusters seldom, if ever, kill proposals that have broad support. Former congressman Bill Frenzel (R-MN), a 20-year veteran of Congress, has argued, "The filibuster has been often indicted for denying the popular will, but over recent history, that point is hard to demonstrate. In the first place, it is not easy to get, and hold, 41 votes in the Senate under any circumstances. It is practically impossible to do against a popular proposal. Filibusters simply do not succeed unless they have popular support or unless there is a lack of enthusiasm for the proposal being filibustered."[16] Congressman Frenzel asserts, "The filibuster surely gives the minority a little more clout, but it does not prevent a majority from passing reasonably popular proposals. It gives a minority the opportunity to negotiate what it believes is an intolerable proposal into one it can live with. That compromise may serve the needs of the majority tolerably well too."[17]

Frenzel was writing in 1995. The abuse of the filibuster as a blunt partisan tool has rendered that 41 threshold easier to reach for a committed minority, but the basic fact is that filibusters are seldom permanently successful in the face of public opinion to the contrary.

The 111th Congress is a case in point. By virtually all vote study measures this was the most polarized, the most partisan Congress since the Reconstruction era of the 1860s and 1870s. However, with the passage of the $787 billion American Recovery and Reinvestment Act of 2009, better known as the stimulus bill, the historic Patient Protection and Affordable Care Act, known as health reform, the financial reform act, and the small business jobs bill, the 111th Congress was more productive than any since the mid-1960s during the Johnson administration.

Each of the four massive and sweeping bills that we have mentioned required overcoming a filibuster with a successful cloture vote in the Senate. The stimulus bill gained the support of three Republicans,[18] the health reform bill gained cloture without minority support,[19] and the financial reform bill received the votes for cloture from three Republicans.[20] And the small business bill required 6 cloture votes on the bill or amendments to it until finally, with the support of two Republicans, cloture was invoked and the bill was passed.[21] Even the START treaty required a cloture vote, which was supported by eleven Republican senators.[22] The lame-duck session repealed the "Don't Ask, Don't Tell" policy after severing it from the Defense authorization bill and then invoking cloture.[23]

It is important to note that in the case of the stimulus bill, given the context of the financial collapse and the deep recession that followed, a filibuster against the motion to proceed to the bill in the Senate—that is, simply a decision just to take it up on the floor for consideration and for amendment—was politically unsustainable. The motion to proceed, unlike many others in the 111th Congress, was adopted by unanimous consent.[24] Similarly, although the motion to proceed to the financial reform bill was initially filibustered by the Republicans and they defeated three efforts to invoke cloture,[25] strong public opinion in favor of financial reform forced the minority to relent and the motion to proceed was adopted by unanimous consent.[26] This is consistent with a pattern of strong national support for a bill trumping filibustering minorities that goes back in the Senate to the early nineteenth century, long before there was even a cloture process to end debate.

By contrast, on health reform, where public opinion was more evenly divided, the Democrats were only able to overcome a vigorous Republican filibuster on the motion to proceed because at that particular point in time, after Senator Arlen Specter (R then D-PA) had switched parties and before the death of Senator Edward Kennedy (D-MA) and the election of Senator Scott Brown (R-MA), they had 60 Democratic votes in the Senate. The cloture vote on the motion to proceed was 60–39.[27]

When the same party controls the White House and Congress, the importance of the filibuster in protecting minority views grows.

Of course, this is exactly the circumstance in which majorities are most exasperated by the filibuster. This is the time when greater efficiency in the Senate suddenly seems more desirable to some.

FILIBUSTER AND THE SEPARATION OF POWERS

Particularly when power is unified as when one party controls the White House and both houses of Congress, the potential to filibuster empowers the minority in the Senate to demand oversight of executive actions. In *The American Senate,* Professor Lindsay Rogers points out the key link between the Senate's supermajority requirements and the separation of powers: "The Senate is the only American institution so organized and articulated as to exert any supervision over the executive, and this function would be impossible were the rules to provide for closure [majority cloture]." He goes on: "The undemocratic, usurping Senate is the indispensable check and balance in the American system, and only complete freedom of debate permits it to play this role . . . Adopt closure in the Senate, and the character of the American government will be profoundly changed."[28]

FILIBUSTER UNDEMOCRATIC?

Although the media, for the most part, have viewed the filibuster as "undemocratic" and almost universally as "obstructionist," Ruth Marcus of the *Washington Post* wrote one of the most eloquent defenses of the filibuster. She wrote: "The existence of the filibuster is, on balance, a good thing . . . The filibuster makes the process—take a deep breath, Democrats—fairer. It enhances the opportunity for real debate. On the major legislation for which its use was meant, the filibuster tends, overall, to create a better end product, one more likely to gain wide acceptance among voters. No doubt, the filibuster has been overused in recent years, snarling Senate action on even the most routine matters. But such abuse is evidence of a deeper problem—the increasing polarization of politics—and not its cause."[29]

Well-known human rights lawyer Joanne Mariner has argued:

The use of the filibuster is undemocratic, and unquestionably so, to the extent that democracy is equated with simple majority rule. But if democracy is seen as a more complex process in which minorities, too, deserve a voice—and which even recognizes that public officials who belong to a political minority may nonetheless represent majority views on certain issues—then filibusters may have a legitimate role to play. Because of its potent nature, the filibuster is a means not simply of counting heads, but of assessing the intensity of views on a given subject . . . An obstructive filibuster, unsupported by popular opinion, is obviously a dangerous game. Were the . . . minority to start cavalierly holding up [majority] legislation and blocking . . . nominees who do not fall into the extremist category, it would likely pay a heavy price in the next elections.[30]

President Lyndon Baines Johnson, speaking as Majority Leader on the Senate floor on March 9, 1949, declared:

If I should have the opportunity to send into the countries behind the iron curtain one freedom and only one, I know what my choice would be. I would send to those nations the right of unlimited debate in their legislative chambers. Peter the Great did not have a Senate with unlimited debate, with power over the purse, when he enslaved hundreds of thousands of men in the building of Saint Petersburg. If we now, in the haste and irritation, shut off this freedom, we shall be cutting off the most vital safeguard which minorities possess against the tyranny of momentary majorities.[31]

BUILDING CONSENSUS

Senator Russell Feingold (D-WI) in a speech on the Senate floor in 2000 argued that the twin pillars of the Senate, the almost unlimited rights to debate and amend, "make every single senator a force to be reckoned with. Every senator—whether a Member of the majority or the minority—can be a player. And Leadership cannot neglect or exclude any single senator without substantial risk. As a result, senators do well never to burn bridges with any other senator. Because any one senator can disrupt the Senate, every senator has good reason to show comity for every other senator."[32]

It is, simply put, the possibility of filibusters that drives senators to reach for consensus. While a simple majority can enact legislation, the supermajority 60 votes are needed to end debate and reach a final vote. In most circumstances this requires at least some portion of the minority party to join with the majority. As a result, in our experience, for example, the senators with whom we have worked, when planning the introduction of a bill or an amendment, will at the very outset ask which of the senators of the opposing party will be their cosponsor.

Political scientist Dick Fenno, in his fascinating book *The Making of a Senator*, describes the efforts of then–freshman senator Dan Quayle (R-IN) to get reauthorization of the highly controversial Comprehensive Employment and Training Act (CETA) through the Senate in 1982. Senator Quayle is quoted: "It's been a bipartisan bill from the beginning . . . I never thought of it in any other way. It's my first piece of legislation and it should be bipartisan."[33]

Fenno observes, "As he explained later, the instinct that governed this view concerned the Senate as well as the committee. When I asked if his preference for bipartisanship grew out of his experience in the House, he laughed."[34] Senator Quayle's response to Fenno was: "Hell no. The House is completely partisan. The Democrats run it and won't let the Republicans do anything. The House is the worst training ground in the world for bipartisanship. If anything, you come out of the House filled with hate—with venom. But, when you get to the Senate you realize immediately that things are different, that the only way anything gets done here, with few exceptions, is through bipartisanship."[35]

Senator Quayle, of course, is talking about the impact of the filibuster and the supermajority requirements imposed by Rule XXII. The ultimate passage of the CETA bill, a Quayle-Kennedy bill in the end, reflects how the Senate really works, at least when it does work. While this consensus-building function is, at times, hampered by the unwillingness of one or both parties to abandon a pure political and/or ideological posture in order to legislate, very often the Senate has been the crucible for moderation, compromise, and eventual consensus.

As the sometimes dysfunctional Senate of the twenty-first century strives to reform its rules to reduce pointless and unproductive tactics, it must take care to protect the balance wheel. The effect that the possibility of filibuster has on tactics, decision making, and ultimately outcomes is woven into the fabric of the Senate. There are many examples. One in which we were both involved is the still ongoing debate over oil and mineral resources in Alaska.

The long struggle over the status of oil and gas drilling in the pristine Arctic National Wildlife Refuge (ANWR) has its roots in a provision of the Alaska National Interest Lands Conservation Act (ANILCA) passed in 1980. One of the authors (Arenberg) played a role in drafting the ANWR provision and the negotiations over final passage of the bill, which President Carter called the most significant land conservation measure in American history. The bill protects over one hundred million acres of federal land in Alaska and more than doubled the size of the National Park System in America.

In fact, it was during the Senate's deliberations over the Alaska bill that the authors first met. Dove was an assistant Senate parliamentarian, and Senator Paul Tsongas's (D-MA) legislative director, Arenberg, was handling the Alaska issue for the senator. Senator Tsongas was the author of the major version of the bill backed by environmental organizations and battling the version reported by the Senate Energy Committee under Senator "Scoop" Jackson (D-WA).

The history of this landmark environmental bill illustrates the key role that the Senate and its filibuster play in shaping consensus on major policy. Senator Mike Gravel (D-AK) threatened and ultimately did filibuster the bill. Senator Tsongas's strategy for passage of the substitute, however, was built on convincing Alaska's senior senator, then the Republican whip in the Senate, Ted Stevens (R-AK) not to filibuster. This strategy led to a unanimous consent agreement that brought the bill to the floor. However, when the first of the major Tsongas amendments surprised opponents by overcoming the Energy Committee's opposition on the floor, Senator Stevens launched a filibuster. This led the majority leader to pull the bill off the floor. Tsongas began several weeks of negotiations with Senators Jackson and Stevens in an effort to find a compromise. These negotiations, which took place in Senator Jackson's "hideaway office" tucked into the third floor of the Capitol building, came to be known by the participants as the "Alaska hostage crisis." The face-to-face negotiations forced by the threat of a protracted filibuster led to a compromise acceptable to all sides. All sides, that is, except Senator Gravel. He launched what was essentially a lone-wolf filibuster against the compromise legislation. Cloture was filed and on August 18, 1980, the Senate invoked cloture on a 63–25 vote. The next day, the Senate passed the bill.

The House, with its Democratic majority in control, insisted on its legislation, which contained even stronger environmental and conservation protections. When President Jimmy Carter was defeated in November by an opponent of the Alaska legislation, Republican Ronald Reagan, the House, led by Mo Udall (D-AZ), quickly accepted the Senate bill. It was signed into law by "lame-duck" President Carter on December 2, 1980, before Reagan took office.

Without the filibuster and its supermajority requirements in the Senate, it's likely that a more aggressive Alaska bill would have been passed by the Democratic majorities in the House and Senate. However, it is equally likely that President Reagan, with the Republican majority that swept into the Senate with him, and his secretary of the interior, the notorious (at least among environmentalists) James Watt, would have been able to roll back much of the bill—maybe repeal it entirely.

Senator Ted Stevens knew and artfully used the Senate rules. He understood what many critics of the filibuster, particularly outside of the Senate, do not. While he knew that pure obstructionism in the face of public support would, in the end, lose out in the Senate, nonetheless the rules gave him leverage to move Tsongas and the environmentalists toward a compromise. They were faced with deadlines. The end of the session and the election were looming on the horizon. And an impatient majority leader would not likely give them enough of the Senate's valuable floor time to wear down an effective filibuster. On the other hand, Stevens did not want to be forced to an all-out showdown that he might lose with all that his state of Alaska and his allies, the oil and gas industry and the mining industry, had at stake.

The dynamic created by the threat of a debilitating filibuster drove both sides into negotiation of a compromise. The bill that did emerge from the process, and that earned the reluctant support of Senator Stevens, has stood the test of time. The official National Park Service history declares, "The act was a milestone in the history of conservation in America. Never before, and surely never again, would lands be preserved on so vast a scale."[36]

While the ANWR language prohibited oil and gas exploration in the protected area of the Alaskan North Slope, it allows for the Congress in an emergency to open the area to exploration and drilling. For the past 30 years, Republican administrations and some in Congress have sought to do just that. Many efforts have been launched in the Congress. Over those years, although most public opinion polling shows large majorities of Americans opposed to drilling in ANWR, the House of Representatives has passed legislation to permit it. At times, there have been substantial majorities in the Senate willing to go along.

Many of the Democrats in the current Senate were there in December of 2005 when Senator Stevens and many Republicans attempted to use the Emergency Supplemental Appropriations bill in the wake of Hurricane Katrina to open up the pristine North Slope to oil drilling. This was only defeated by a filibuster led by Senator Maria Cantwell (D-WA). The effort to invoke cloture and defeat the Cantwell filibuster failed to get the necessary 60 votes, but a considerable majority of the Senate supported Stevens. The cloture vote was 56–44 (fifty-seven senators supported cloture; Majority Leader Frist [R-TN] voted no for parliamentary reasons so that he was eligible under the rules to ask for reconsideration of the vote). Thirty-two Democratic senators who voted against cloture remain in the Senate today (President Obama, Vice President Biden, and Secretaries Clinton and Salazar, all members of the Senate at the time, also voted against cloture).

In 2002, the Democratic majority easily beat off a cloture attempt on an amendment offered by Senator Lisa Murkowski (R-AK) to open up ANWR to drilling, 46–54, denying the amendment an up-or-down vote. In 1991, when the Republicans did have the majority, it was a filibuster led by liberal hero Senator Paul Wellstone (D-MN) that blocked ANWR on a 50–44 cloture vote. The supermajority requirement saved the day. Eight of the Democratic senators who voted against cloture on that occasion are still in the Senate, including filibuster opponent Senator Tom Harkin (D-IA). (Vice President Biden also voted against cloture.)

In March of 2003, an effort by Stevens to use the budget reconciliation process to circumvent the need for a supermajority to overcome opposition to the environmental protections in place for ANWR was narrowly defeated in the Senate by a 52–48 vote because some senators who otherwise supported the oil drilling were opposed to circumventing the filibuster rule. Six Republican senators had written a letter to Majority Leader Frist declaring, "Because the opening of the Arctic refuge to drilling raises a host of policy concerns, including serious environmental ramifications, we do not believe this issue should be injected in the budget process."[37] All six, including Senator John McCain (R-AZ), voted against the use of reconciliation to permit the opening of ANWR to oil drilling.

THE FILIBUSTER HAS BEEN ABUSED, BUT EFFORTS TO REFORM CAN BE DANGEROUS

The Alaska example is part of a long history. When Democrats are intent on gutting the filibuster they should recall moments such as (among many others) those addressing the Gingrich-led "Contract with America" in 1995, thwarting the Bush effort to privatize social security in 2005–2006, negotiating a power-sharing arrangement in the evenly divided 50–50 Senate of 2000 (Republicans had the majority by virtue of Vice President Cheney's tie-breaking vote), holding back Republican flat tax proposals, defeating Bush's efforts to make the elimination of the estate tax permanent, negotiation of the rules and procedures for the Clinton impeachment trial in the Senate, thwarting Republican efforts to enact national "right to work" legislation, defeating Bush right-wing judges in 2005, a strong bipartisan condemnation of the Reagan administration's Iran-Contra by the Senate's Select Committee, and blocking Republican efforts to instruct the federal courts to issue a stay in the Terri Schiavo case.

And Republicans, when they regain the majority, as they surely will, must face down the temptation to eliminate the filibuster as a stumbling block to their agenda. They, then, must remember that the gavel will again change hands and they should recall mostly Democratic-supported ideas like single-payer health insurance, the banning of assault weapons, "cap and trade" bills and other global warming legislation, gay marriage, the Employment Non-Discrimination Act (ENDA), the Employee Free Choice Act (so-called "card check" elections), and comprehensive immigration reform.

Lee Rawls, who served former majority leader Bill Frist (R-TN) as his chief of staff, put it well: "What the American legislative system does not provide is a cure-all of a bipartisan tool for rapid structural change. But this is the vain hope of theory, not reality."[38] He then reminds us of the words of James Madison in *The Federalist* No. 51, "If men were angels, no government, would be necessary."[39]

For much of the Senate's history, the use of tactics like the filibuster were held in check by the mores of the Senate and the conviction of its individual members. Political scientist Donald Matthews wrote about the Senate culture in 1960, "It's just a matter of I won't be an S.O.B. if you won't be one. A few, by exercising their right to filibuster, can block the passage of all bills."[40] Then, as now, the rules existed that could be abused to obstruct the majority's agenda. At the time, it took a two-thirds vote, an even higher bar than today's 60 votes, to end a filibuster. Yet, as Matthews observed, "While these and other similar powers always exist as a potential threat, the amazing thing is that they are rarely utilized. The spirit of reciprocity results in much, if not most, of the senators' actual power not being exercised. If a senator does push his formal powers to the limit, he has broken the implicit bargain and can expect, not cooperation from his colleagues, but only retaliation in kind."[41]

These mores of the Senate are gone or dying. Increasingly, new senators come to the Senate from the House. In the 111th Congress there were forty-nine senators who had previously served in the House,[42] and a similar proportion of the previous four Congresses served in the House before being elected to the Senate. The newly arriving senators are accustomed to the rough-and-tumble of the hyper-partisan House.

Those new senators who find themselves in the minority feel no constraint on the use of their new, more powerful procedural tools. Political scientists Sean Theriault and Davis Rohde, who have studied party polarization in the Congress, argue that the "Senate's increased [partisan] polarization was mostly due to the effect" of the group of senators who previously served in the House with Newt Gingrich between 1995 and 1999. They term this group the "Gingrich Senators."[43] Professors Nicol Rae and Colton Campbell write, "Many came from the House, after having been baptized by former whip Newt Gingrich into relentless and combative partisanship."[44]

Those new senators who arrive in the majority, having never experienced and developed a sense of the value of these protections for the minority, see and feel only the frustration and the apparent obstructionism. Senator Chris Dodd (D-CT), who met with the Democratic freshmen of the 111th Congress in 2010 to convince them to back off support for eliminating the filibuster, said, "Those ideas are normally being promoted by people who haven't been here in the minority and don't understand how the rules, if intelligently used, can help protect against the tyranny of the majority and cause things to slow down."[45]

HYPER-PARTISANSHIP AND POLARIZATION ARE THE CHALLENGE

Debate, competition, and even political combat between the parties are a healthy part of our democratic structure. In the 1950s, 1960s, early 1970s, political scientists and other commentators worried about the lack of clear ideologies and well-delineated and coherent parties. But, beginning with the Vietnam War and the cultural and political divisions that it helped to spawn, our political parties have gradually become more homogeneous, ideological, and polarized. This is particularly true of political activists in both parties. Whereas 50 years ago the elites in each party were likely to be more moderate, or at least pragmatic, today Democratic activists are, for the most part, among the most liberal elements of the party, and Republican activists are among the most conservative in theirs.

These trends are accelerated and deepened by the 24-hour news cycle, cable media, and the information explosion on the internet. In the 1950s and 1960s, most Americans watched evening news daily on one of the three networks. CBS, NBC, and ABC maintained vast news organizations dedicated to the pursuit of objectivity and the highest standards of broadcast journalism. This created a shared base of "facts." You might question the objectivity of a particular report, but these organizations, at the least, *strived* for a professional standard of objective news reporting. The political debate was informed by the shared consensus. Today, one might watch Fox News for an hour, switch to MSNBC for another hour, and find not a single shared fact. The standard appears to be advocacy, not objectivity.

The fragmentation of information on the internet allows people to seek out sources of information with which they largely agree. This creates a circumstance in which although Americans are arguably better informed about politics, and the Congress for that matter, than ever before, liberals are able to gain information almost exclusively from liberal sites and conservatives from conservative sites. This creates a kind of "stovepiping" in which many are too seldom exposed to views contrary to their own. As we have seen, this polarization is reflected in the national legislature.

The long-term solutions for the underlying problems of extreme and excessive party polarization and the decline in civility that has accompanied it are beyond the scope of this book. But it is clear that these solutions must engage not only members of Congress but also political elites and activists, the media, and voters themselves. The degree of polarization is evident not only in the legislative body but in the broader political culture.

Of course, the true protection against frivolous filibusters rests in the hands of the electorate. Filibusters that do not command considerable support are a dicey matter for senators to undertake. For example, as tempting as it may have been for Democrats to attempt to block President Bush's Supreme Court nominees John Roberts and Samuel Alito, Roberts was not filibustered, and although a cloture vote (an overwhelming 72–25 vote to end debate) was required on Alito,[46] no true committed effort to filibuster the nominee took place. The broad support for both of these nominees made such filibusters politically risky. On the other side of the aisle, the same circumstance developed with President Obama's Supreme Court nominees Sonia Sotomayor and Elena Kagan.

Members of Congress will respond if they are held accountable by an electorate that demands that the parties engage each other. Most Americans favor greater bipartisanship. At the same time, however, voters are easily drawn into the partisan wars. In campaigns, we hear over and over that the electorate is sick of negative campaign ads and partisan attacks, and yet they continue to predominate. This is because they "move the numbers." That is, the electorate responds and they are effective. This type of approach has leached into governance. Congressional debate increasingly sounds like campaign sloganism—bumper-sticker politics.

PUBLIC OPINION MUST LEAD THE WAY

If there is to be major change in the rules regarding filibustering in the Senate, public opinion will need to lead the way. If the rules of the Senate are followed, it will take a two-thirds vote to end the debate and vote on a major rules change. The 67 necessary votes can only be found if there is a broad public consensus.

Even with the increased attention that the filibuster has received, public opinion in support of filibuster reform remains lukewarm at best. A poll conducted for the Aspen Ideas Festival, in July 2010, found 53 percent of Americans want to "do away with the filibuster." This contrasts, however, with 66 percent in the same poll who want to impose a retirement age for members of Congress and 74 percent who want to abolish the Electoral College. Roughly the same level of support (51%) was expressed for imposing a retirement age on the president and for electing Supreme Court justices.[47] In fact, the respondents favored by 49 percent to 41 percent allowing changes to the Constitution by popular referendum—in our view, a horrifying idea.

A CBS News/*New York Times* poll in February 2010 showed about 44 percent of Americans thought the filibuster "should remain in place." Fifty percent disagreed.[48] But in January of that year when the Pew Research Center poll asked how many senators "are needed to break a filibuster," 62 percent of those polled either thought it was fifty-one or acknowledged that they did not know. Only 26 percent answered correctly, fewer than could identify the chairman of the Republican National Committee or identify Stephen Colbert in that poll.[49]

SOME PROPOSALS FOR REFORM

No one disputes that the filibuster tactic is being abused in the contemporary Senate. However, tinkering with the Senate rules will not eliminate the problem. For that, we need a return to the kind of respect for the Senate itself, its history, and its rules that will restrain senators of both parties from exploiting rights embedded in the rules just because they can.

Barack Obama, while still a senator from Illinois, recognized that abandoning the filibuster is not a solution. He declared on the Senate floor: "The American people want less partisanship in this town, but everyone in this chamber knows that if the majority chooses to end the filibuster—if they choose to change the rules and put an end to democratic debate—then the fighting and the bitterness and the gridlock will only get worse."[50]

However, a considerable amount of the misuse, abuse, delay, and obstruction could be addressed by some changes in the rules. Having said all of that, what reforms are possible and advisable? Recognizing that in this area of Senate rules reform, there is truly nothing new under the sun, here is what we would recommend.

First, *oppose the proposal to reduce cloture to a simple majority.* We have emphasized the many reasons why we believe weakening the rights of minorities and of the senators themselves by reducing the requirement to end debate to a simple majority—even over a period of time—would be a profound mistake. This would weaken individual senators and leave them incapable of protecting minority rights, challenging an imperial presidency, and/or playing their rightful role in the federal system by protecting the interest of their states, and it would undermine the incentive for members of the majority to seek consensus with at least a part of the minority.

Second, *support the Senate's historic view that it is a continuing body. Reject the "constitutional option."* Do not succumb to the temptation to permit a simple majority to rewrite the entire Senate rulebook at the outset of every Congress. This is a slippery slope. It will almost inevitably lead to strict majority rule of debate and amendment, turning the Senate into a smaller and less significant shadow of the House of Representatives. The Senate, like the upper body of most all democracies around the world, would shrink in significance as compared to its more populous lower body. Although proponents will argue that the "constitutional option" can be used to adopt moderate, reasonable rules changes that protect minority rights, we believe that this is an illusion. Once a majority is able to change the rules at will, they will inevitably take firmer control of the body.

Third, *reduce or eliminate debate on the motion to proceed to a bill.* This would greatly reduce the number of purely obstructionist filibusters. Once consideration of a bill takes place, the minority would retain their right to filibuster the substance of the legislation. The decision about whether to take a bill up for consideration and amendment could be determined with 2 hours of debate or less. It is already possible for a motion to proceed that is non-debatable and therefore cannot be filibustered to be made under Senate Rule VIII. This route has, for some reason that escapes us, fallen out of favor with modern majority leaders (since Robert Byrd used it). Nonetheless, this is a somewhat cumbersome path, and we would support making the motion to proceed a non-debatable motion (as it already is with respect to nominations and treaties on the Executive Calendar).

Fourth, *eliminate filibusters on the three procedural motions necessary to send a bill to conference committee with the House.* These motions, the motion to disagree with the House, the motion to request a conference with the House, and the motion to appoint Senate conferees, are currently all debatable and therefore subject to filibuster. Making these actions non-debatable motions, together with the elimination of filibusters on the motion to proceed, would lessen the unnecessary loss of time and energy by reducing the number of filibusters possible on any one measure from six to two. Each piece of legislation is currently subject to six separate potential filibusters, on the motion to proceed, the bill itself, the three motions necessary to send a bill to conference with the House mentioned above, and then the conference report when it returns.[51]

Fifth, *regularize the use of holds by creating clear guidelines and eliminating all secret holds.* The Senate acted in January 2011 to attempt to eliminate secret holds. As we have argued, it falls to the leaders of both parties to police this transparency and to impose moderation on overall use of holds. It is within the power of the majority and minority leaders to reduce the numbers and duration of holds.

Sixth, *reform the majority's tactic of "filling the amendment tree."* Senate rules expert Norman Ornstein has suggested, for example, the possibility of providing the minority with the right to offer a non-debatable motion to set aside a filled amendment tree and offer one amendment.[52] The right of the minority to participate in the amendment process must be protected. Majority Leader Harry Reid and Minority Leader Mitch McConnell have forged an agreement, discussed in detail in the epilogue, that should lead to a marked reduction in the use of this tactic.

Seventh, the Senate should undertake a serious effort to *curb or eliminate the expedited procedures afforded to reconciliation legislation.* This particular reform would require greater study and evaluation by the Senate, but the continued abuse and distortion of the reconciliation process as a means to circumvent the normal rules is not desirable and sometimes leads to unintended consequences. Reconciliation was never intended to serve as a gaping hole in the regular Senate rules, including filibusters; was never intended to increase the size of deficits; and certainly was never intended for the passage of major authorization bills.

Eighth, if the current expedited procedures are not curtailed, *address the vote-a-rama, so that amendments can be seriously considered and voted upon.* The current spectacle demeans the Senate's process of debate and consideration. Debate on a reconciliation bill is limited to 20 hours. At the expiration of 20 hours—which can be further reduced by a simple majority vote with a non-debatable motion—the Senate proceeds to vote without further debate on any amendments that have been filed and called up. This sometimes leads to what have been called "vote-a-ramas." The number of amendments offered to reconciliation bills generally has increased over the history of the reconciliation process. Only a few amendments were offered to the earliest reconciliation bills, but dozens of amendments have been offered to reconciliation bills more recently. In 2001, fifty-nine amendments were voted on, and in 2003, it reached sixty-five. These nonsensical vote-a-ramas also occur during the Senate's consideration of the annual budget resolution. In 2008, 44 roll-call votes, with virtually no debate, occurred on amendments to a budget resolution in one day![53]

Ninth, *limit debate on executive branch nominations below the cabinet level.* The president is entitled to staff his administration, and the functions of government rely on filling those positions in a timely manner. We would retain senators' right to fully debate judicial nominations. Federal judges serve for life. It is not unreasonable to expect nominees to have the support of at least some part of the minority.

These changes would be constructive, moderate, and go some of the way to a reduction in obstructionism. Further, most are well within the kind of adjustment to the rules that the Senate has historically been more comfortable with. They avoid the kind of wrenching changes that some have proposed. As Senator Byrd, not long before his death, declared, "The Senate has been the last fortress of minority rights and freedom of speech in this Republic for more than two centuries. I pray that Senators will pause and reflect before ignoring that history and tradition in favor of the political priority of the moment."[54]

We believe that one way to maximize the chances that a sensible and sustainable reform package could be put together would be for the majority leader and minority leader to meet and gather with some senior members of the Senate, "old bulls," and others who have been active in the rules reform debate. The bipartisan group could be tasked to put together a filibuster reform package that could be supported by both parties.

When an agreement is reached on a bipartisan reform package, implementation could be delayed for several years—for one or perhaps two Congresses. This would introduce uncertainty about which party would be the majority and which the minority. This would encourage the members of each party to examine any change from the perspective of being both in the majority and in the minority. Finding a solution, it seems to us, requires that both parties think in terms larger than their short-term advantage, This is a lot like the old parents' trick of heading off children's arguments over who gets the larger slice of cake by letting one child slice and the other choose.

We propose this mechanism because, as we have pointed out, most members of the Senate today and across the whole sweep of Senate history tend to adopt positions that are very sensitive to the partisan advantages of the moment. That is, senators who find themselves in the majority want to reform the filibuster in order to more efficiently enact their agenda. Senators who find themselves in the minority have, naturally, a more acute appreciation for the rights of the minority, the dangers of overzealous majorities, and the horrors of one-party government. Majorities tend to hate the filibuster. Minorities revere it.

In the words usually credited to Nelson Mandela, "Where you stand depends on where you sit." Delaying the actual implementation of a new filibuster rule encourages members of both parties to think through where they may sit in the near future.

Marty Paone, who served the Senate Democrats for 29 years alternately as secretary of the majority and secretary of the minority, remembers that "following an election, if there was a change in the Majority, I would joke with my Republican counterpart that, in addition to handing over the presiding book, we would also trade speech folders: One accused the other of being an obstructionist, while the second complained of the trampling of the Minority's rights."[55]

Even with the reforms that we have recommended, the Senate will be left to struggle with the ongoing abuse of its filibuster rules as long as its polarized parties are tempted to place combat in the political arena above solving the nation's problems.

PBS reporter Gwen Ifill once asked former Senate majority leader George Mitchell whether the filibuster then occurring over President George W. Bush's judicial nominees to the U.S. Circuit Court was "strategic, tactical, necessary? Is it useful?" Mitchell replied, "I think the real issue is the decline of comity in the Senate, the increase of partisanship, and the loss of institutional loyalty on both sides. And I think the way to deal with this is to try to restore that—overall not just on judicial nominations."[56]

We believe that it is the responsibility of senators to restore that loyalty to the Senate and when called upon, in the interest of the nation, to rise above the demands of partisan conflict. This may seem impossibly high-minded or even naïve. However, we believe that a recommitment to the deliberative process by senators of both parties, a return to the willingness to come to the table and forge tough compromises, is needed. In such an environment the role of unlimited debate and unfettered amendment in the Senate will again become clearer.

Then-senator Obama, speaking against the "nuclear option," said on the Senate floor, "We need to rise above an 'ends justify the means' mentality because we're here to answer to the people—all of the people—not just the ones wearing our party label."[57]

The United States of America has weathered periods of hyper-partisanship before. The Senate has as well. Its rules can be difficult and cumbersome. The filibuster, in particular, imposes many inefficiencies on how the Senate functions. However, in the end, it is the privilege of debate and amendment that protects the minority, encourages consensus, and establishes the Senate as the stabilizing force in our national politics.

★ ★ ★

Epilogue

As the new year dawned, the opening salvos of the 2011 filibuster reform battle were fired in the *Washington Post*, the *New York Times*, the *Boston Globe*, and other newspapers across the country. Senator Tom Udall (D-NM), writing in the *Washington Post*, declared the Senate dysfunctional and "broken." He asserted the "constitutional option," maintaining that "on the first day of the new session, the rules can be changed under a simple, rather than two-thirds, majority."[1] Senator Udall threw down the challenge to his colleagues, urging them to "recognize the obstruction that has prevented us from doing our jobs and join me in reforming Senate rules for the good of our country."[2]

In the *New York Times*, former vice president Walter "Fritz" Mondale, calling the Senate "arguably more dysfunctional than at any time in recent history," called for use of the "constitutional option," raising a familiar argument: "If changing Senate rules really required a two-thirds supermajority, it would effectively prevent a simple majority of any Senate from ever amending its own rules, which would be unconstitutional ... The document is very explicit about the few instances where a supermajority vote is needed—and changing the Senate's procedural rules is not among them. In all other instances it must be assumed that the Constitution requires only a majority vote."[3]

Of course, this is the same Fritz Mondale who told senators less than a decade earlier that the Senate must protect the right of any individual senator to "stop everything" and "rip open an issue in a way that no other institution in America can."[4] And, in 1993, he told a select Joint Committee on the Organization of Congress that eliminating the filibuster would be "a tragedy."[5]

Senate Minority Leader Mitch McConnell (R-KY) fired back in the *Washington Post*: "Any rule change aimed at making it easier for one party to force legislation through the Senate with only a slim partisan majority would undermine the Senate's unique role as a moderating influence and put a permanent end to bipartisanship."[6]

The ranking Republican on the Rules Committee, Senator Lamar Alexander (R-TN), speaking to the Heritage Foundation, declared, "Those who want to create a freight train running through the Senate today, as it does in the House, might think about whether they will want that freight train in two years when the freight train might be the Tea Party Express . . . The reform the Senate needs is a change in behavior, not a change in rules."[7]

Earlier, late in the lame-duck session at the end of 2010, all of the Democratic senators who would be returning for the 112th Congress in January lit the fuse by writing a letter to Majority Leader Harry Reid (D-NV) calling for filibuster reform. They wrote: "We believe the current abuse of the rules by the minority threatens the ability of the Senate to do the necessary work of the nation, and we urge you to take steps to bring these abuses of our rules to an end."[8]

The letter left the impression, at least with many outside of the Senate, that the Democratic caucus was unified. Some took it as an indication that Democrats might attempt the "constitutional option." In reality, the unity was illusory. A number of competing packages of rules reforms were being proposed and there was no consensus on whether the simple majority "constitutional option" was appropriate. Many senators were keeping their "powder dry" on this point, unwilling to commit without a caucus consensus on what specific changes might be made.

Other senators, students of the Senate, knew that past filibuster reforms had come about through compromise under the simple threat of the creation of a "constitutional option" precedent. Some of these senators wanted to repeat that experience, but without actually using the stratagem.

Meanwhile, the Senate leadership, Majority Leader Reid and Minority Leader McConnell, acting through Rules Committee Chairman Chuck Schumer (D-NY) and Ranking Republican Alexander, launched negotiations aimed at finding steps in the direction of reform that might be taken on a bipartisan basis.

On January 5, 2011, the Senate held its first session of the 112th Congress. This was the "first legislative day," the day that proponents of the "constitutional option" insist is the special opportunity for the Senate to write its own rules. They maintain that on that day it can be accomplished by simple majority vote.

The lead modern-day proponent, Senator Tom Udall, rose and told the Senate, "The constitutional option is our chance to fix rules that are being abused—rules that have encouraged obstruction like none ever seen before in this Chamber. Amending our rules will not, as some have contended, make the Senate no different than the House. While many conservatives claim that the Democrats are trying to abolish the filibuster, our resolution maintains the rule but addresses its abuse. But, more importantly, the filibuster was never part of the original Senate. The Founders made this body distinct from the House in many ways, but the filibuster is not one of them."[9]

Senator Tom Harkin (D-IA) was even more direct. In 1994, he had told the Senate that the filibuster was "unconstitutional."[10] On this day, he rose to respond to Minority Leader McConnell, who had pointed out that the Senate had never changed its rules except by use of its existing rules. Senator Harkin vehemently disagreed: "The rules set down by a . . . Senate a long time ago, said that in order to change the rules, you need a two-thirds vote of the Senate. I submit that is unconstitutional."[11]

So, both in 1994 and 2011, Senator Harkin had declared Senate rules unconstitutional. But, in the interim, in 2005, when the Republican majority sought to change the rules by a simple majority with a version of the "constitutional option" then labeled "the nuclear option," Senator Harkin told the Senate: "It will be like an out-of-control virus. If 51 Senators can change any rule at any time for any reason, then anything is possible . . . the majority leader is letting the genie out of the bottle and there will be no putting that genie back once it is out. It will wreak destruction in ways no one now can predict or foresee."[12]

Senator Harkin, showing how profoundly he understood the dangers, defended the right of senators to be able to speak for as long they want, declaring, "That has been our right since the founding of the Senate."[13] Senator Harkin raised one of the tried and true traditional arguments advanced by the Senate minority: "The filibuster is a more than 200-year-old tradition in the Senate; it has withstood the test of time . . . We understand the danger of majorities acting without check or restraint, running roughshod over those who would disagree . . . The rules of the Senate and the rule of extended debate give the minority that absolute safety. You take that away and you take away the minority rights in the Senate. Most Americans understand that checks and balances are the key to preserving our liberty."

Senator Harkin continued: "Under the rules of the Senate, it takes 67 votes to change the rules, 60 votes to end debate on a judicial nominee. But by resorting to this parliamentary gimmick, this nuclear option, the majority would change this rule with only 51 votes. The result would be to destroy any check or restraining influence on the power of the majority. This is not the American way. It is certainly not the wishes of the American people." He concluded: "The majority party in the Senate, whether Democratic or Republican, has always been frustrated by the minority's use of the filibuster. But I submit that frustration is the necessary byproduct of an effective system of checks and balances. It is the price we pay to safeguard minority right."[14]

As the seemingly timeless arguments back and forth on both sides echoed once again in 2011, as they had in 1917, 1949, 1953, 1957, 1975, and many times in between, we thought of Senator J. William Fulbright

(D-AR). Fulbright during the 1957 floor debate declared: "[Proponents of the 'constitutional option'] seek to leave the impression that majority rule is an ingredient—even a principal characteristic—of our Constitution. It is no such thing. I think one of the distinguishing characteristics of our Constitution is the denial of rule by the majority . . . I think it is quite inaccurate and very mischievous to leave the impression that majority rule in some way is a distinguishing characteristic of our Constitution, or to equate majority rule with democracy, as [the proponents] have so fervently attempted to do. "[15]

During the 1953 debate on this subject, Senator Richard Russell (D-GA), who knew the Senate's rules better than any of his era, called the "constitutional option" an effort to create a "shortcut" to amending the rules. He told the Senate, "If the theory can apply to the rules, it can apply to amendments to the Constitution and our entire government, without any orderly processes, can be driven into chaos."[16] Majority Leader Robert Taft (R-OH), selected as one of the five greatest senators in the body's history[17] replied, "It seems perfectly clear to me that the Senate rules simply continue in effect, although they are subject to change by the Senate."[18]

This time in 2011, it was Senate Minority Leader McConnell who made the counter-argument on the floor to those who intended to attempt to change the rules with only a simple majority: "What is being considered is unprecedented. No Senate majority has ever changed the rules except by following those rules; that is, with the participation and the agreement of the minority . . . The Founders crafted the Senate to be different. They crafted it to be a deliberate, thoughtful place. Changing the rules in the way that has been proposed would unalterably change the Senate itself. It will no longer be the place where the whole country is heard and has the ability to have its say, a place that encourages consensus and broad agreement."[19]

Speaking to reporters the next day, Senator McConnell said, "We don't think the Senate rules are broken."[20]

The Senate agreed to recess until January 25 for the Martin Luther King holiday. Under the Senate rules, by recessing rather than adjourning, the Senate remained in the same "legislative day" as distinguished from a "calendar day." This meant that the Senate when it returned would remain in its "first legislative day," thereby not prejudicing the decision of the Senate on the "constitutional option." There was much comment about this maneuver in the media, the *Washington Post* called it "a parliamentary trick to leave the chamber in a state of suspended animation."[21] But it had been done in the Senate many times before. In fact, in 1980, Majority Leader Robert Byrd (D-WV) had kept the Senate in one very long legislative day from January 3 to June 12.

The purpose for the delay was to give Majority Leader Reid the time he needed to seek a bipartisan agreement with Minority Leader McConnell in order to head off the "Young Turks" intent on use of the "constitutional option," a step that the leaders knew would sweep away the filibuster.

As senators returned to Washington, it became clear that the Democratic caucus was split and that there would be no unified support for attempting to establish the precedent of the "constitutional option." Senators Reid and McConnell were nearing a bipartisan "gentleman's agreement"[22] to support several rules changes to reduce the incidence of obstructionism.

The day before the Senate returned, Senator Tom Udall acknowledged that the threat seemed to have generated the willingness to compromise. "It's shaking things up a lot," he commented.[23] The *New York Times* reported that "top senators were hoping it would be sufficient to persuade their colleagues to halt any attempt on the floor to change the rules with a strict majority vote—an effort that lawmakers on both sides have warned could cripple the Senate. Democrats fear that such a vote—even if it were to fail—would scuttle any deal with Republicans. They also say it could leave them open to more wide-ranging changes should Republicans win control of the Senate in 2012."[24]

Senators Tom Udall, Tom Harkin, and Jeff Merkley (D-OR), the lead firebrands in the Democratic caucus, pressed for a showdown vote. However, since their resolutions had been offered and, under the Senate rules, required unanimous consent to be taken up and considered on the same day, the Republicans objected and the reform resolutions were forced "over under the rule" which meant that they could not be voted on until at least the next legislative day—no longer the first day.

The reality, however, was that a majority simply did not exist for the "constitutional option" and beyond that, there was no majority for the "Harkin ratchet" proposal or Senator Merkley's "talking filibuster."[25] And with the leadership now supporting a bipartisan agreement, it would be difficult even to get a vote on their proposals.

In the end, a unanimous consent agreement was worked out providing for five roll-call votes. The first two would occur, with a 60-vote threshold,[26] on proposals by Senators Ron Wyden (D-OR) and Chuck Grassley (R-IA) to eliminate secret holds and by Senator Mark Udall (D-CO) to end the practice of demanding that the clerks read amendments aloud. These senators had built a broad bipartisan base of support for their changes and seemed likely to succeed.

The three more aggressive major rules change proposals, by Senators Harkin, Tom Udall, and Merkley, which appeared to have no Republican support and which would have been subject to a filibuster requiring a two-thirds vote for cloture, would, under the unanimous consent agreement, be given roll-call votes with two-thirds vote thresholds. They were obviously doomed to failure. The 2-year struggle over filibuster reform finally came to a head as the Senate roll was called. The Wyden-Grassley resolution to end secret holds was adopted overwhelmingly, 92–4. Senator Mark Udall's commonsense proposal to end the stalling tactic of requiring amendments to be read on the floor also was adopted by a strong bipartisan vote of 81–15.

The more radical reforms were rejected. Senator Tom Udall's effort to eliminate filibusters on the motion to proceed and to guarantee amendments for the minority was defeated, 44–51. The Merkley "talking filibuster" was defeated 46–49. The Senate most clearly rejected Senator Harkin's effort to sweep away the filibuster in the Senate by a resounding 12–84 vote. This was an even smaller number of votes in support of the Harkin proposal than the 19 it had received in 1995.

Senator Tom Udall, speaking for those who supported more substantial changes to the rules, expressed the commitment to continue the battle: "While I'm disappointed this body lacks the necessary will to

enact truly substantive reforms, we have certainly succeeded in bringing reform to the forefront and shining a light on the sources of our
dysfunction . . . I'm committed to making sure the Senate is more than
just a graveyard for good ideas and we are able to address the challenges
we face as a nation."[27]

Then, in a formal colloquy on the Senate floor, the Senate's leaders,
Senator Reid and Senator McConnell, cemented the deal that they had
forged:

SENATOR REID: "The Senate was always intended to be, has always been,
and should always remain, the saucer that allows the boiling tea to cool to
ensure rash actions do not get enacted into law; to ensure that laws reflect
the cold rationality of reason and not the heat of perhaps misplaced passion. But, there has been concern in recent years that the Senate rules have
been abused—that a very few have turned rules designed to ensure careful
examination into a simple bottleneck for parochial purposes. Some have
even expressed concerned that the Senate is broken."

SENATOR MCCONNELL: "Senators in both of our parties agree that there
has been a significant breakdown in the Senate, though I am sure there are
different perspectives on the causes of the breakdown . . . But, I know that
the Majority Leader and I both care about this institution and the vital role
it plays in our democracy."

SENATOR REID: "Yes, we both would like to see a different Senate this
year—with fewer filibusters and procedural delays and more opportunities
for debate and amendments. In many cases, the problem is not necessarily
in the Senate rules, it is in the lack of restraint in the exercise of prerogatives
under the rules . . . Senator McConnell, I have discussed with you that many
Senators in the Majority have been very unhappy at the excessive use of the
filibuster the last two Congresses, particularly on motions to proceed but
also at other times when a matter that has bipartisan support is filibustered
purely for delay."

SENATOR MCCONNELL: "And, in my Caucus, I have many Senators who
have complained that the Majority Leader has abused his ability to 'fill the
amendment tree,' preventing Senators from offering and debating amendments that they believe are important, especially when a matter has not
gone through committee or cloture is filed too quickly."

Senator Reid: "As we have discussed, in the interests of comity and more
open process in the Senate, we have agreed that we should use these pro-

cedural options of filling the amendment tree and filibustering the motion to proceed infrequently."

SENATOR MCCONNELL: "I agree that both sides should do their best to reinstitute regular order, where bills come to the floor and Senators get amendments. Of course, there will be times when there is no consensus and when either side may want to use all its rights to defeat a bill. But we should endeavor to work together to follow the regular order where practicable and use our procedural options with discretion."[28]

The leaders went on to express their bipartisan joint rejection of the use of the "constitutional option":

SENATOR MCCONNELL: "I want to close by clearly reaffirming my view that if we are going to change Senate rules, we must do so within those rules. *As Rule 5 states, the Senate is a continuing body, and the rules continue unless changed within the parameters of the Rules.* I strongly reject this notion that a simple majority can muscle their way to new rules at the beginning of a new Congress. I believe this is a flawed approach. Majorities come and go. My Democratic colleagues should be wary of attempting this maneuver because they will not always be in the Majority. The Senate is not the House of Representatives, and our Founding Fathers never intended it to be. What some of my colleagues in the Majority propose would damage the institution and turn the Senate into a legislative body like the House where a simple Majority can run roughshod over the Minority. *I would oppose such an effort to change the rules with a simple majority in this Congress or the next Congress, regardless of which political party is in the majority.* I ask the Majority Leader to join me in rejecting this effort." (emphasis ours)

SENATOR REID: "I know that there is a strong interest in rules changes among many in my Caucus. In fact, I would support many of these changes through regular order. But, I agree that the proper way to change Senate rules is through the procedures established in those rules, and *I will oppose any effort in this Congress or the next to change the Senate's Rules other than through the regular order."*[29] (emphasis ours)

When the smoke cleared, two things were apparent. First, the Senate had rejected the idea that debate in the Senate should be ended by a simple majority. And second, once again the Senate had recoiled at the idea of allowing the majority party in the Senate—whichever party it might be—to change the Senate's rules without the support of at least some of the minority.

By its unwillingness to create the precedent of a "constitutional option," the Senate reinforced its status as a continuing body. By creating 67-vote thresholds by unanimous consent, it honored the provisions of Rule XXII requiring a two-thirds vote to end debate on a rules change and it operated under the Rule V requirement that rules changes be made under the existing rules.

Senator Tom Udall, gracious in his acceptance of the outcome of the Senate debate and votes, nonetheless raised vigorous exception to the inclusion of the opposition to the "constitutional option" in the majority leader's and minority leader's colloquy. "I strongly disagree that they could take away other senators' constitutional rights," he told *Politico* outside the Senate chamber. "As long as they're leaders, I assume they'll hold to it. That doesn't mean that 51 of us can't join together and say, 'We want reform on the floor.' That's all it takes."[30] The outcome will be seen by some as surrender, a failure of the forces of reform. *Politico's* headline the next morning screamed "Filibuster Reform Goes Bust." The article began, "The youth of the Senate lost a fierce fight to the filibuster Thursday, proving once again that the institution can still crush the whims of the moment. If there's any doubt that tradition trumped the fast-paced era, look to how the deal is described: a 'gentleman's agreement.'"[31] The *Los Angeles Times* headline declared, "Drive to Alter Filibusters Fizzles as Senate Adopts Modest Fixes,"[32] and Newark, New Jersey's, *Star Ledger* headlined its lead editorial, "Democrats Wimp Out on Filibuster Reform."[33]

In our view, this gets it wrong. In reality, the compromises that resulted—small incremental steps—are consistent with the long history of the Senate's struggle with the filibuster rules. Faced with those who would sweep the filibuster away, either by design or unintended consequence, the Senate acted to make some incremental changes in its rules. The route to reform of the abuse of the filibuster lies not in rewiring the Senate rules (although some changes are desirable) but in the behavior of senators themselves. The commitment of the leaders to restrain their respective caucus' use of the filibuster on the motion to proceed (in the case of the minority) and the use of the filling of the amendment tree to block amendments (in the case of the majority) was a step in the right direction. This is the kind of outcome in a Senate crisis that the former giants of the Senate would recognize.

The agreement passed its first important test in the 112th Congress. The Republican majority was able to offer a completely non-germane and politically potent amendment to an aviation bill, titled "Repealing the Job-Killing Health Care Law Act,"[34] to repeal President Obama's signal health reform bill, an action the Republican-controlled House of Representatives had already adopted. The Democratic majority, consistent with the agreement between Majority Leader Reid and Minority Leader McConnell, did not block the amendment. (Although, by unanimous consent, 60 votes were required for the amendment to succeed.) The minority Republicans did not filibuster proceeding to the bill and a debate and roll-call vote took place. Democrats defeated the amendment on a party-line 47–51 vote.[35]

"It worked," said Senator John Barrasso (R-WY). "No shenanigans."[36] Fellow Republican leader Senator Lamar Alexander added, "This is the way the Senate ought to work . . . An important bill got to the floor. It is getting a whole variety of amendments on everything from the Davis-Bacon Act to health care. We will end up passing a bill and take a step that we should have taken some time ago. Truth is, it is not taking any longer than it used to because we were just sitting around doing nothing."[37]

Former congressman Lee Hamilton, who now heads the Center on Congress at Indiana University, wrote:

> Here's what's most notable about the whole thing: the sky didn't fall. The health-care amendment got voted down, the Senate moved on to the substance of the aviation bill, and senators on both sides agreed that the atmosphere in the Senate had benefited from this break in the ongoing partisan wars. There's a lesson here, and it's a simple one. Basic fairness in legislative procedure is essential to the smooth running of Congress and to the achievement of consensus . . . [T]he Senate is to be commended for taking a break from the partisan wars. Let's hope it lasts, and that the House

follows its example. We now have an entire generation of politicians on Capitol Hill who've known little besides the frustration and anger of "let's ram it through" politics, and they need a chance to learn what fair process looks like—and how much they might be able to get done if they allow it to flourish.[38]

Even in the most dramatic moment of the year, the passage of the legislation to avoid a default by the federal government by lifting the debt ceiling, the opponents shied away from a filibuster. In an illustration of how the importance of the moment and the emerging public consensus can restrain even the most strident minorities, Senator Jim DeMint (R-SC), one of the Senate's most notorious practitioners of the filibuster, explained: "If we had done that, then you guys in the media would have concluded . . . that we are just trying to just obstruct the whole process, when that's not what we've done. That's the way they try to marginalize you: If you're not for the grand deal, you're a right-wing nut."[39]

The Senate can build on this. The route to broader reforms is to seek a bipartisan approach. The rules demand it. But, more importantly, the historical role of the U.S. Senate requires it. We think this is achievable if the effective date of the reforms is far enough in the future that neither party caucus views the decision from the perspective of solely the majority or the minority.

But on the subject of the Senate's filibuster, there is only one certainty. The subject of filibuster reform will be back—again and again. Senator Tom Udall has promised as much and most every majority, particularly when they have a president of their party in the White House, will seek a more "efficient" route to the enactment of its agenda. They will decry the filibuster. The opposition will accuse them of seeking a "power grab" and the battle will again be joined.

Already in October 2011, another rules crisis arose. When Majority Leader Reid was able to invoke cloture on a Chinese currency bill, the Republicans continued to bog down consideration of the bill by using the parliamentary maneuver of offering motions to suspend Rule XXII in order to offer non-germane amendments. Although suspending the rules requires a two-thirds vote (no motion to suspend the rules has succeeded since 1941), the minority in this way forces a vote. Majority Leader Reid became frustrated by a series of such efforts, the last straw being the minority's effort to embarrass the Democrats by forcing a vote on the original version of President Obama's jobs bill, which contained provisions that some members of the Democratic caucus opposed. In response, Senator Reid led the Democratic majority onto the slippery slope with a "nuclear option"–like ploy. Senator Reid raised a point of order that motions to suspend the rules were not in order post-cloture, arguing that they were dilatory. The presiding officer, Senator Mark Begich (D-AK), acting on the advice of Senate Parliamentarian Alan Frumin, ruled against the point of order. On appeal, the Senate by a near-party-line vote, 51–48, overturned the ruling. This creates the precedent in the Senate that post-cloture motions to waive the rules are not in order. The danger is that Senator Reid's successful maneuver will encourage future Senate majorities to use a less narrowly drawn "nuclear option" to eviscerate the filibuster. Former Senate majority secretary Marty Paone, who spent many years as the principal parliamentary advisor to Senate Democrats, said, "It's a can of worms they took down off the shelf—it's always been there . . . Hopefully they'll put it on the back shelf and forget about it again."[40]

In December 2011 and January 2012, a series of events raised the issue of obstruction of presidential nominations once more. First, the Senate Republicans held hostage the nomination of Richard Cordray for director of the Consumer Financial Protection Bureau based not on his qualifications but on their unwillingness to accept the existence of the agency, which was created as a part of last year's Dodd-Frank financial regulatory reform legislation.

Second, the president threatened to exercise his powers in a way the Constitution's Framers likely would have found surprising if not troubling when he circumvented the Senate's "advice and consent" responsibilities by making a recess appointment.

Third, the Republican minority forced the president's hand by its use of sham "pro forma" Senate sessions every few days to avoid a congressional recess and thus frustrate Obama's ability to make a recess appointment.

Finally, in a highly controversial action the president brushed aside long-standing precedent and ignored these sessions, treated the Senate as if it were in recess even if it said it wasn't, and made the recess appointments of Cordray and three members of the National Labor Relations Board.

The use of the filibuster for such unbridled obstructionism—in our judgment an abuse of the Senate rules—reignited demands for limits. President Obama, in his State of the Union address, called for a reform that would limit debate on confirmation of presidential nominations.

In these times of polarized partisan warfare in the Congress, it will be difficult but all the more important that senators avoid abusing the filibuster and related tactics, so that it can better serve its functions of protecting the minority and fostering consensus. We have called it "the soul of the Senate." In the oft-cited *Mr. Smith Goes to Washington,* famed broadcaster H. V. Kaltenborn, playing himself broadcasting from the Senate galleries, declares: "Half of official Washington is here to see democracy's finest show, the filibuster, the right to talk your head off, the American privilege of free speech in its most dramatic form."[41]

APPENDIX A. COMPARISON OF LIBERAL-CONSERVATIVE VOTE SCORES

			ARENBERG MEASURE	NATIONAL JOURNAL	SENATE CONSERVATIVE FUND	ADA	CQ BUSH OPPOSE	DW-NOMINATE SCORES
Levin	MI	D	100.0%	80.2%	100.0%	100.0%	69%	−0.467
Akaka	HI	D	97.2%	86.8%	100.0%	100.0%	70%	−0.491
Bingaman	NM	D	97.2%	88.2%	100.0%	100.0%	72%	−0.367
Stabenow	MI	D	96.2%	83.2%	98.1%	100.0%	69%	−0.441
Durbin	IL	D	96.2%	85.7%	98.1%	100.0%	69%	−0.542
Cardin	MD	D	96.2%	85.7%	96.2%	100.0%	69%	−0.487
Biden	DE	D	96.1%	84.8%	100.0%	80.0%	67%	−0.331
Murray	WA	D	96.1%	92.7%	100.0%	95.0%	72%	−0.417
Kerry, John	MA	D	96.1%	74.2%	98.0%	95.0%	70%	−0.471
Kennedy	MA	D	96.0%	*	100.0%	*	82%	−0.523
Clinton	NY	D	95.4%	82.2%	94.4%	*	62%	−0.461
Leahy	VT	D	95.2%	82.3%	96.2%	100.0%	70%	−0.481
Schumer	NY	D	94.8%	85.7%	98.1%	100.0%	70%	−0.446
Reed	RI	D	94.8%	91.5%	96.2%	95.0%	65%	−0.512
Brown, Sherrod	OH	D	94.8%	75.8%	96.2%	95.0%	70%	−0.570
Casey	PA	D	94.8%	79.3%	96.2%	90.0%	65%	−0.391
Wyden	OR	D	94.7%	76.8%	94.2%	95.0%	72%	−0.425
Kohl	WI	D	94.4%	81.7%	98.1%	95.0%	63%	−0.365

			ARENBERG MEASURE	NATIONAL JOURNAL	SENATE CONSERVATIVE FUND	ADA	CQ BUSH OPPOSE	DW-NOMINATE SCORES
Dodd	CT	D	94.3%	82.8%	96.2%	100.0%	69%	-0.440
Klobuchar	MN	D	94.2%	65.0%	88.7%	100.0%	69%	-0.371
Lautenberg	NJ	D	94.1%	88.3%	98.1%	100.0%	70%	-0.522
Boxer	CA	D	94.0%	90.2%	98.1%	95.0%	70%	-0.567
Cantwell	WA	D	93.9%	81.0%	94.3%	100.0%	72%	-0.388
Tester	MT	D	93.8%	63.0%	90.6%	85.0%	70%	-0.347
Menendez	NJ	D	93.7%	82.2%	98.1%	100.0%	72%	-0.512
Harkin	IA	D	93.7%	76.5%	96.1%	95.0%	75%	-0.541
Sanders	VT	I	93.4%	82.3%	96.2%	100.0%	70%	-0.712
Baucus	MT	D	93.4%	68.3%	94.3%	80.0%	65%	-0.211
Dorgan	ND	D	93.2%	68.3%	92.5%	90.0%	70%	-0.358
Mikulski	MD	D	92.7%	72.7%	98.1%	90.0%	58%	-0.421
Webb	VA	D	92.3%	63.8%	94.3%	95.0%	58%	-0.251
Conrad	ND	D	92.2%	64.7%	100.0%	90.0%	60%	-0.305
Whitehouse	RI	D	92.0%	80.3%	96.2%	90.0%	59%	-0.531
Feinstein	CA	D	91.9%	81.0%	98.1%	100.0%	62%	-0.359
Salazar	CO	D	91.5%	67.8%	98.1%	95.0%	57%	-0.293
Nelson, Bill	FL	D	91.4%	79.3%	96.2%	95.0%	58%	-0.310
Rockefeller	WV	D	91.3%	70.8%	100.0%	85.0%	55%	-0.390
Obama	IL	D	90.8%	*	92.3%	*	72%	-0.451
Reid	NV	D	90.0%	77.3%	96.2%	70.0%	57%	-0.433
Inouye	HI	D	89.4%	69.5%	98.0%	85.0%	54%	-0.377

			ARENBERG MEASURE	NATIONAL JOURNAL	SENATE CONSERVATIVE FUND	ADA	CQ BUSH OPPOSE	DW-NOMINATE SCORES
Byrd, Robert	WV	D	89.2%	77.7%	97.1%	*	69%	−0.374
Lieberman	CT	D/I	89.1%	59.3%	96.2%	85.0%	48%	−0.312
Lincoln	AR	D	88.2%	65.5%	90.6%	80.0%	59%	−0.246
Johnson	SD	D	87.8%	55.8%	92.5%	80.0%	56%	−0.306
Pryor, Mark	AR	D	87.2%	56.8%	96.2%	85.0%	54%	−0.268
Feingold	WI	D	86.9%	65.0%	79.2%	100.0%	70%	−0.769
Carper	DE	D	86.7%	64.7%	92.5%	85.0%	55%	−0.263
McCaskill	MO	D	86.6%	51.8%	75.0%	80.0%	55%	−0.296
Nelson, Ben	NE	D	85.0%	49.8%	86.8%	75.0%	52%	−0.072
Bayh, Evan	IN	D	80.9%	47.3%	76.0%	70.0%	53%	−0.204
Landrieu	LA	D	80.6%	50.7%	79.2%	65.0%	47%	−0.234
Snowe	ME	R	78.8%	50.8%	83.0%	80.0%	52%	0.045
Smith, Gordon	OR	R	71.1%	45.7%	63.5%	60.0%	51%	0.149
Collins	ME	R	73.2%	49.0%	62.3%	75.0%	41%	0.074
Specter	PA	R	66.5%	44.8%	55.8%	45.0%	42%	0.092
Coleman	MN	R	63.7%	39.0%	50.9%	45.0%	42%	0.168
Stevens	AK	R	59.6%	41.0%	54.0%	30.0%	31%	0.270
Dole, Elizabeth	NC	R	58.2%	39.2%	46.0%	40.0%	42%	0.409
Voinovich	OH	R	57.5%	38.7%	49.1%	25.0%	26%	0.225
Cochran	MS	R	57.5%	34.3%	41.5%	15.0%	26%	0.354
Murkowski, Lisa	AK	R	57.0%	42.2%	50.0%	25.0%	28%	0.249
Martinez	FL	R	56.0%	37.5%	42.3%	30.0%	33%	0.357

			ARENBERG MEASURE	NATIONAL JOURNAL	SENATE CONSERVATIVE FUND	ADA	CQ BUSH OPPOSE	DW-NOMINATE SCORES
Domenici	NM	R	55.2%	33.8%	45.8%	20.0%	27%	0.282
Lugar	IN	R	55.0%	38.2%	36.5%	25.0%	13%	0.259
Hagel	NE	R	52.7%	40.2%	40.4%	10.0%	21%	0.340
Roberts	KS	R	52.2%	29.8%	29.8%	20.0%	35%	0.387
Bennett, Bob	UT	R	51.0%	34.2%	39.6%	15.0%	15%	0.375
Warner, John	VA	R	50.8%	40.2%	45.7%	40.0%	28%	0.261
Sununu	NH	R	47.8%	34.2%	25.5%	25.0%	21%	0.429
Alexander	TN	R	47.7%	21.5%	30.2%	25.0%	23%	0.355
Hutchison, Kay	TX	R	47.6%	19.7%	20.8%	20.0%	33%	0.371
Bond	MO	R	46.5%	14.7%	21.6%	20.0%	22%	0.346
Hatch	UT	R	46.2%	25.2%	24.5%	10.0%	20%	0.333
Grassley	IA	R	46.0%	17.7%	22.6%	25.0%	28%	0.416
Isakson	GA	R	45.9%	21.7%	22.6%	25.0%	28%	0.507
Corker	TN	R	45.9%	22.2%	20.8%	20.0%	28%	0.409
Shelby	AL	D/R	45.2%	26.3%	22.6%	15.0%	26%	0.422
Brownback	KS	R	45.1%	24.0%	19.2%	5.0%	22%	0.446
Wicker	MS	R	44.8%	21.3%	24.5%	10.0%	30%	0.424
Craig	ID	R	44.2%	20.3%	21.6%	15.0%	35%	0.455
McConnell	KY	R	44.1%	14.7%	20.8%	20.0%	24%	0.486
Chambliss	GA	R	43.8%	16.3%	20.8%	25.0%	28%	0.515
Thune	SD	R	43.6%	11.2%	15.1%	10.0%	24%	0.492
Graham, Lindsey	SC	R	42.3%	15.5%	16.3%	15.0%	28%	0.500

			ARENBERG MEASURE	NATIONAL JOURNAL	SENATE CONSERVATIVE FUND	ADA	CQ BUSH OPPOSE	DW-NOMINATE SCORES
Crapo	ID	R	41.9%	17.3%	17.0%	15.0%	24%	0.503
Cornyn	TX	R	41.8%	16.5%	18.0%	20.0%	27%	0.559
Sessions	AL	R	38.2%	20.8%	9.4%	20.0%	26%	0.588
Burr	NC	R	36.8%	11.8%	13.5%	5.0%	19%	0.594
Gregg	NH	R	36.2%	21.0%	15.4%	15.0%	18%	0.459
McCain	AZ	R	35.7%	*	23.1%	5.0%	11%	0.423
Bunning	KY	R	35.3%	9.7%	9.6%	5.0%	21%	0.659
Enzi	WY	R	34.3%	6.8%	3.8%	5.0%	22%	0.626
Vitter	LA	R	33.5%	10.0%	9.4%	5.0%	24%	0.617
Allard	CO	R	33.3%	8.7%	5.9%	5.0%	28%	0.623
Barrasso	WY	R	33.3%	6.8%	1.9%	5.0%	24%	0.625
Ensign	NV	R	32.8%	6.8%	4.0%	0.0%	17%	0.627
Inhofe	OK	R	30.6%	9.3%	3.9%	5.0%	25%	0.741
Kyl	AZ	R	28.2%	6.8%	1.9%	0.0%	17%	0.653
Coburn	OK	R	25.4%	8.0%	3.8%	0.0%	15%	0.930
DeMint	SC	R	21.9%	7.7%	0.0%	0.0%	16%	0.843

APPENDIX B. COMPARISON OF LIBERAL-CONSERVATIVE VOTE SCORE RANKINGS

			ARENBERG MEASURE	NATIONAL JOURNAL	SENATE CONSERVATIVE FUND	ADA	CQ BUSH OPPOSE	DW-NOMINATE SCORES
Levin	MI	D	1	21	1	1	20	16
Akaka	HI	D	2	6	1	1	9	12
Bingaman	NM	D	2	5	1	1	3	32
Stabenow	MI	D	4	11	9	1	20	20
Durbin	IL	D	4	7	9	1	20	5
Cardin	MD	D	4	7	22	1	20	13
Biden	DE	D	7	10	1	39	27	37
Murray	WA	D	7	1	1	17	3	25
Kerry, John	MA	D	7	29	19	17	9	15
Kennedy	MA	D	10	*	1	*	1	8
Clinton	NY	D	11	15	35	*	32	17
Leahy	VT	D	12	13	22	1	9	14
Schumer	NY	D	13	7	9	1	9	19
Reed	RI	D	13	2	22	17	28	10
Brown, Sherrod	OH	D	13	28	22	17	9	3
Casey	PA	D	13	22	22	28	28	26

			ARENBERG MEASURE	NATIONAL JOURNAL	SENATE CONSERVATIVE FUND	ADA	CQ BUSH OPPOSE	DW-NOMINATE SCORES
Wyden	OR	D	17	26	39	17	3	23
Kohl	WI	D	18	17	9	17	31	33
Dodd	CT	D	19	12	22	1	20	21
Klobuchar	MN	D	20	37	46	1	20	31
Lautenberg	NJ	D	21	4	9	1	9	9
Boxer	CA	D	22	3	9	17	9	4
Cantwell	WA	D	23	18	36	1	3	28
Tester	MT	D	24	41	44	33	9	36
Menendez	NJ	D	25	15	9	1	3	10
Harkin	IA	D	25	27	34	17	2	6
Sanders	VT	I	27	13	22	1	9	3
Baucus	MT	D	27	33	36	39	28	49
Dorgan	ND	D	29	33	40	28	9	35
Mikulski	MD	D	29	30	9	28	37	24
Webb	VA	D	31	40	36	17	37	46
Conrad	ND	D	32	39	1	28	34	41
Whitehouse	RI	D	33	20	22	28	35	7
Feinstein	CA	D	34	18	9	1	32	34
Salazar	CO	D	35	35	9	17	40	43
Nelson, Bill	FL	D	36	22	22	17	37	39
Rockefeller	WV	D	37	31	1	33	43	27
Obama	IL	D	38	*	43	*	3	18

			ARENBERG MEASURE	NATIONAL JOURNAL	SENATE CONSERVATIVE FUND	ADA	CQ BUSH OPPOSE	DW-NOMINATE SCORES
Reid	NV	D	39	25	22	46	40	22
Inouye	HI	D	40	32	19	33	46	29
Byrd, Robert	WV	D	41	24	21	*	20	30
Lieberman	CT	D/I	42	43	22	33	52	38
Lincoln	AR	D	43	36	44	39	35	47
Johnson	SD	D	44	45	40	39	42	40
Pryor, Mark	AR	D	45	44	22	33	46	44
Feingold	WI	D	46	37	49	1	9	1
Carper	DE	D	47	42	40	33	43	45
McCaskill	MO	D	48	46	52	39	43	42
Nelson, Ben	NE	D	49	49	47	45	49	51
Bayh, Evan	IN	D	50	51	51	47	48	50
Landrieu	LA	D	51	48	49	48	53	48
Snowe	ME	R	52	47	48	39	49	52
Smith, Gordon	OR	R	53	52	53	49	51	55
Collins	ME	R	54	50	54	45	57	53
Specter	PA	R	55	53	55	50	54	54
Coleman	MN	R	56	59	57	50	54	56
Stevens	AK	R	57	55	56	54	62	61
Dole, Elizabeth	NC	R	58	58	60	52	54	72
Voinovich	OH	R	59	60	59	56	74	57
Cochran	MS	R	59	63	64	72	74	66

		ARENBERG MEASURE	NATIONAL JOURNAL	SENATE CONSERVATIVE FUND	ADA	CQ BUSH OPPOSE	DW-NOMINATE SCORES
Murkowski, Lisa	AK	R	61	54	58	56	64	58
Martinez	FL	R	62	62	63	54	60	68
Domenici	NM	R	63	66	61	64	72	62
Lugar	IN	R	64	61	67	56	99	59
Hagel	NE	R	65	56	65	79	88	64
Roberts	KS	R	66	67	69	64	58	71
Bennett, Bob	UT	R	67	64	66	72	97	70
Warner, John	VA	R	68	56	62	52	64	60
Sununu	NH	R	69	64	70	56	88	78
Alexander	TN	R	70	73	68	56	84	67
Hutchison, Kay	TX	R	71	78	80	64	60	69
Bond	MO	R	72	84	77	64	85	65
Hatch	UT	R	73	69	71	79	91	63
Grassley	IA	R	74	79	74	56	64	74
Isakson	GA	R	75	72	74	56	64	86
Corker	TN	R	75	71	79	64	64	72
Shelby	AL	D/R	77	68	74	72	74	75
Brownback	KS	R	78	70	83	83	85	79
Wicker	MS	R	79	74	71	79	63	77
Craig	ID	R	80	77	77	72	58	80
McConnell	KY	R	81	84	80	64	79	82
Chambliss	GA	R	82	82	80	56	64	87

			ARENBERG MEASURE	NATIONAL JOURNAL	SENATE CONSERVATIVE FUND	ADA	CQ BUSH OPPOSE	DW-NOMINATE SCORES
Thune	SD	R	83	87	88	79	79	83
Graham, Lindsey	SC	R	84	83	86	72	64	84
Crapo	ID	R	85	80	85	72	79	85
Cornyn	TX	R	86	81	84	64	72	88
Sessions	AL	R	87	76	91	64	74	89
Burr	NC	R	88	86	89	83	92	90
Gregg	NH	R	89	75	87	72	93	81
McCain	AZ	R	90	*	73	83	100	76
Bunning	KY	R	91	89	90	83	88	97
Enzi	WY	R	92	94	95	83	85	94
Vitter	LA	R	93	88	91	83	79	91
Allard	CO	R	94	91	93	83	64	92
Barrasso	WY	R	94	94	98	83	79	93
Ensign	NV	R	96	94	94	92	94	95
Inhofe	OK	R	97	90	96	83	78	98
Kyl	AZ	R	98	94	98	92	94	96
Coburn	OK	R	99	92	97	92	97	100
DeMint	SC	R	100	93	100	92	96	99

NOTES

1. SOUL OF THE SENATE

1. "Senate's Abuse of Filibuster Rule Threatens Democracy," *San Jose Mercury News,* January 28, 2010.

2. Paul Krugman, "A Dangerous Dysfunction," *New York Times,* December 20, 2009, A31.

3. "Filibuster Abuse: Founding Fathers Didn't Plan It This Way," *Patriot-News* (Harrisburg, Pa.), February 16, 2010, accessed July 1, 2011, http://www.pennlive.com/editorials/index.ssf/2010/02/filibuster_abuse_founding_fath.html.

4. "Filibuster, Gone Rogue: A Senate Rule That Cripples Our Democracy," *Star-Ledger* (Newark, N.J.), January 10, 2010, accessed July 1, 2011, http://blog.nj.com/njv_editorial_page/2010/01/filibuster_gone_rogue_a_senate.html.

5. Clay Dumas, "Tyranny of the Minority," *Harvard Crimson* (Cambridge, Mass.), February 17, 2010, accessed July 1, 2011, http://www.thecrimson.com/article/2010/2/17/year-filibuster-republicans-democrats/.

6. Thomas Geoghegan, "Mr. Smith Rewrites the Constitution," *New York Times,* January 10, 2010, A17.

7. Lloyd Cutler, "The Way to Kill Senate Rule XXII," *Washington Post,* April 19, 1993, A23.

8. "Time to Retire the Filibuster," *New York Times,* January 1, 1995, accessed July 1, 2011, http://www.nytimes.com/1995/01/01/opinion/time-to-retire-the-filibuster.html.

9. Ryan Grim, "Pelosi: End the Filibuster," *Huffington Post,* July 1, 2010, accessed July 5, 2011, http://www.huffingtonpost.com/2010/07/01/pelosi-end-the-filibuster_n_632851.html.

10. From its earliest known sources, the liquid is sometimes reported as tea. sometimes as coffee. According to Senator Robert Byrd, the story's first known appearance is in an 1871 letter from constitutional law professor Francis Lieber to Ohio representative and later president James A. Garfield (*Congressional Record,*

April 24, 2006). According to the Jefferson Encyclopedia on the Monticello website: "To date, no evidence has surfaced that such a conversation actually took place. The earliest known appearance of this story is in *Harper's New Monthly Magazine* in 1884 ... It was repeated by M. D. Conway in his *Omitted Chapters of History Disclosed in the Life and Papers of Edmund Randolph,* first published in 1888. Since then, the story has appeared many times in print, usually prefaced by the phrase, 'the story goes . . .' or something similar. There is no definitive proof that this story is not true. However, one possible indication that it is apocryphal is the fact that, to all appearances, Jefferson was not against the idea of a bicameral legislature. He wrote to the Marquis de Lafayette in 1789, '. . . for good legislation two houses are necessary . . .'" (http://wiki.monticello.org/mediawiki/index.php/ Senatorial_Saucer#_note-2).

11. U.S. Senate website, www.senate.gov.

12. Sarah A. Binder and Steven S. Smith, *Politics or Principle? Filibustering in the United States Senate* (Washington, D.C.: Brookings Institution Press, 1997), 1, 4.

13. Senator Tom Harkin, *Congressional Record,* February 11, 2010, S571.

14. William Ewart Gladstone, *Gleanings of Past Years, 1875–8,* vol. 1 (London: John Murray, 1879), 220.

15. See chapter 2: the Senate's previous question motion, even when it did exist (1789–1806) very likely did not serve the purpose of ending debate and bringing the matter to vote.

16. Martin B. Gold, *Senate Procedure and Practice,* 2nd ed. (Lanham, Md.: Rowman & Littlefield, 2008), 48.

17. Roy Ulrich, "A Critique of the Senate Filibuster," *Huffington Post,* May 2, 2009, accessed June 5, 2011, http://www.huffingtonpost.com/roy-ulrich/a-critique-of-the-senate_b_193861.html.

18. Senator Orville Platt, *Congressional Record,* September 21, 1893, 1636.

19. U.S. Senate website, www.senate.gov.

20. "Legislative Bomb," *Nation,* April 25, 2005, accessed July 1, 2011, http://www.thenation.com/article/legislative-bomb.

21. Vice President Joseph Biden, *Face the Nation,* February 14, 2010.

22. Some historians think it was Alexander Hamilton who wrote *The Federalist* No. 51.

23. James Madison, *The Federalist* No. 51, February 6, 1788.

24. Lindsay Rogers, *The American Senate* (New York: Knopf, 1926), 16.

25. Walter F. Mondale, U.S. Senate Leaders' Lecture Series, September 4, 2002, U.S. Senate website, www.senate.gov.

26. Walter F. Mondale, "Testimony of Hon. Walter F. Mondale," Joint Committee on the Organization of Congress hearing, July 1, 1993, 20.

27. Walter F. Mondale, "Resolved: Fix the Filibuster," *New York Times,* January 2, 2011, WK10.

2. FILIBUSTER, CLOTURE, AND UNFETTERED AMENDMENT

1. Robert C. Byrd, *The Senate 1789–1989: Addresses on the History of the United States Senate,* vol. 1 (Washington, D.C.: U.S. Government Printing Office, 1988), 93. Byrd cites John Langhorne and William Langhorne, *Plutarch's Lives* (1855), 499.

2. Franklin L. Burdette, *Filibustering in the Senate* (Princeton, N.J.: Princeton University Press, 1940), 13.

3. U.S. Senate website, www.senate.gov.

4. Under certain circumstances, such as appropriations bills, when cloture has been invoked on legislation, budget resolutions, reconciliation bills, and other legislation given expedited procedures under law, amendments must be germane.

5. Walter J. Oleszek, "'Holds' in the Senate," Congressional Research Service, May 19, 2008, 1.

6. Senator Tom Harkin, *Congressional Record,* January 4, 1995, S33.

7. Martin Gold, counsel to the Senate Republican Leader, 1979–1982, 2003–2004, oral history interview, 2004, Senate Historical Office, U.S. Senate website, www.senate.gov.

8. Senator Harry Reid, *Congressional Record,* December 15, 2010, S10261.

9. Such use of obstructive tactics has grown year by year, and the Republicans who are most recently in the minority have engaged in these tactics even more extensively. We explore this in the next chapter.

10. Barbara Sinclair, "The New World of U.S. Senators," in *Congress Reconsidered,* ed. Lawrence Dodd and Bruce Oppenheimer (Washington, D.C.: CQ Press, 2009), 7.

11. Orrin Hatch, *Square Peg: Confessions of a Citizen Senator* (New York: Basic Books, 2002), 26–27.

12. Ibid., 27.

13. Ibid.

14. Senator Carl Levin, *Congressional Record,* May 20, 2005, S5560.

15. Senator George J. Mitchell, U.S. Senate Leaders' Lecture Series, June 16, 1999, U.S. Senate website, www.senate.gov.

3. HISTORY OF THE FILIBUSTER

1. Joseph Cooper, *The Previous Question: Its Standing as a Precedent for Cloture in the United States Senate* (Washington, D.C.: U.S. Government Printing Office, 1962), 26.

2. Ibid., 15–26.

3. Byrd, *The Senate,* vol. 1, 48.

4. Mary-Jo Kline and Joanne Wood Ryan, eds., *Political Correspondence and Public Papers of Aaron Burr,* vol. 2 (Princeton, N.J.: Princeton University Press, 1983), 912.

5. Robert C. Byrd, *The Senate 1789–1989: Addresses on the History of the United States Senate,* vol. 2 (Washington, D.C.: U.S. Government Printing Office, 1991), 96–97.

6. Ibid., 97.

7. U.S. Senate website, "Art and History," www.senate.gov.

8. Byrd, *The Senate,* vol. 2, 105–106.

9. Burdette, *Filibustering,* 23.

10. Ibid.

11. Richard A. Baker, *The Senate of the United States: A Bicentennial History* (Malabar, Fla.: Krieger, 1988), 43.

12. Thomas Hart Benton, *Thirty Years' View: A History of the Working of the American Government for Thirty Years, from 1820 to 1850,* vol. 2 (New York: Appleton and Company, 1873), 255.

13. Ibid.

14. Ibid.

15. Ibid.

16. Gregory J. Wawro and Eric Schickler, *Filibuster: Obstruction and Lawmaking in the U.S. Senate* (Princeton, N.J.: Princeton University Press, 2006), 76.

17. *Oxford English Dictionary,* 2nd ed., 1989; online version, September 2011. http://www.oed.com/view/Entry/70179; accessed 20 September 2011. Earlier version first published in *New English Dictionary,* 1896.

18. Ibid.

19. In 1959, the Senate, based on a recommendation from a special committee headed by then senator John Kennedy, honored its five "most outstanding" members in history. Portraits of each were painted on the walls of the Senate Reception Room. The five senators were Henry Clay, John C. Calhoun, Daniel Webster, Robert Taft, and La Follette.

20. Burdette, *Filibustering,* 120.

21. Ibid.

22. Ibid.

23. Ibid., 121. "Sine die" is generally the final adjournment of a session of Congress. Technically it means "without a day certain for reconvening."

24. Ibid.

25. "Text of the President's Statement to the Public," *New York Times,* March 5, 1917, accessed July 2, 2011, http://query.nytimes.com/mem/archive-free/pdf?res=F1 0815FE3F5E11738DDDAC0894DB405B878DF1D3.

26. U.S. Constitution, Article II, Section 3 provides: "[the president] may, on extraordinary occasions, convene both Houses, or either of them . . ."

27. U.S. Senate website, www.senate.gov.

28. U.S. Senate website, "Reference," www.senate.gov.

29. Ibid.

30. Ibid. (through the end of the 111th Congress in 2010).

31. On October 19, 2000, the Senate voted to add the portraits of Arthur Vandenberg and Robert Wagner to those of the "Famous Five" in the Senate Reception Room.

32. Senator Arthur Vandenberg, *Congressional Record*, August 2, 1948, S9603.

33. Ibid.

34. Floyd M. Riddick, oral history interview, 1979, Senate Historical Office, U.S. Senate website, www.senate.gov.

35. Senator Carl Levin, *Congressional Record*, May 12, 2005, S10533.

36. Ibid.

37. Ibid.

38. For a time at the outset of the 111th Congress, the seats of former Senators Obama (who, of course, had been elected president), Biden (vice president), Salazar (secretary of the interior), and Clinton (secretary of state) were temporarily vacant and therefore cloture under Rule XXII required 59 votes at the time.

4. POLARIZED POLITICS AND THE USE AND ABUSE OF THE FILIBUSTER

1. Jean Edward Smith, "Filibusters: The Senate's Self Inflicted Wound," *New York Times*, March 1, 2009, A16.

2. It has even been used to set a 67-vote threshold on rules changes for the same reason.

3. Senator Harry Reid, *Congressional Record*, February 11, 2008, S845.

4. 57–41, Senate roll-call vote #13, February 12, 2008.

5. Sinclair, "The New World," 11.

6. Ezra Klein, "The Rise of the Filibuster: An Interview with Barbara Sinclair," *Washington Post*, December 26, 2009, accessed July 17, 2011, http://voices.washington post.com/ezra-klein/2009/12/the_right_of_the_filibuster_an.html.

7. Norman J. Ornstein, Thomas E. Mann, and Michael J. Malbin, *Vital Statistics on Congress, 2008* (Washington, D.C.: Brookings Institution Press, 2008).

8. U.S. Senate website, www.senate.gov.

9. Ibid.

10. Ibid.

11. Ibid.

12. Ibid.

13. Ibid.

14. David Lightman, "Senate Republicans: Filibuster Everything to Win in November?" McClatchy Newspapers, February 12, 2010, accessed July 2, 2011, http://www.mcclatchydc.com/2010/02/12/84487/senate-republicans-filibuster.html.

15. Gregory Koger, *Filibustering: A Political History of Obstructionism in the House and Senate* (Chicago: University of Chicago Press, 2010), 133.

16. Bruce I. Oppenheimer, "Changing Time Constraints on Congress: Historical Perspectives on the Use of Cloture," in *Congress Reconsidered,* 3rd ed., ed. Lawrence S. Dodd and Bruce I. Oppenheimer (Washington, D.C.: CQ Press, 1985), 393–413.

17. Averages are based on data from the Senate Daily Digest, Office of the Secretary of the Senate.

18. Ornstein, Mann, and Malbin, *Vital Statistics,* 74. Data was updated to include the 2008 election by co-author Michael Malbin on the website of the Campaign Finance Institute, www.cfinst.org.

19. Ibid.

20. Spending totals from the 2008 campaign are from the Federal Election Commission website, www.fec.gov.

21. E. J. Dionne, "Chris Dodd, the Senate's Happy Warrior," *Washington Post,* August 9, 2010, accessed July 2, 2011, http://www.washingtonpost.com/wp-dynyn/content/article/2010/08/08/AR2010080802395.html.

22. Eric Redman, *The Dance of Legislation* (Seattle: University of Washington Press, 2001), 8.

23. Joint Committee on the Organization of Congress, *Organization of the Congress—Final Report.* Washington, D.C.: U.S. Government Printing Office, 1993, 1, accessed July 2, 2011, http://www.rules.house.gov/Archives/jcoc2p.htm.

24. Barbara Sinclair, "Examining the Filibuster: Legislative Proposals to Change Senate Procedures," U.S. Senate Committee on Rules and Administration, hearings, July 28, 2010.

25. Ibid.

26. During the tumultuous Reconstruction period, President Andrew Johnson was impeached on a party line vote. Like Clinton, he was acquitted. President Richard Nixon resigned in the face of sure impeachment by a bipartisan majority.

27. The House votes were 228–206 on the grounds of perjury to a grand jury and 221–212 on obstruction of justice. Two additional articles were defeated by the House.

28. Thomas E. Mann and Norman J. Ornstein, *The Broken Branch: How Congress Is Failing America and How to Get It Back on Track* (New York: Oxford University Press, 2006), 9.

29. Adam Clymer, "No Deal; Politics and the Dead Arts of Compromise," *New York Times,* October 22, 1995, accessed July 2, 2011, http://www.nytimes.com/1995/10/22/weekinreview/no-deal-politics-and-the-dead-arts-of-compromise.html?pagewanted=3&src=pm.

30. Ibid.

31. Richard E Cohen, Kirk Victor and David Bauman, "The State of Congress," *National Journal,* January 10, 2004, 83–84.

32. Ibid., 84.

33. Charles Babington, "Ethics Panel Rebukes DeLay: Majority Leader Offered Favor to Get Peer's Vote," *Washington Post,* October 1, 2004, A01.

34. *Congressional Record,* July 19, 2007, S9581–S9582.

35. Ibid.

36. Senator Mitch McConnell, *Congressional Record,* July 19, 2007, S9582–S9583.

37. Ibid., S9583.

38. Ibid.

39. This is pursuant to Article I, Section 5 of the Constitution, which provides that each House may authorize less than a quorum "to compel the attendance of absent Members, in such manner, and under such penalties as each House may provide."

40. Helen Dewar, "Midnight Manhunt in the Senate; 'Banana Republic' Dragnet Hit After Packwood's Arrest in Filibuster," *Washington Post,* February 25, 1988, A1.

41. Senator Harry Reid, *Congressional Record,* July 21, 2010, S6041.

42. "Toward a More Responsible Two-Party System," *American Political Science Review* 44 (September 1950).

43. Ibid.

44. "Massachusetts: The Gentleman from Martin, Mr. North Attleboro," *Time,* March 15, 1968.

45. Barbara Sinclair, "Tip O'Neill and Contemporary House Leadership," in *Masters of the House: Congressional Leaders Over Two Centuries,* ed. Roger H. Davidson, Susan Webb Hammond, and Raymond W. Smock (Boulder, Colo.: Westview Press, 1998), 313.

46. Elizabeth Drew, *Showdown: The Struggle between the Gingrich Congress and the Clinton White House* (New York: Simon & Schuster, 1996), 26.

47. Ibid., 39.

48. Roger H. Davidson, Walter J. Oleszek, and Frances E. Lee, *Congress and Its Members,* 12th ed. (Washington, D.C.: CQ Press, 2010), 193.

49. Sinclair, "Tip O'Neill," 188.

50. Guy Gugliotta and Juliet Eilperin, "Gingrich Steps Down in Face of Rebellion," *Washington Post,* November 7, 1998, A1.

51. Kathryn Pearson and Eric Schickler, "The Transition to Democratic Leadership in a Polarized House," in *Congress Reconsidered,* 9th ed., ed. Lawrence C. Dodd and Bruce I. Oppenheimer (Washington, D.C.: CQ Press, 2009), 186.

52. Ronald Kessler, *Inside Congress: The Shocking Scandals, Corruption, and Abuse of Power Behind the Scenes on Capitol Hill* (New York: Simon & Schuster, 1997), 58–59.

53. Warren B. Rudman, *Combat: Twelve Years in the U.S. Senate* (New York: Random House, 1996), 242–243.

54. Lightman, "Senate Republicans."

55. Arenberg worked as Senator Levin's legislative director and deputy chief of staff between 1994 and 2009.

56. Scores were listed by SCF as percentages of conservative votes. We have translated those numbers into percentages of liberal votes for purposes of rough

comparison. The SCF describes itself on its website: "SCF is a political action committee dedicated to electing strong conservatives to the United States Senate. We do not support liberal Republicans and we are not affiliated with the Republican Party or any of its campaign committees."

57. For purposes of comparison, presidential support percentages have been translated into presidential opposition scores.

58. Jack L. August, Jr., "Wanted: A Civil Legislature," *Arizona Republic,* January 11, 2009, accessed July 2, 2011, http://www.azcentral.com/arizonarepublic/viewpoints/articles/2009/01/10/20090110august11-vip.html.

59. Senator Howard Baker, U.S. Senate Leaders' Lecture Series, July 14, 1998, U.S. Senate website, www.senate.gov.

60. Eileen Shanahan, "Equal Rights Amendment Is Approved by Congress," *New York Times,* March 23, 1972, A1.

61. Constitutional amendments require a two-thirds vote of both houses of Congress and ratification by three-fourths of the states. Only thirty-five of the necessary thirty-eight states ratified the ERA prior to the 1979 deadline.

62. The scores of liberal Republican senator Jacob Javits and conservative Democrat/independent senator Harry Byrd (VA) dropped as outriders because they were anomalies in their respective parties in terms of voting behavior.

63. Davidson, Oleszek, and Lee, *Congress and Its Members,* 12th ed., 193, citing Elizabeth Shogren, "Will Welfare Go Way of Health Reform?" *Los Angeles Times,* August 10, 1995, A18.

64. "The result has been a noticeable erosion of the comity traditionally associated with that institution." Roger H. Davidson and Colton C. Campbell, "The Senate and the Executive," in *Esteemed Colleagues: Civility and Deliberation in the U.S. Senate,* ed. Burdette A. Loomis (Washington, D.C.: Brookings Institution Press, 2000), 196.

65. Manu Raju, "Corker Bucks GOP without Regrets," *Politico,* May 5, 2010.

66. Susan Crabtree, "Obama: Compromise Is Not a Dirty Word," *TPM,* July 25, 2011, accessed August 1, 2011, http://tpmdc.talkingpointsmemo.com/2011/07/obama-compromise-is-not-a-dirty-word.php.

67. Barbara Sinclair, "Examining the Filibuster: Legislative Proposals to Change Senate Procedures," U.S. Senate Committee on Rules and Administration hearings, July 28, 2010.

68. Jerry Harkavy, "Snowe Says Polarization Hurts the Senate," *Bangor Daily News,* April 4, 2009, accessed May 17, 2010, http://bangordailynews.com/2009/04/12/news/snowe-says-polarization-hurts-senate/.

5. CRITICISMS OF THE FILIBUSTER

1. Binder and Smith, *Politics or Principle?* 19–20.
2. Ibid., 211.

3. Jim Abrams, "New Senators Look to Update Old Senate Ways," *Washington Times,* August 19, 2010, A1.

4. Carl Hulse, "Democrats Seek Changes to Senate Procedures," *New York Times,* December 24, 2010, A2.

5. Interview with former congressman Lee Hamilton (D-IN) by Richard Arenberg at the Center on Congress at Indiana University, Bloomington, January 6, 2011.

6. Ibid.

7. "Committee of the Whole" refers to the membership of the House of Representatives in the form in which it debates and amends bills on the House floor. When the debate and amendment process is complete, the Committee of the Whole House is said to "rise" and become the House of Representatives, which then votes on final passage.

8. Walter J. Oleszek, "Self-Executing Rules Reported by the House Committee on Rules," Congressional Research Service, December 21, 2006.

9. 110th Congress House Rules Manual—House Document No. 110-162. Washington, D.C.: U.S. Government Printing Office, 2009.

10. Erik Wasson, "Dems Rip Proposed Rule Giving New Power to GOP Budget Chairman," *The Hill,* December 30, 2010, accessed January 7, 2011, http://thehill.com/blogs/on-the-money/budget/135451-budget-skirmish-starts-over-ryan-rule.

11. In 2005, a pact among fourteen senators, seven from each party, averted the crisis over the so-called "nuclear option." The "Gang of 14" included Senators Robert Byrd (D-WV), Danny Inouye (D-HI), Joe Lieberman (D-CT), Ben Nelson (D-NE), Mary Landrieu (D-LA), Mark Pryor (D-AR), Ken Salazar (D-CO), Olympia Snowe (R-ME), John McCain (R-AZ), John Warner (R-VA), Lindsey Graham (R-SC), Mike DeWine (R-OH), Susan Collins (R-ME), and Linc Chafee (R-RI). See also the discussion of the "Gang of 14" in chapters 6 and 11.

12. Wawro and Schickler, *Filibuster,* 263.

13. Ibid., 280.

14. Interview with Senator Tom Udall (D-NM) by Richard Arenberg at Hart Senate Office Building, Washington, D.C., December 9, 2010.

15. Koger, *Filibustering,* 39.

16. Binder and Smith, *Politics or Principle?* 20.

17. Sarah A. Binder and Thomas E. Mann, "Slaying the Dinosaur: The Case for Reforming the Senate Filibuster," *Brookings Review* 13 (Summer 1995): 42–46.

18. The subtitle of George Packer's critique of the Senate in the *New Yorker* is "Just How Broken Is the Senate?" Congressional scholar Norm Ornstein wrote a 2008 article in the American Enterprise Institute's journal, the *American,* called "Our Broken Senate." Senators Jeff Merkley (D-OR) and Tom Udall (D-NM), among others, have called the Senate "broken."

19. Jonathan Martin, "Tom Daschle to Barack Obama: Meet, Eat, with GOP Leaders," *Politico,* January 16, 2011, accessed January 19, 2011, http://www.politico.com/news/stories/0111/47224.html. [video interview]

20. Marin Cogan, "Steny Hoyer Criticizes the Senate," *Politico,* March 2, 2010, accessed August 15, 2010, http://www.politico.com/news/stories/0310/33767.html.

21. Ben Smith, "Pelosi Vents to Obama, Reid on Energy Bill," *Politico,* July 27, 2010, accessed August 15, 2010, http://www.politico.com/blogs/bensmith/0710/ Aides_Pelosi_chides_Reid_on_energy_bill.html.

22. Congressman David Obey (D-WI) press release, accessed December 12, 2010, http://www.obey.house.gov/index.php?option=com_ content&view=article&id=924%3A-statement-by-congressman-david-r- obey&catid=47&Itemid=203.

23. Marty Paone speaking on May 17, 2010, at the Brookings Institution at a conference organized by the Brookings Institution and the Weidenbaum Center of Washington University on prospects for reforming the filibuster in light of mounting criticism of the Senate and calls for reform of the chamber's rules.

24. "Fear Cannon May Lift House Above Senate," *New York Times,* May 8, 1904, 7.

25. Interview with former congressman Lee Hamilton (D-IN) by Richard Arenberg.

26. Glenn Greenwald, "What Happened to the Senate's '60-Vote Requirement?'" *Salon,* November 9, 2007, accessed May 8, 2010, http://www.salon.com/ news/opinion/glenn_greenwald/2007/11/09/filibuster.

27. "Senators in Need of a Spine," *New York Times,* January 26, 2006, accessed April 17, 2010, http://www.nytimes.com/2006/01/26/opinion/26thur1.html?page wanted=print.

28. "Along the NAACP Battlefront," *Crisis Magazine,* November 1951, 601.

29. Senator Tom Harkin, *Congressional Record,* March 1, 1994, S2159.

30. Two additional supermajority requirements were added by constitutional amendment: a provision of the Fourteenth Amendment requiring a two-thirds vote of both houses to allow former federal officeholders who joined the Confederacy to return to federal office; and provision of the Twenty-fifth Amendment requiring a two-thirds vote of both Houses to declare the president is unable to discharge the powers and duties of his office.

31. It should be pointed out that the Constitution also provides in Article V "that no State, without its Consent, shall be deprived of its equal Suffrage in the Senate." This creates, in effect, a unanimous consent requirement.

32. The letter, dated December 2, 2010, was signed by Sarah Binder, Professor of Political Science at George Washington University; Gregory Koger, Associate Professor of Political Science at the University of Miami; Thomas Mann, W. Averell Harriman Chair & Senior Fellow, Governance Studies, The Brookings Institution; Norman Ornstein, Resident Scholar, American Enterprise Institute for Public Policy Research; Eric Schickler, Jeffrey & Ashley McDermott Endowed Chair & Professor of Political Science, University of California, Berkeley; Barbara Sinclair, Marvin Hoffenberg Professor of American Politics Emerita, University of California, Los Angeles; Steven S. Smith, Kate M. Gregg Distinguished Professor of Social Sciences

& Professor of Political Science, Washington University; and Gregory J. Wawro, Deputy Chair & Associate Professor of Political Science, Columbia University.

33. Although they refer to the "Framers," the seven instances actually include the Fourteenth and Twenty-fifth Amendments to the Constitution, obviously written later.

34. December 2, 2010, letter.

35. U.S. Constitution, Article I, Section 5.

36. Ibid.

37. Catherine Fisk and Erwin Chemerinsky, "The Filibuster," *Stanford Law Review* 49, no. 181 (January 1997): 253.

38. Eric A. Posner and Adrian Vermeule, "Legislative Entrenchment: A Reappraisal," *Yale Law Journal* 111 (April 30, 2002): 1665.

39. Ibid., 1666.

40. David E. Lockwood and George Siehl, "Military Base Closures: A Historical Review from 1988 to 1995," Congressional Research Service, October 18, 2004, 4.

41. Ibid., 11.

42. Supreme Court of the United States. *John H. Dalton, Secretary of the Navy, et al., Petitioners v. Arlen Specter et al.* Concurring opinion written by Justice Souter, with whom Justice Blackmun, Justice Stevens, and Justice Ginsburg joined. May 23, 1994.

43. Thomas Jefferson, *The Autobiography of Thomas Jefferson* (Chehalis, Wash.: Big Fish Publishing, 2010) 93 (originally published 1821).

44. Tom Daschle, *Like No Other Time: The 107th Congress and the Two Years That Changed America Forever* (New York: Crown Publishers, 2003), 32.

45. Burdette, *Filibustering*, 240.

46. Charles Whalen and Barbara Whalen, *The Longest Debate: A Legislative History of the 1964 Civil Rights Act* (Washington, D.C.: Seven Locks Press, 1985), 132–133.

47. Dirksen Congressional Center quoting the *Peoria Journal Star* on June 10, 2004, accessed July 1, 2011, http://www.congresslink.org/print_basics_histmats_civilrights64_cloturespeech.htm.

48. Whalen and Whalen, *The Longest Debate*, 199.

49. *Peoria Journal Star,* June 10, 2004.

50. Ibid.

6. THE DANGERS OF OVERZEALOUS REFORM

1. Letter from James Madison to James Monroe, October 5, 1786, Library of Congress website, www.loc.gov.

2. Madison, *The Federalist* No. 51.

3. Donald A. Ritchie, *The U.S. Congress: A Very Short Introduction* (New York: Oxford University Press, 2010), 3.

4. David McCullough, *John Adams* (New York: Simon & Schuster, 2001), 443–444.

5. Bill Dauster, "The Monster That Ate the Senate," remarks at the Washington College of Law, American University, Washington, D.C., January 13, 1998. Reprinted in *Public Budgeting and Finance* 18, no. 2 (Summer 1998): 87–93.

6. Margaret Talev, "Constant Filibuster Threat Is Tying Senate in Knots," *Seattle Times,* July 20, 2007, accessed December 17, 2010, http://seattletimes .nwsource.com/html/nationworld/2003800474_filibuster22.html.

7. Senator Robert Byrd, *Congressional Record,* January 4, 1995, S40–S41.

8. Library of Congress THOMAS, accessed January 20, 2012, http://thomas .loc.gov/cgi-bin/query/D?c107:1:./temp/~c107RCAM1b.

9. Daschle, *Like No Other Time,* 244.

10. Senator Robert Byrd, *Congressional Record,* October 10, 2002, S20382.

11. Wil S. Hylton, "The Angry One," *GQ,* January, 2007.

12. Senator Tom Daschle, *Congressional Record,* October 10, 2002, S20385.

13. Senator Barbara Boxer, *Congressional Record,* October 10, 2002, S20398.

14. As Senator Levin's legislative director at the time, author Arenberg was directly involved.

15. Senator Carl Levin, *Congressional Record,* March 17, 2005, S2927.

16. Ibid.

17. Senator Carl Levin, *Congressional Record,* March 20, 2005, S3100.

18. Ibid.

19. Senator Bill Frist, *Congressional Record,* March 20, 2005, S3100.

20. *Schiavo v. Schiavo,* U.S. Court of Appeals for the Eleventh Circuit, D.C. Docket No. CV-05-00530-T, March 23, 2005.

21. Jeffrey Toobin, *The Nine: Inside the Secret World of the Supreme Court* (New York: Doubleday, 2007), 248.

22. Ibid.

23. Ibid., 249.

24. Jeffrey Goldberg, "Party Unfaithful: The Republican Implosion," *New Yorker,* June 4, 2007, accessed July 10, 2011, http://www.newyorker.com/ reporting/2007/06/04/070604fa_fact_goldberg?currentPage=all.

25. U.S. Senate website, Senate roll-call vote #1, January 5, 1995, www.senate .gov. The vote came on a motion to table the Harkin amendment. The 76–19 vote to table killed the amendment.

26. Senator Harkin and Independent senator Joe Lieberman of Connecticut. Senator Lieberman, who continues to caucus with the Democrats, now lists himself as an Independent Democrat. Ironically, Lieberman used the threat of filibuster to great effect during the 2009–2010 health reform debate in the Senate.

27. Helen Dewar, "Winds of Political Change Blow More Softly in Senate; Filibusters and Lobbyists' Gifts Survive," *Washington Post,* January 6, 1995, A1.

28. Sixty votes would still be required to invoke cloture on the first motion, 57 on the second, 54 on the third, and finally a 51-vote majority on the fourth.

29. Tom Harkin, "Examining the Filibuster: Legislative Proposals to Change Senate Procedures," U.S. Senate Committee on Rules and Administration hearings, September 22, 2010.

30. Senator George G. Wright, *Congressional Record,* March 19, 1873, S114.

31. Senator Thomas F. Bayard, *Congressional Record,* March 19, 1873, S114.

32. Ibid.

33. He was chosen by Grover Cleveland, who was running for reelection in 1888. They received more popular votes but lost in the Electoral College, and Benjamin Harrison was elected president.

34. Senator Allen Thurman, *Congressional Record,* March 19, 1873, S115.

35. Ibid.

36. Ibid., S116.

37. George Packer, "The Empty Chamber: Just How Broken Is the Senate?" *New Yorker,* August 9, 2010, accessed September 1, 2010, http://www.newyorker.com/reporting/2010/08/09/100809fa_fact_packer.

38. Dionne, "Chris Dodd."

39. Andrew Rotherham and Robert Saldin, "In Defense of the Filibuster," *New York Daily News,* March 3, 2010, accessed September 1, 2010, http://www.nydaily news.com/opinions/2010/03/03/2010-03-03_in_defense_of_the_filibuster.html.

40. Average since 1992 is 4.6, since 1994 is 3.5; dropping the 1997 vote, the average is .8 senators.

41. Lee H. Hamilton, "Why Polarization Hurts Us," Center on Congress at the Indiana University, November 16, 2010, accessed November 17, 2010, http://www .centeroncongress.org/radio_commentaries/why_polarization_hurts_us.php.

42. An open rule in the House of Representatives permits all germane amendments to be offered on the floor.

43. John Boehner, "Congressional Reform and the 'People's House': An Address by House Minority Leader John Boehner," American Enterprise Institute for Public Policy Research, " September 30, 2010, accessed January 7, 2011, http://www.american.com/archive/2010/september/congressional-reform-and-the-peoples-house.

44. Lorraine H. Tong, "Senate Committee Party Ratios: 94th–110th Congresses," Congressional Research Service, November 18, 2008.

45. Daschle, *Like No Other Time,* 33–34.

46. Ibid., 39–40.

47. Trent Lott, *Herding Cats: A Life in Politics* (New York: HarperCollins, 2005), 210.

48. Ibid.

49. Christopher J. Deering and Steven S. Smith, *Committees in Congress* (Washington, D.C.: CQ Press, 1997), 227.

50. Richard F. Fenno, Jr., *Congressmen in Committee* (Boston: Little, Brown, 1973), 172–173.

51. Jim McClure and Malcolm Wallop. "Don't Go Nuclear: There Are Other Options for Fighting Democratic Obstructionism," *Wall Street Journal,* March 20, 2005.

7. RELATED TACTICS: HOLDS

1. They are also sometimes referred to as "time agreements." It is something of a curiosity that they are usually referred to in the academic literature as "UCAs," although we have never seen that terminology used in Congress, where they are universally called "UCs."

2. Ironically, although the Senate rules lack a general germaneness requirement, when germaneness is imposed in the Senate, under its precedents, germaneness is interpreted very tightly. As rules expert Martin Gold describes it in *Senate Procedure and Practice,* "Germaneness is a tight standard, and the Senate sometimes operates under a looser requirement, that of "'relevance.' The relevance standard can be imposed only by unanimous consent . . . the test will be whether such amendments relate to the subject of the measure to which they attach and do not contain any significant matter not addressed in the measure" (108).

3. Oleszek, "'Holds' in the Senate," 1.

4. Carl Hulse, "Senate May End an Era of Cloakroom Anonymity," *New York Times,* August 2, 2007, accessed July 2, 2011, http://www.nytimes.com/2007/08/02/washington/02ethics.html.

5. Koger, *Filibustering,* 174.

6. Joint Committee on the Organization of Congress, *Organization of the Congress—Final Report.*

7. Oleszek, "'Holds' in the Senate," 1.

8. Carl Hulse, "Senate May End an Era of Cloakroom Anonymity."

9. John E. Sununu, "Democrats Err in Bid to Muzzle Senators," *Boston Globe,* January 3, 2011, accessed July 12, 2011, http://articles.boston.com/2011-01-03/bostonglobe/29338587_1_cloture-filibuster-reform-unlimited-debate.

10. C. Lawrence Evans, "Requiring Public Disclosure of Notices of Objections ('Holds') to Proceedings to Motions or Measures in the Senate." U.S. Senate Committee on Rules and Administration hearings, June 17, 2003.

11. Barbara Sinclair, "The 60-Vote Senate: Strategies, Process, and Outcomes," in *U.S. Senate Exceptionalism,* ed. Bruce I. Oppenheimer (Columbus: Ohio State University Press, 2002), 250.

12. Thomas W. Lippman, "Holbrooke Hits Yet Another Snag; Grassley Puts Hold on Nomination in Dispute with State Dept.," *Washington Post,* June 26, 1999, A5.

13. Walter Pincus, "Lott and McConnell Also Have 'Hold' on Holbrooke; Appointment to Election Panel at Stake," *Washington Post,* July 7, 1999, A4.

14. Thomas E. Mann, "Examining the Filibuster: Silent Filibusters, Holds, and the Senate Confirmation Process," U.S. Senate Committee on Rules and Administration hearings, June 23, 2010. (Mann cites "You Really Got A Hold on Me," National Public Radio, June 2, 2010.)

15. Anne Joseph O'Connell, "Waiting for Leadership: President Obama's Record in Staffing Key Agency Positions and How to Improve the Appointments Process," Center for American Progress, April 21, 2010, 2.

16. Walter J. Oleszek, "Proposals to Reform 'Holds' in the Senate," Congressional Research Service, December 20, 2007, 2.

17. Lott, *Herding Cats,* 284–285.

18. C. Lawrence Evans and Walter J. Oleszek, "Message Politics and Senate Procedure," in *The Contentious Senate: Partisanship, Ideology, and the Myth of Cool Judgment,* ed. Colton C. Campbell and Nicol C. Rae (Lanham, Md.: Rowman & Littlefield, 2001), 125.

19. "'Don't Ask' Repeal Blocked Despite Majority Views," ABC News, September 21, 2010, accessed September 27, 2010, http://abcnews.go.com/Politics/senate-vote-repeal-ban-gays-military/story?id=11685658&page=2.

20. Senator Collins's vote was crucial because Senator Reid voted with the prevailing side only to retain his procedural right to enter a motion to reconsider the vote, and many observers believed that the two Democrats from Arkansas might well vote to take up the bill if their votes were the deciding votes. This would make Senator Collins's vote the potential 60th vote necessary to proceed to the bill.

21. The Senate went on to pass the repeal of DADT by a 65–31 vote with eight Republicans voting aye.

22. Charles Pope, "Ron Wyden and Charles Grassley Fight Senate Secret Holds," *Oregonian,* June 8, 2010, accessed June 29, 2010, http://www.oregonlive.com/politics/index.ssf/2010/06/oregons_ron_wyden_and_iowas_ch.html.

23. Ibid.

24. Senator Paul Wellstone, *Congressional Record,* October 31, 2001, S11274. Note: Barbara Sinclair cites Senator Wellstone's speech in *Party Wars: Polarization and the Politics of National Policy Making* (Norman: University of Oklahoma Press, 2006), 209.

25. Sinclair, "The 60-Vote Senate," 251.

26. Again in January of 2011, the Senate acted to eliminate secret holds, adopting a Wyden-Grassley resolution, S Res. 28, setting up a new procedure to require that holds be made public. As of this writing, the new requirements have not yet been implemented.

27. Evans, "Requiring Public Disclosure."

28. Dan Friedman and Megan Scully, "Shelby Puts Blanket Hold on Presidential Nominees," *Congress Daily,* February 5, 2010.

29. Ibid.

30. Interview with Senator Jack Reed (D-RI) by Richard Arenberg at Cranston, R.I., November 9, 2010.

8. RELATED TACTICS: FILLING THE AMENDMENT TREE

1. The "tree" diagrams can be seen at "Riddick's Senate Procedure," Government Printing Office, 74, accessed July 2, 2011, http://www.gpoaccess.gov/riddick/index.html.

2. More often than not, the tree is filled in this fashion, with amendments that are not substantively very different from each other. They may perhaps merely have differing dates of enactment, for example.

3. Walter J. Oleszek, *Congressional Procedures and the Policy Process*, 8th ed. (Washington, D.C.: CQ Press), 2011, 265–266.

4. Sinclair, "The New World." 16.

5. Ibid.

6. Ritchie, *The U.S. Congress*, 76.

7. Senator Byron Dorgan, *Congressional Record*, May 8, 1996, S4818.

8. Senator Tom Daschle, *Congressional Record*, May 8, 1996, S4818.

9. Senator Byron Dorgan, *Congressional Record*, May 8, 1996, S4818.

10. Senator Robert Dole, *Congressional Record*, May 8, 1996, S4820.

11. Ibid.

12. Senator Tom Daschle, *Congressional Record*, May 8, 1996, S4820.

13. Ibid.

14. Senator Byron Dorgan, *Congressional Record*, May 8, 1996, S4820.

15. Ibid.

16. Senator Susan Collins, *Congressional Record*, September 21, 2010, S7234.

17. Senator Carl Levin, *Congressional Record*, September 21, 2010, S7235.

18. Ibid.

19. Senator John McCain, *Congressional Record*, September 21, 2010, S7245.

20. Data from the Congressional Research Service.

21. As reported by the Senate Republican Policy Committee, "Senate Democrats Threaten Unprecedented Power Grab," January 4, 2011. Footnote cites "CRS research provided to author."

22. Senator Charles Grassley, *Congressional Record*, September 15, 2010, S7124.

23. Senator John Thune, *Congressional Record*, November 15, 2007, S14574.

24. Ibid., S14574–S14575.

25. Senator Chris Dodd, *Congressional Record*, September 29, 2006, S10613.

26. Ibid.

27. In the 100th Congress, at the time Senator Specter first proposed reform of the practice of filling the amendment tree, he was still a member of the Republican Party. Senator Specter moved to the Democratic caucus on April 30, 2009.

28. In this instance, Majority Leader Harry Reid (D-NV).

29. Senator Arlen Specter, *Congressional Record*, February 7, 2007, S1668.

30. Ibid.

31. Ibid., S1668–1669.

32. Ibid.

33. The amendment was actually formally filed a week later. *Congressional Record*, February 15, 2007, S2112.

34. Senator Arlen Specter, *Congressional Record*, February 8, 2007, S1764.

35. Senator Harry Reid, *Congressional Record*, February 28, 2008, S1522–1523.

36. Ibid., S1523.

37. Norman J. Ornstein, "Examining the Filibuster: Ideas to Reduce Delay and Encourage Debate in the Senate," U.S. Senate Committee on Rules and Administration hearings, September 29, 2010.

38. Ibid.

39. Ibid.

9. CIRCUMVENTING THE FILIBUSTER: RECONCILIATION

1. The "Gang of 14" were Senators Linc Chafee (R-RI), John McCain (R-AZ), Lindsey Graham (R-SC), Mike DeWine (R-OH), Susan Collins (R-ME), Olympia Snowe (R-ME), John Warner (R-VA), Robert Byrd (D-WV), Daniel Inouye (D-HI), Mary Landrieu (D-LA), Ben Nelson (D-NE), Joseph Lieberman (D-CT), Ken Salazar (D-CO), and Mark Pryor (D-AR).

2. Carrie Budoff Brown and Chris Frates, "Democrats: No Thanks to New 'Gang of 14,'" *Politico*, March 10, 2010, accessed March 11, 2010, http://www.politico.com/news/stories/0310/34165_Page2.html.

3. Karl Rove, "Democrats Can't Filibuster ObamaCare Repeal: The GOP Needs 51 Senate Votes, and a New President, to Get It Done," *Wall Street Journal*, February 10, 2011, accessed February 15, 2011, http://online.wsj.com/article/SB10001424052748704858404576134161926945334.html.

4. Including one of the authors, Robert B. Dove.

5. The budget act anticipated a process with two annual budget resolutions. A second budget resolution was adopted in each of the first 7 years. Since that time, the second budget resolution has fallen into disuse.

6. Senator Edmund Muskie, *Congressional Record*, March 20, 1974, S7480.

7. Senator Lee Metcalf, *Congressional Record*, March 20, 1974, S7530.

8. Senator Howard Baker, *Congressional Record*, June 22, 1981, S13209.

9. Ibid.

10. Senator Robert Byrd, *Congressional Record*, February 15, 2001, S1534.

11. Ibid., S1536.

12. Robert Keith, "Budget Reconciliation Process: The Senate's 'Byrd Rule'," Congressional Research Service, updated March 20, 2008. Quoted is letter from Representative Martin Olav Sabo to Representative Lee H. Hamilton, October 26, 1993.

13. Senator Robert Byrd, *Congressional Record*, April 29, 2009, S4874–S4875. Senator Byrd did support the more modest reconciliation bill that later facilitated the broad health reform bill that passed the Senate March 25, 2010, by a 56–43 vote.

This was because the narrower use of reconciliation amended only matters with a direct budgetary impact.

14. Dauster, "The Monster That Ate the United States Senate."

10. REFORMING THE FILIBUSTER: THE CONSTITUTIONAL OPEN

1. U.S. Constitution, Article I, Section 3 states: "Immediately after they shall be assembled in Consequence of the first Election, they shall be divided as equally as may be into three Classes. The Seats of the Senators of the first Class shall be vacated at the Expiration of the second Year, of the second Class at the Expiration of the fourth Year, and of the third Class at the Expiration of the sixth Year, so that one third may be chosen every second Year."

2. Richard S. Beth, "'Entrenchment' of Senate Procedure and the 'Nuclear Option' for Change: Possible Proceedings and Their Implications," Congressional Research Service, March 28, 2005.

3. Ibid.

4. U.S. Constitution, Article I, Section 5, Clause 2 states: "Each House may determine the Rules of its Proceedings."

5. Text of S Res. 396 as introduced by Senator Tom Udall of New Mexico.

6. Tom Udall, "Amending the Filibuster Rule," *Politico*, March 5, 2010, accessed March 6, 2010, http://www.politico.com/news/stories/0310/33936_Page2.html.

7. "Along the NAACP Battlefront," *Crisis Magazine*, November 1951, 601.

8. *Congressional Record*, January 3, 1953, S11.

9. Floyd M. Riddick, oral history interview, 1979, Senate Historical Office, U.S. Senate website, www.senate.gov.

10. Senator Robert Taft, *Congressional Record*, January 6, 1953, S198.

11. *Congressional Record*, January 7, 1953, S232.

12. *Congressional Record*, January 4, 1957, S215.

13. *Congressional Record*, January 7, 1959, S207.

14. Binder and Smith, *Politics or Principle?* 176.

15. Senate Rule V, Paragraph 2.

16. *Congressional Record*, January 18, 1967, S918.

17. Lindsay Rogers, *The American Senate* (New York: Johnson Reprint Corp., 1968), xv. The quote appears in the introduction of the reprint of the book, originally published in 1926.

18. Ibid.

19. Byrd, *The Senate*, vol. 2, 133.

20. Senator Byrd died on June 28, 2010.

21. Actually, the three named senators were the only members of the Senate who were then in the Senate. Others (Senators Baucus, Cochran, Harkin, and Grassley) were in the House of Representatives in 1975 but would not have voted on a Senate rules change.

22. Byrd, *The Senate,* vol. 2, 104.

23. *The Youth's Companion* was a popular religious youth magazine founded in Boston in 1827 that grew in popularity until about the turn of the twentieth century. The article appeared in the November 13, 1890, edition.

24. Senator Francis Cockrell, *Congressional Record,* January 22, 1891, S1680.

25. Benjamin Harrison, *This Country of Ours* (New York: Charles Scribner's Sons, 1897), 51–52.

26. Senator Thomas Walsh, *Congressional Record,* March 6, 1917, S8–S9.

27. Vice President Thomas Marshall, *Congressional Record,* March 6, 1917, S9.

28. Senator Thomas Walsh, *Congressional Record,* March 6, 1917, S9.

29. Martin B. Gold and Dimple Gupta, "The Constitutional Option to Change Senate Rules and Procedures: A Majoritarian Means to Overcome the Filibuster," *Harvard Journal of Law & Public Policy* 28, no. 1 (2004).

30. CQRollCall.com, accessed December 8, 2009, http://corporate.cqrollcall .com/wmspage.cfm?parm1=227.

31. Ibid.

32. Ibid.

33. Senator Warren Harding, *Congressional Record,* March 7, 1917, S16.

34. Ibid., S18.

35. Senator Francis Warren, *Congressional Record,* March 7, 1917, S17.

36. U.S. Senate Rule V, Section 2.

37. Norman Ornstein, "Time to Reassess Filibuster to Keep Senate Functioning," *Roll Call,* January 20, 2010, 6.

38. Tom Udall, "Amending the Filibuster Rule," *Politico,* March 5, 2010, accessed March 6, 2010, http://www.politico.com/news/stories/0310/33936_Page2.html.

39. Interview with Senator Tom Udall (D-NM) by Richard Arenberg at Hart Senate Office Building, Washington, D.C., December 9, 2010.

40. Rule V, Paragraph 2, U.S. Senate Rules, U.S. Senate Rules Committee website, rules.senate.gov.

41. *Congressional Quarterly Almanac* (1953), 313.

42. Martin Gold, oral history interview, 2004, Senate Historical Office, U.S. Senate website, www.senate.gov.

43. Senator Robert Byrd, "Examining the Filibuster: The Filibuster Today and Its Consequences," U.S. Senate Committee on Rules and Administration hearings, May 19, 2010.

44. The Senate parliamentarian sits on the Senate dais and advises the presiding officer on the interpretation of its rules and procedures.

45. Senator Joseph Biden, *Congressional Record,* May 23, 2005, S5735–S5736.

46. Ibid., S5736–S5737.

47. Byrd, *The Senate,* vol. 2, 132.

48. Senator Sam Ervin, *Congressional Record,* January 18, 1967, S925–S926.

49. Senator Ted Stevens, *Congressional Record,* April 16, 2002, S4609.

50. U.S. Constitution, Article V, Section 5.

51. James Morton Smith, ed., *The Republic of Letters: The Correspondence between Thomas Jefferson and James Madison 1776–1826* (New York: W. W. Norton, 1995), accessed January 8, 2010, http://www.constitution.org/jm/17900204_tj.txt.

52. John W. Dean and Barry M. Goldwater, Jr., *Pure Goldwater* (New York: Palgrave Macmillan, 2008), 90–91.

53. Senator Mike Mansfield, *Congressional Record,* January 18,1967, S921–S922.

11. REFORMING THE FILIBUSTER: THE NUCLEAR OPTION

1. Senator Lott was referring to President George W. Bush's nomination of Charles W. Pickering to be a judge in the U.S. Court of Appeals for the Fifth Circuit. The nomination was filibustered by Senate Democrats, and Republicans failed in an effort to invoke cloture. The nomination was withdrawn in December of 2004, although Pickering did serve on the court from January to December of 2004, having been given a recess appointment by President Bush. (Recess appointments are temporary.)

2. Lott, *Herding Cats,* 288.

3. Ibid., 289.

4. Charles Babington, "GOP Moderates Wary of Filibuster Curb: A Few Holdouts Could Block Move to Cut Off Debate on Judicial Nominees," *Washington Post,* January 16, 2005, A05.

5. Norman J. Ornstein, "Abe Fortas Hangs Over Discussion of Judicial Filibusters," *Roll Call,* December 13, 2004, accessed March 12, 2011, http://www.aei.org/article/21700.

6. Ibid.

7. "The Senate on the Brink," *New York Times,* March 6, 2005, accessed January 3, 2011, http://www.nytimes.com/2005/03/06/opinion/05sun1.html.

8. Judging the Environment: Fair Courts for a Healthy Environment, http://www.judgingtheenvironment.org/assets/files/filibuster_nuclear_option_editorials.doc.

9. Colbert I. King, "The Filibuster: A Tool for Good and Bad," *Washington Post,* June 18, 2005, accessed January 3, 2011, http://www.washingtonpost.com/wp-dyn/content/article/2005/06/17/AR2005061701212.html.

10. Sheryl Gay Stolberg, "Senators Who Averted Showdown Face New Test in Court Fight," *New York Times,* July 14, 2005, accessed January 3, 2011, http://www.nytimes.com/2005/07/14/politics/14gang.html.

11. "Democrats: No Thanks to New 'Gang of 14,'" *Politico,* March 10, 2010, accessed March 11, 2010, http://www.politico.com/news/stories/0310/34165.html.

12. "Why We Need the Filibuster," *Chicago Tribune,* May 27, 2003, accessed December 18, 2010, http://articles.chicagotribune.com/2003-05-27/news/0305270167_1_pricilla-owen-filibuster-miguel-estrada.

13. "Legislative Bomb," *Nation,* April 25, 2005, accessed July 1, 2011, http//www
.thenation.com/article/legislative bomb.

14. "Bring on the Filibuster," *Nation,* February 22, 2010, accessed July 1, 2011,
http://www.thenation.com/article/bring-filibuster.

15. "Legislative Bomb," *Nation,* April 25, 2005.

16. Ibid.

17. Paul Kane, "Some Democrats Seek Change in Filibuster Rules, but Others Are Wary," *Washington Post,* February 8, 2010, accessed December 15, 2010,
http://www.washingtonpost.com/wp-dyn/conctent/article/2010/02/07/
AR2010020702403_2html.

18. Ibid.

12. BRING IN THE COTS

1. Karen Tumulty, "Doris Kearns Goodwin: 'Let Them Filibuster,'" *Time
.com,* January 29, 2010, accessed February 3, 2010, http://swampland.blogs.time
.com/2010/01/29/doris-kearns-goodwin-let-them-filibuster/.

2. Patrick O'Connor and John Bresnahan, "Hoyer to Pelosi: Stand Up to
Senate," *Politico,* February 17, 2009, accessed January 11, 2010, http://www.politico
.com/news/stories/0209/18925.html.

3. Naftali Bendavid, "Filibuster Threat? Start Talking: Democrats Say Obstructing Republicans Should Have to Stick It Out on Senate Floor," *Wall Street
Journal,* March 9, 2010, A3.

4. Ibid.

5. Ibid.

6. Ibid.

7. Kate O'Beirne, "Let 'Em Talk! The Case for Real, Not Fake, Filibusters,"
National Review, February 24, 2003, accessed January 15, 2010, http://www.national
review.com/articles/205862/let-em-talk/kate-obeirne#.

8. Ibid.

9. Ibid.

10. "Sine die adjournment" refers to the end of the congressional session. It
means literally "without a day" set for the next meeting.

11. U.S. Senate website, www.senate.gov.

12. Ibid.

13. "The Art of Filibustering," *New York Times,* January 31, 1915, accessed January 15, 2010, http://query.nytimes.com/mem/archive-free/pdf?res=F10712F83A5A1
2738FDDA80B94D9405B858DF1D3.

14. John Saar, "Paul Tsongas Prepares His Ultimate Weapon on Arms Control:
A Senate Filibuster," *People,* April 11, 1983, 41–42.

15. Burdette, *Filibustering,* 210.

16. Ibid.

17. Ibid., 216–217.

18. Elizabeth Drew, "Enough with the Misleading Words about Congress," *Politico,* September 7, 2010, accessed September 9, 2010, http://www.politico.com/news/stories/0910/41701.html.

19. CQRollCall.com, accessed February 17, 2010, http://corporate.cqrollcall.com/wmspage.cfm?parm1=227.

20. Ibid.

21. Byrd, *The Senate,* vol. 2, 158.

22. Ibid.

23. Jesse Holland, "Senate Readying Itself for All-Night Talkathon on Judges," Associated Press, November 12, 2003, accessed July 2, 2011, http://www.freerepublic.com/focus/f-news/1020114/posts.

24. Ibid.

25. Neil A. Lewis, "Angered by Filibusters on Nominees, Republicans Stage Their Own Protest," *New York Times,* November 13, 2003, accessed January 12, 2010, http://www.nytimes.com/2003/11/13/us/angered-by-filibusters-on-nominees-republicans-stage-their-own-protest.html?src=pm.

26. Ibid.

27. Ibid.

28. "Filibusters Passe, Way Needed to End Judge Logjam, Frist Says," *Washington Times,* October 26, 2003, accessed January 12, 2010, http://www.washingtontimes.com/news/2003/oct/26/20031026-114807-8012r/.

29. Ibid.

30. Ibid.

31. Senator Harry Reid, *Congressional Record,* July 16, 2007, S9231.

32. Senator Harry Reid (D-NV) press release, July 17, 2007, accessed January 11, 2010, http://reid.senate.gov/newsroom/pr_071707_iraq.cfm.

33. Shailagh Murray and Paul Kane, "Democrats Won't Force War Vote: Effort Halted After GOP Blocks Proposal," *Washington Post,* July 19, 2007, accessed January 10, 2010, http://www.washingtonpost.com/wp-dyn/content/article/2007/07/18/AR2007071800482.html.

34. Sridhar Pappu, "Slumber Party Politics on the Hill: The Democrats Take the Iraq War Strategy to the Mattresses," *Washington Post,* July 18, 2007, accessed January 10, 2010, http://www.washingtonpost.com/wp-dyn/content/article/2007/07/17/AR2007071702163.html.

35. Ibid.

36. Ibid.

37. Kiki Ryan, "Reid Tweets Lady Gaga Over DADT," *Politico,* September 14, 2010, accessed September 19, 2010, http://www.politico.com/click/stories/1009/reid_tweets_lady_gaga_over_dadt.html.

38. Christina Wilkie, "Celebrities Enlist Followers in Lobbying Congress on 'Don't Ask, Don't Tell' Vote," *The Hill,* September 19, 2010, accessed September 19,

2010, http://thehill.com/homenews/senate/119651-celebrities-enlist-followers-in-lobbying-congress-on-dont-ask-dont-tell-vote.

39. Elise Viebeck, "McCain on Lady Gaga: 'I'm Glad She's Paying Attention,'" *The Hill*, September 17, 2010, accessed September 19, 2010, http://thehill.com/blogs/twitter-room/other-news/119417-mccain-on-lady-gaga-im-glad-shes-paying-attention.

40. *Washington Post*/ABC News poll, December 9–12, 2010, accessed December 27, 2010, http://www.washingtonpost.com/wp-srv/politics/polls/postpoll_12132010.html.

13. DEFENDING THE FILIBUSTER

1. In February–March 2010, Senator Bunning blocked efforts to extend unemployment insurance benefits because he objected to further deficit spending. The filibuster proved so unpopular even many Republicans, including Kentucky's other senator, Minority Leader McConnell (R-KY), refused to defend him. *The Hill* reported: "Democratic press aides had a field day with Bunning's filibuster, blasting out several press releases calling attention to the situation, including distributing an editorial criticizing Bunning in the Louisville *Courier-Journal*" (J. Taylor Rushing, "Bunning Filibuster Ends, Jobless Benefits Will Be Extended," *The Hill*, March 2, 2010).

2. We will discuss in the epilogue specific proposals made recently by Senators Tom Harkin (D-IA) and Tom Udall (D-NM). The Senate Committee on Rules and Administration led by Senator Chuck Schumer (D-NY) held a series of hearings in 2010 on changes to the filibuster rule. One of the authors (Dove) testified at one of those hearings.

3. Senator Thomas Hardwick, *Congressional Record*, March 8, 1917, S35–S36.

4. Carl Hulse, "True Test of Senate Compromise Lies Ahead," *New York Times*, June 10, 2005, accessed August 1, 2011, http://www.nytimes.com/2993/06/19/politics/10assess.html.

5. Sam Stein, "Durbin Launches Online Petition to Reform the Filibuster," *Huffington Post*, February 26, 2010, accessed August 1, 2011, http://www.huffingtonpost.com/2010/02/26/durbin-launches-online-pe_n_478225.html.

6. Senator Bill Frist, *Congressional Record*, January 4, 2005, S14.

7. Senator Bill Frist, *Real Time with Bill Maher*, HBO, aired June 11, 2010.

8. Ben Eidelson, "Let the Majority Rule: Why the Filibuster Is OK for Democrats but Not for Republicans," *Slate*, February 8, 2010, accessed February 11, 2010, http://www.slate.com/id/2244060/.

9. Ibid.

10. Rogers, *The American Senate*, 175.

11. Senator Lawrence Sherman, *Congressional Record*, June 8, 1918, S7539.

12. Senator Robert Byrd, *Congressional Record*, January 4, 1995, S40.

13. Robert A. Caro letter to Senate Rules Committee Chairman, Senator Trent Lott, and Ranking Member, Senator Chris Dodd, June 8, 2003.

14. Smith, "Filibusters," A16.

15. U.S. Constitution, Article V.

16. Bill Frenzel, "Defending the Dinosaur: The Case for Not Fixing the Filibuster," *Brookings Review,* Summer 1995, 47–49.

17. Ibid.

18. 60–38 vote on February 13, 2009 on the conference report, and earlier 61–36 on the Senate bill on February 9, 2009. Senator Susan Collins (R-ME), Senator Olympia Snowe (R-ME), and then-Republican Senator Arlen Specter of Pennsylvania voted for cloture on both occasions.

19. 60–39 vote on December 23, 2009. No Republican senator voted for cloture.

20. 60–40 vote on May 20, 2010. Senators Susan Collins (R-ME), Olympia Snowe (R-ME), and Scott Brown (R-MA) voted for cloture. Senators Russ Feingold (D-WI) and Maria Cantwell (D-WA) voted against cloture.

21. 61–38 vote on September 16, 2010. Senator George Voinovich (R-OH) and Senator George LeMieux (R-FL) voted for cloture.

22. 67–28 vote on December 21, 2010. Senators Susan Collins (R-ME), Olympia Snowe (R-ME), Scott Brown (R-MA), Bob Bennett (R-UT), Johnny Isakson (R-GA), Richard Lugar (R-IN), Lamar Alexander (R-TN), Bob Corker (R-TN), Thad Cochran (R-MS), Lisa Murkowski (R-AK), and George Voinovich (R-OH) voted for cloture.

23. 63–33 vote on December 18, 2010. Senators Susan Collins (R-ME), Olympia Snowe (R-ME), Scott Brown (R-MA), Mark Kirk (R-IL), Lisa Murkowski (R-AK), and George Voinovich (R-OH) voted for cloture.

24. *Congressional Record,* February 2, 2009, S1237.

25. 57–41, April 26, 2010; 57–41, April 27, 2010; 56–42, April 28, 2010, U.S. Senate website, www.senate.gov.

26. *Congressional Record,* April 28, 2010, S2750.

27. *Congressional Record,* November 21, 2009, S11967.

28. Rogers, *The American Senate,* viii–ix.

29. Ruth Marcus, "Why the Filibuster Is Frustrating but Necessary," *Washington Post,* January 27, 2010, accessed January 28, 2010, http://www.washingtonpost.com/wp-dyn/content/article/2010/01/26/AR2010012603433.html.

30. Joanne Mariner, "A Good Tool for a Good Fight: In Defense of the Filibuster," *Counter Punch,* November 26, 2002, accessed July 8, 2010, http//www.counterpunch.org/mariner1126.html.

31. Byrd, *The Senate,* vol. 2, 162.

32. Senator Russell Feingold, *Congressional Record,* May 18, 2000, S4172.

33. Richard F. Fenno, Jr., *The Making of a Senator: Dan Quayle* (Washington, D.C.: CQ Press, 1989), 44.

34. Ibid.

35. Ibid.

36. G. Frank Williss, "Do Things Right the First Time: Administrative History, the National Park Service and the Alaska National Interest Lands Conservation Act of 1980," U.S. Department of the Interior, September 1985, chapter 4.

37. Tom Doggett, "Six Republican Senators Turn Against Bush on ANWR," Reuters News, January 31, 2003, accessed July 8, 2010, http://www.freerepublic.com/focus/news/833505/posts.

38. W. Lee Rawls, *In Praise of Deadlock: How Partisan Struggle Makes Better Laws* (Baltimore: Johns Hopkins University Press, 2009), 115.

39. Madison, *The Federalist* No. 51.

40. Donald Matthews, *U.S. Senators and Their World* (Chapel Hill: University of North Carolina Press, 1960), 100–101.

41. Ibid.

42. Jennifer Manning, "Membership of the 111th Congress: A Profile," Congressional Research Report for Congress, February 4, 2010, 5n17.

43. Sean M. Theriault and David Rohde, "The Gingrich Senators and Their Effect on the U.S. Senate," paper prepared for delivery at the American Political Science Association Annual Meeting, July 26, 2010, accessed July 2, 2011, http://citeseerx.ist.psu.edu/viewdoc/summary?doi=10.1.1.173.3142.

44. Nicol C. Rae and Colton C. Campbell, "Party Politics and Ideology in the Contemporary Senate," in *The Contentious Senate: Partisanship, Ideology, and the Myth of Cool Judgment* (Lanham, Md.: Rowman & Littlefield, 2001), 8.

45. Ryan Grim, "Dodd Presses Senate Freshmen to Back Off Effort to End Filibuster," *Huffington Post*, August 4, 2010, accessed August 5, 2010, http://www.huffingtonpost.com/2010/08/04/dodd-presses-senate-fresh_n_670433.html.

46. January 30, 2006, Senate roll-call vote #1.

47. Penn Schoen Berland (PSB) poll conducted for the Aspen Ideas Festival: "Does the US Constitution Still Work for 21st Century," July 9, 2010, accessed November 10, 2010, http://www.slideshare.net/tarekrizk/psb-constitution-poll-for-aspen-ideas.

48. The *New York Times*/CBS News poll, February 5–10, 2010, 21, accessed November 10, 2010, http://documents.nytimes.com/new-york-times-cbs-news-poll.

49. Pew Research Center for the People & the Press, January 17, 2010, accessed November 10, 2010, http://pewresearch.org/pubs/1478/political-iq-quiz-knowledge-filibuster-debt-colbert-steele.

50. Senator Barack Obama, *Congressional Record*, April 13, 2005, S3511.

51. Proceeding to the conference report is a privileged matter and not debatable. Therefore, proceeding to the conference report cannot be filibustered.

52. Norman J. Ornstein, "Examining the Filibuster: Ideas to Reduce Delay and Encourage Debate in the Senate," U.S. Senate Committee on Rules and Administration hearings, September 29, 2010.

53. March 13, 2008. The final roll calls occurred after midnight on March 14.

54. Senator Robert Byrd, "Examining the Filibuster: The Filibuster Today and Its Consequences," U.S. Senate Committee on Rules and Administration hearings, May 19, 2010.

55. Martin Paone, "Examining the Filibuster: Ideas to Reduce Delay and Encourage Debate in the Senate," U.S. Senate Committee on Rules and Administration hearings, September 29, 2010.

56. *News Hour with Jim Lehrer,* PBS, November 12, 2003.

57. Senator Barack Obama, *Congressional Record,* April 13, 2005, S3511–S3512.

EPILOGUE

1. Tom Udall, "Senate New Year's Resolution: Fixing a Broken Set of Rules," *Washington Post,* January 4, 2011, accessed January 4, 2011, http://www.washingtonpost.com/wp-dyn/content/article/2011/01/03/AR2011010302449.html. What Senator Udall presumably meant was that debate on changing the rules could be ended by a simple majority and *then* the majority could change the rules. This is an important distinction because, under the existing Senate rules, the rules can be changed by a simple majority. It is ending the debate on a rules change that requires a two-thirds vote in order to reach that final vote on changing the rules.

2. Ibid.

3. Mondale, "Resolved: Fix the Filibuster."

4. Mondale, U.S. Senate Leaders' Lecture Series.

5. Mondale, "Resolved: Fix the Filibuster."

6. Mitch McConnell, "A Power Grab Democrats Should Avoid," *Washington Post,* January 5, 2011, accessed January 5, 2011, http://www.washingtonpost.com/wp-dyn/content/article/2011/01/04/AR2011010402032.html.

7. Lamar Alexander speaking on January 4, 2011, to the Heritage Foundation, accessed January 10, 2011, http://www.myheritage.org/news/sen-lamar-alexander-comes-to-heritage-to-defend-the-filibuster/.

8. Carl Hulse, "Democrats Seek Changes to Senate Procedures."

9. Senator Tom Udall, *Congressional Record,* January 5, 2011, S34.

10. Senator Tom Harkin, *Congressional Record,* March 1, 1994, S2159.

11. Senator Tom Harkin, *Congressional Record,* January 5, 2011, S24.

12. Senator Tom Harkin, *Congressional Record,* May 19, 2005, S5461–S5462.

13. Ibid.

14. Ibid.

15. Senator J. William Fulbright, *Congressional Record,* January 4, 1957, S203.

16. Senator Richard Russell, *Congressional Record,* January 6, 1953, S115.

17. U.S. Senate website, www.senate.gov.

18. Senator Robert Taft, *Congressional Record,* January 6, 1953, S115.

19. Senator Mitch McConnell. *Congressional Record,* January 5, 2011, S17.

20. Manu Raju and Scott Wong, "Filibuster Talks to Drive Senate Recess," *Politico*, January 6, 2011, accessed January 6, 2011, http://www.politico.com/news/stories/0111/47186.html.

21. Paul Kane, "Senate in Long Recess as Leaders Seek to Rein in Democrats' Filibuster Rebellion," *Washington Post*, January 22, 2011, accessed January 22, 2011, http://www.washingtonpost.com/wp-dyn/content/article/2011/01/22/AR2011012203920.html.

22. It was referred to in this way to the chagrin of some of the Senate's women.

23. Carl Hulse, "Senate Nears Compromise to Ease Slowdown Tactics," *New York Times*, January 24, 2011, A15.

24. Ibid.

25. The idea of the "talking filibuster" was described by the *Washington Post* (Paul Kane, "Senate Closer to Compromise on Proposal to Overhaul Rules," *Washington Post,* January 25, 2011):

> If the majority failed to get 60 votes, the minority would have to hold the floor with an old-fashioned "Mr. Smith Goes to Washington"–style filibuster. Once the minority no longer had speakers to hold the floor, the Senate would move toward a final vote. Such a proposal was considered too much change by all Republicans and many Democrats, particularly veteran Democrats who are fearful of altering rules now that would lessen their powers if they lose the majority in two years. "That's part of the minority's right, to extend the debate," said Sen. Carl Levin (D-MI), a 32-year veteran who supports more modest steps to alter the rules.

26. The 60-vote threshold was created by unanimous consent to avoid having to invoke cloture with the delays inherent in that. The 60-vote level reflected that these were proposed "standing orders" and not rules changes which would require a two-thirds vote of the Senate to invoke cloture.

27. Carl Hulse, "Senate Democrats Drop Campaign to Limit Filibuster," *New York Times*, January 26, 2011, A20.

28. Senator Mitch McConnell and Senator Harry Reid, *Congressional Record*, January 26, 2011, S324–S325.

29. Ibid.

30. Manu Raju, "Filibuster Reform Goes Bust," *Politico*, January 28, 2011, accessed January 28, 2011, http://www.politico.com/news/stories/0111/48325.html.

31. Ibid.

32. Lisa Mascaro, "Drive to Alter Filibusters Fizzles as Senate Adopts Modest Fixes," *Los Angeles Times*, January 27, 2011, accessed January 27, 2011, http://www.post-gazette.com/pg/11028/1121203-84.stm?cmpid=nationworld.xml.

33. "Democrats Wimp Out on Filibuster Reform," *Newark Star-Ledger,* January 30, 2011, accessed January 31, 2011, http://blog.nj.com/njv_editorial_page/2011/01/post_27.html.

34. *Congressional Record*, February 1, 2011, S428.

35. U.S. Senate website, www.senate.gov, February 2, 2011.

36. Carl Hulse, "Meant to Be Broken? Maybe Not This Time," *New York Times*, February 5, 2011, A21.

37. Ibid.

38. Lee H. Hamilton, "Congress Needs to Build a Culture of Fairness," Center on Congress at Indiana University, February 18, 2011, accessed February 18, 2011, http://congress.indiana.edu/congress-needs-build-culture-fairness.

39. Lindsey Boerma, "Passing on the Tea," *National Journal*, August 3, 2011, accessed August 4, 2011, http://www.nationaljournal.com/daily/passing-on-the-tea-20110802.

40. Manu Raju and Scott Wong, "Dems Change Rules; Senate in Chaos," *Politico*, October 6, 2011, accessed October 9, 2011, http://www.politico.com/news/stories/1011/65383.html.

41. *Mr. Smith Goes to Washington*, Columbia Pictures, 1939.

SELECTED BIBLIOGRAPHY

Abrams, Jim. "New Senators Look to Update Old Senate Ways." *Washington Times,* August 19, 2010.

Allen, Mike. "GOP Plans 'Marathon' on Judges; Debate to Spotlight Blocked Nominees." *Washington Post,* November 8, 2003.

Amar, Vikram David. "With a Potential Supreme Court Nomination at Stake, Questions of the Filibuster's Constitutionality Linger." Findlaw.com, June 27, 2003, accessed July 2, 2011, http://writ.news.findlaw.com/amar/20030613.html.

Amer, Mildred L. "The First Day of a New Congress: A Guide to Proceedings on the Senate Floor." Congressional Research Service, November 1, 2000.

Arsenault, Mark. "Democrats Seek to Curb Filibusters: Senators Frustrated by Delaying Tactics." *Boston Globe,* December 31, 2010.

Asbel, Bernard. *The Senate Nobody Knows.* Garden City, N.Y.: Doubleday, 1978.

August, Jack L., Jr. "Wanted: A Civil Legislature." *Arizona Republic,* January 11, 2009.

Babington, Charles. "Ethics Panel Rebukes DeLay: Majority Leader Offered Favor to Get Peer's Vote." *Washington Post,* October 1, 2004.

———. "GOP Moderates Wary of Filibuster Curb: A Few Holdouts Could Block Move to Cut Off Debate on Judicial Nominees." *Washington Post,* January 16, 2005.

Bach, Stanley. "The Senate's Compliance with Its Legislative Rules: The Appeal of Order." *Congress and the Presidency* 18, no. 1 (1991): 77–92.

Bailey, Stephen K., and Howard Samuel. *Congress at Work.* New York: Henry Holt and Company, 1952.

Baker, Richard A. *The Senate of the United States: A Bicentennial History.* Malabar, Fla.: Krieger, 1988.

Baker, Ross K. *House and Senate.* 4th ed. New York: W.W. Norton, 2008.

Bawn, Kathleen, and Gregory Koger. "Effort, Intensity and Position Taking: Reconsidering Obstruction in the Pre-Cloture Senate." *Journal of Theoretical Politics* 20, no. 1 (2008): 67–92.

Bayh, Evan. "Why I'm Leaving the Senate." *New York Times,* February 20, 2010.

Beeman, Richard. "Unlimited Debate in the Senate: The First Phase." *Political Science Quarterly,* 83, no. (1968): 419–434.

Bendavid, Naftali. "Filibuster Threat? Start Talking: Democrats Say Obstructing Republicans Should Have to Stick It Out on Senate Floor." *Wall Street Journal,* March 9, 2010.

Benen, Steve. "Dodd Won't Help Reform Filibuster." *Washington Monthly,* February 17, 2010.

———. "The GOP—Grand Obstructionist Party." *Carpetbagger Report,* September 19, 2007, accessed July 2, 2011, http://www.thecarpetbaggerreport.com/archives/12938.html.

Benton, Thomas Hart. *Thirty Years' View: A History of the Working of the American Government for Thirty Years, from 1820 to 1850.* Vol. 2. New York: Appleton and Company, 1873.

Bernstein, Jonathan. "Our Dysfunctional Senate." *Washington Post,* June 1, 2010, accessed July 2, 2011, http://voices.washingtonpost.com/ezra-klein/2010/06/our_dysfunctional_senate.html.

———. "Talking Heads: Why Reviving the Live Filibuster in the Senate is a Terrible Idea." *New Republic,* January 29, 2011, accessed July 2, 2011, http://www.tnr.com/article/politics/82413/senate-live-filibuster-reform.

Beth, Richard S. "'Entrenchment' of Senate Procedure and the 'Nuclear Option' for Change: Possible Proceedings and Their Implications." Congressional Research Service, March 28, 2005.

———. "How Unanimous Consent Agreements Regulate Senate Floor Action." Congressional Research Service, April 30, 2003.

Beth, Richard S., and Stanley Bach. "Filibusters and Cloture in the Senate." Congressional Research Service, March 2003.

Binder, Sarah. A. *Minority Rights, Majority Rule: Partisanship and the Development of Congress.* New York: Cambridge University Press, 1997.

———. "The Senate as a Black Hole: Lessons Learned from the Judicial Appointment Experience." *Brookings Review* 19, no. 2 (2001).

———. *Stalemate: Causes and Consequences of Legislative Gridlock.* Washington, D.C.: Brookings Institution Press, 2003.

Binder, Sarah A., and Thomas E. Mann. "Slaying the Dinosaur: The Case for Reforming the Senate Filibuster." *Brookings Review* 13 (Summer 1995).

Binder, Sarah A., and Steven S. Smith. "Political Goals and Procedural Choice in the Senate." *Journal of Politics* 60, no. 2 (1998): 398–416.

———. *Politics or Principle? Filibustering in the United States Senate.* Washington, D.C.: Brookings Institution Press, 1997.

Bloch, Susan Low. "Congressional Self-Discipline: The Constitutionality of Supermajority Rules." *Constitutional Commentary* 14 (Spring 1997).

Bluestein, Greg, "Carter Laments 'Unprecedented' Partisan Divide." Associated Press, March 17, 2010.

Boaz, David. "Filibuster Flip-Flops." *American Spectator,* April 25, 2005.

Boehner, John. "Congressional Reform and the 'People's House': An Address by House Minority Leader John Boehner." American Enterprise Institute for Public Policy Research, September 30, 2010.

Boerma, Lindsey. "Passing on the Tea," *National Journal,* August 3, 2011.

Bolton, Alexander. "Filibuster Reform Is Short of Needed Votes." *The Hill,* July 28, 2010.

Bond, Jon R., and Richard Feisher, eds. *Polarized Politics: Congress and the President in a Partisan Era.* Washington, D.C.: CQ Press, 2000.

Bresnahan, John. "Reid Puts Blanket Hold on Bush Nominees." *Roll Call,* June 11, 2004.

Broder, David. "The Party's Over." *Atlantic Magazine,* March 1972.

———. "The Senate, Running on Empty." *Washington Post,* August 5, 2010.

Brown, Carrie Budoff, and Chris Frates. "Democrats: No Thanks to New 'Gang of 14.'" *Politico,* March 10, 2010.

Brownstein, Ronald. "One for the Books." *National Journal,* December 23, 2010, accessed July 2, 2011, http://www.nationaljournal.com/columns/political-connections/one-for-the-books-20101223.

———. *The Second Civil War: How Extreme Partisanship Has Paralyzed Washington and Polarized America.* New York: Penguin Press, 2007.

Bruhl, Aaron-Andrew P. "Burying the 'Continuing Body' Theory of the Senate." *Iowa Law Review* 95 (September 14, 2010): 1401.

Burdette, Franklin L. *Filibustering in the Senate.* Princeton, N.J.: Princeton University Press, 1940.

Burke, Edmund. "Speech to the Electors of Bristol," *The Founders' Constitution.* Vol. 1, Chapter 13, Document 7. Chicago: University of Chicago Press, 1987.

Byrd, Robert C. "Examining the Filibuster: The Filibuster Today and Its Consequences." U.S. Senate Committee on Rules and Administration hearings, May 19, 2010.

———. *The Senate 1789–1989: Addresses on the History of the United States Senate.* Vol. 1. Washington, D.C.: U.S. Government Printing Office, 1988.

———. *The Senate 1789–1989: Addresses on the History of the United States Senate.* Vol. 2. Washington, D.C.: U.S. Government Printing Office, 1991.

Calmes, Jacqueline. "Dilatory Debate: A Tactic as Old as the Senate." CQ *Weekly Online.* September 5, 1987, 2119, accessed April 12, 2010 http://library.cqpress.com/cqweekly/WR100401669.

———. "'Trivialized' Filibuster Is Still a Potent Tool." CQ *Weekly Online.* September 5, 1987, 2115–2120, accessed April 12, 2010 http://library.cqpress.com/cqweekly/WR100401678.

Caro, Robert A. *The Years of Lyndon Johnson: Master of the Senate.* New York: Knopf, 2002.

Cater, Douglass. *Power in Washington: A Critical Look at Today's Struggle to Govern in the Nation's Capital.* New York: Vintage Books, 1964.

Chait, Jonathan. "Senate Dems Throw in the Towel." *New Republic,* January 24, 2011.

Chapman, Steve. "Bipartisan Hypocrisy on the Filibuster." *Chicago Tribune,* April 3, 2005.

Chicago Tribune. "Why We Need the Filibuster." May 27, 2003.

Clymer, Adam. "No Deal; Politics and the Dead Arts of Compromise." *New York Times,* October 22, 1995.

Cohen, Richard E. "Democrats Push to Speed Up Slow Senate." *Politico,* December 23, 2010.

Cohen, Richard E., Kirk Victor, and David Bauman. "The State of Congress." *National Journal,* January 10, 2004.

Congressional Quarterly Almanac. Washington, D.C.: Congressional Quarterly Books, 1949, 1953, 1957, 1959, 1963, 1975.

Cooper, Joseph. *The Previous Question: Its Standing as a Precedent for Cloture in the United States Senate.* Washington, D.C.: U.S. Government Printing Office, 1962.

Cornyn, John. "Our Broken Judicial Confirmation Process and the Need for Filibuster Reform." *Harvard Journal of Law & Public Policy* 27, no. 1 (September 2003).

Cost, Jay. "Democrats, Keep the Filibuster!" *RealClearPolitics HorseRaceBlog,* August 25, 2010, www.realclearpolitics.com.

Crabtree, Susan. "Obama: Compromise Is Not a Dirty Word." *TPM,* July 25, 2011.

Cutler, Lloyd. "The Way to Kill Senate Rule XXII." *Washington Post,* April 19, 1993.

Dahl, Robert A. *Preface to Democratic Theory.* Chicago: University of Chicago Press, 1956.

Daschle, Tom. *Like No Other Time: The 107th Congress and the Two Years That Changed America Forever.* New York: Crown Publishers, 2003.

Dauster, Bill. "It's Not 'Mr. Smith Goes to Washington'—Senate Filibusters." *Washington Monthly,* November 1996.

———. "The Monster That Ate the Senate." Remarks at the Washington College of Law, American University, Washington, D.C., January 13, 1998. Reprinted in *Public Budgeting and Finance* 18, no. 2 (Summer 1998): 87–93.

Davidson, Roger H., and Colton C. Campbell. "The Senate and the Executive." In *Esteemed Colleagues: Civility and Deliberation in the U.S. Senate,* edited by Burdette A. Loomis. Washington, D.C.: Brookings Institution Press, 2000.

Davidson, Roger H., Susan Webb Hammond, and Raymond W. Smock, eds. *Masters of the House: Congressional Leaders Over Two Centuries.* Boulder, Colo.: Westview Press, 1998.

Davidson, Roger H., Walter J. Oleszek, and Frances E. Lee. *Congress and Its Members.* 12th ed. Washington, D.C.: CQ Press, 2010.

Davis, Christopher. "Filling the Amendment Tree in the Senate." Congressional Research Service, April 2, 2008.

Dean, John W., and Barry M. Goldwater, Jr. *Pure Goldwater.* New York: Palgrave Macmillan, 2008.

Deering, Christopher J., and Steven S. Smith. *Committees in Congress.* Washington, D.C.: CQ Press, 1997.

Dionne, E. J. "Chris Dodd, the Senate's Happy Warrior." *Washington Post,* August 9, 2010.

Dodd, Lawrence C., and Bruce I. Oppenheimer, eds. *Congress Reconsidered,* 3rd ed. Washington, D.C.: CQ Press. 1985.

———, eds. *Congress Reconsidered,* 9th ed. Washington, D.C.: CQ Press, 2009.

Dove, Robert B. *Enactment of a Law: Procedural Steps in the Legislative Process.* Washington, D.C.: U.S. Government Printing Office, 1982.

Drew, Elizabeth. "Enough with the Misleading Words about Congress." *Politico.* September 7, 2010.

———. *Senator.* New York: Simon & Schuster, 1978.

———. *Showdown: The Struggle between the Gingrich Congress and the Clinton White House.* New York: Simon & Schuster, 1996.

Drum, Kevin. "Resist the Filibuster Fiat." *Washington Post,* January 31, 2005.

Edgar, Bob. "Senate Should Fix, Not Kill, the Filibuster." *Cap Times,* December 26, 2010, accessed July 2, 2011 http://host.madison.com/ct/news/opinion/column/article_d5bbfa73-7c8f-5952-a5fb-787b41d41c4f.html.

Edwards, Mickey. "The Dysfunctional Senate." *Atlantic,* February 7, 2010.

Eidelson, Ben. "Let the Majority Rule: Why the Filibuster Is OK for Democrats but Not for Republicans." *Slate,* February 8, 2010.

Evans, C. Lawrence. "Requiring Public Disclosure of Notices of Objections ('Holds') to Proceedings to Motions or Measures in the Senate." U.S. Senate Committee on Rules and Administration hearings, June 17, 2003.

Evans, C. Lawrence, and Walter J. Oleszek. "Message Politics and Senate Procedure." In *The Contentious Senate: Partisanship, Ideology, and the Myth of Cool Judgment,* edited by Colton C. Campbell and Nicol C. Rae, 107–127. Lanham, Md.: Rowman & Littlefield, 2001.

———. "The Procedural Context of Senate Deliberation." In *Esteemed Colleagues: Civility and Deliberation in the U.S. Senate,* edited by Burdette A. Loomis. Washington, D.C.: Brookings Institution Press, 2000.

Fallows, James. "The Filibuster: Let's Talk about It." *Atlantic,* December 20, 2009.

Farrand, Max. *The Record of the Federal Convention of 1787.* New Haven, Conn.: Yale University Press, 1966.

Fenno, Richard F., Jr. *Congressmen in Committee.* Boston: Little, Brown, 1973.

———. *The Making of a Senator: Dan Quayle.* Washington, D.C.: CQ Press, 1989.

———. "The Senate Through the Looking Glass: The Debate Over Television." *Legislative Studies Quarterly* 14, no. 3 (August 1989): 313–348.

———. *The United States Senate: A Bicameral Perspective.* Washington, D.C.: American Enterprise Institute, 1982.

Fisk, Catherine, and Erwin Chemerinsky. "The Filibuster." *Stanford Law Review* 49, no. 181 (January 1997); 181–254.

Frenzel, Bill. "Defending the Dinosaur: The Case for Not Fixing the Filibuster." *Brookings Review,* Summer 1995.

Friedman, Dan. "Fixing the Filibuster." *National Journal Daily,* June 23, 2011, accessed June 24, 2011 http://www.nationaljournal.com/columns/looking-in/fixing-the-filibuster-20110623?mrefid=site_search.

———. "Senate's Returning Democrats Unanimously Favor Filibuster Reform." *National Journal,* December 22, 2010.

Friedman, Dan, and Megan Scully. "Shelby Puts Blanket Hold on Presidential Nominees." *Congress Daily,* February 5, 2010.

Frum, Eric. "Is the Senate to Blame for Obama's Stalled Agenda?" *FrumForum.com,* August 4, 2010, accessed August 7, 2010, http://www.frumforum.com/is-the-senate-to-blame-for-obamas-stalled-agenda.

Galloway, George B. *The Legislative Process in Congress.* New York: Crowell, 1953.

Geoghegan, Thomas. "The Case for Busting the Filibuster." *Nation,* August 31, 2009.

———. "The Infernal Senate: The Real Source of Gridlock." *New Republic,* November 21, 1994.

———. "Mr. Smith Rewrites the Constitution." *New York Times,* January 11, 2010.

Gibson, Joseph. *A Better Congress: Change the Rules, Change the Results, A Modest Proposal.* Alexandria, Va.: Two Seas Media, 2010.

Gold, Martin B. Oral History Interview, 2004. Senate Historical Office, U.S. Senate website, www.senate.gov.

———. *Senate Procedure and Practice.,* 2nd ed. Lanham, Md.: Rowman & Littlefield, 2008.

Gold, Martin B., and Dimple Gupta. "The Constitutional Option to Change Senate Rules and Procedures: A Majoritarian Means to Overcome the Filibuster." *Harvard Journal of Law & Public Policy* 28, no. 1 (2004).

Goldberg, Jeffrey. "Party Unfaithful: The Republican Implosion." *New Yorker,* June 4, 2007.

Gordon v. Lance, 403 U.S. 1, 12 (1971), U.S. Supreme Court, June 7, 1971.

Greenwald, Glenn. "What Happened to the Senate's '60–Vote Requirement'?" *Salon,* November 9, 2007.

Griffith, Ernest S,. and Francis R. Valeo. *Congress: Its Contemporary Role.* 5th ed. New York: New York University Press, 1975.

Grim, Ryan. "Dodd Presses Senate Freshmen to Back Off Effort to End Filibuster." *Huffington Post,* August 4, 2010.

———. "Pelosi: End the Filibuster." *Huffington Post,* July 1, 2010.

Gugliotta, Guy, and Juliet Eilperin. "Gingrich Steps Down in Face of Rebellion." *Washington Post,* November 7, 1998.

Hale, Dennis, ed. *The United States Congress: Proceedings of the Thomas P. O'Neill, Jr. Symposium.* Boston: Boston College Trustees, 1981.

Hamilton, Lee H. "Congress Needs to Build a Culture of Fairness." Center on Congress at the Indiana University, February 18, 2011, accessed February 26, 2011, http://congress.indiana.edu/congress-needs-build-culture-fairness.

———. *How Congress Works and Why You Should Care.* Bloomington: Indiana University Press, 2004.

———. *Strengthening Congress.* Bloomington: Indiana University Press, 2009.

———. "Why Polarization Hurts Us." Center on Congress at the Indiana University, November 16, 2010.

Harkavy, Jerry. "Snowe Says Polarization Hurts the Senate." *Bangor Daily News,* April 4, 2009.

Harkin, Tom. "Examining the Filibuster: Legislative Proposals to Change Senate Procedures." U.S. Senate Committee on Rules and Administration hearings, September 22, 2010.

———. "Filibuster Reform: Curbing Abuse to Prevent Minority Tyranny in the Senate." Brennan Center for Justice website, June 21, 2010, accessed July 1, 2010, http://www.brennancenter.org/content/resource/filibuster_reform_curbing_abuse_to_prevent_minority_tyranny_in_the_sen/.

———. "Fixing the Filibuster." *Huffington Post,* February 12, 2010.

Harrison, Benjamin. *This Country of Ours.* New York: Charles Scribner's Sons, 1897.

Hatch, Orrin. *Square Peg: Confessions of a Citizen Senator.* New York: Basic Books, 2002.

Hatfield, Mark O. *Vice Presidents of the United States, 1789–1993.* Washington, D.C.: U.S. Government Printing Office, 1997.

Heniff, Bill, Jr., and Justin Murray. "Congressional Budget Resolutions: Historical Information." Congressional Research Service, January 29, 2010.

Hertzberg, Hendrik. "Oh, Shut Up." *New Yorker,* January 10, 2011.

Hilley, John L. *The Challenge of Legislation: Bipartisanship in a Partisan World.* Washington, D.C.: Brookings Institution Press, 2008.

Hylton, Wil S. "The Angry One." *GQ,* January 2007.

Hook, Janet. "Some Democrats Want to Rein in the Filibuster., *Los Angeles Times,* January 10, 2010.

Hulse, Carl. "Democrats Seek Changes to Senate Procedures." *New York Times,* December 24, 2010.

———. "Meant to Be Broken? Maybe Not This Time." *New York Times,* February 5, 2011.

———. "Senate Democrats Drop Campaign to Limit Filibuster." *New York Times,* January 26, 2011.

———. "Senate Nears Compromise to Ease Slowdown Tactics." *New York Times,* January 24, 2011.

Isenberg, Nancy. *Fallen Founder: The Life of Aaron Burr.* New York: Penguin Books, 2007.

Isenstadt, Alex. "Boehner Miffed by Committee Ratios." *Politico,* January 12, 2009, http://www.politico.com/news/stories/0109/17356.html.

Jefferson, Thomas. *The Autobiography of Thomas Jefferson.,* Chehalis, Wash.: Big Fish Publishing, 2010 (originally published 1821).

Joint Committee on the Organization of Congress. *Organization of the Congress—Final Report.* Washington, D.C.: U.S. Government Printing Office, 1993.

Kane, Paul. "Senate in Long Recess as Leaders Seek to Rein in Democrats' Filibuster Rebellion." *Washington Post,* January 22, 2011.

———. "Senate Leaders Agree to Filibuster Changes." *Washington Post,* January 27, 2011.

———. "Some Democrats Seek Change in Filibuster Rules, but Others Are Wary." *Washington Post,* February 8, 2010.

Keith, Robert. "Budget Reconciliation Process: The Senate's 'Byrd Rule.'" Congressional Research Service, March 20, 2008.

Kessler, Ronald. *Inside Congress: The Shocking Scandals, Corruption, and Abuse of Power Behind the Scenes on Capitol Hill.* New York: Simon & Schuster, 1997.

Killian, Linda. "The Senate Filibuster Isn't Going Anywhere." *U.S. News and World Report,* October 4, 2010.

King, Colbert I. "The Filibuster: A Tool for Good and Bad." *Washington Post,* June 18, 2005.

Klein, Ezra. "The Fifty Vote Senate: Could an Obscure Senate Rule Free Barack Obama from the Filibuster and Enable Health Care Reform?" *American Prospect,* March 23, 2009, accessed January 15, 2010, http://www.prospect.org/cs/articles?article=the_fifty_vote_senate.

———. "Reid Promises Filibuster Reform." *Washington Post,* March 10, 2010.

———. "The Rise of the Filibuster: An Interview with Barbara Sinclair." *Washington Post,* December 26, 2009.

———. "Sen. Jeff Merkley: 'This Isn't a Question of Filibuster or No Filibuster.'" *Washington Post,* December 23, 2010, accessed December 24, 2010, voices .washingtonpost.com/ezra-klein/2010/12/sen_jeff_merkley_this_isnt_a_q.html.

Kline, Mary-Jo, and Joanne Wood Ryan, eds. *Political Correspondence and Public Papers of Aaron Burr.* Vol. 2. Princeton, N.J.: Princeton University Press, 1983.

Koger, Gregory. "The Case for Filibustering: or, How I Learned to Stop Worrying and Love Mitch McConnell." *Monkey Cage,* September 23, 2009, accessed February 12, 2010, http://www.themonkeycage.org/2009/09/the_case_for_filibustering_or.html.

———. "Examining the Filibuster: Legislative Proposals to Change Senate Procedures." U.S. Senate Committee on Rules and Administration hearings, July 28, 2010.

———. *Filibustering: A Political History of Obstructionism in the House and Senate.* Chicago: University of Chicago Press, 2010.

Kosar, Kevi R. "Shutdown of the Federal Government: Causes, Effects, and Process." Congressional Research Service, September 20, 2004.

Krehbiel, Keith. "Pivotal Politics: A Theory of U.S. Lawmaking." Chicago: University of Chicago Press, 1998.

Krugman, Paul. "America Is Not Yet Lost." *New York Times,* February 8, 2010.

———. "A Dangerous Dysfunction." *New York Times,* December 20, 2009.

Lee, Frances E. *Beyond Ideology: Politics, Principles and Partisanship in the U.S. Senate.* Chicago: University of Chicago Press, 2009.

Lee, Frances E., and Bruce I. Oppenheimer. Sizing *Up the Senate: The Unequal Consequences of Equal Representation.* Chicago: University of Chicago Press, 1999.

Lewis, Neil A. "Angered by Filibusters on Nominees, Republicans Stage Their Own Protest." *New York Times,* November 13, 2003.

Lightman, David. "Senate Republicans: Filibuster Everything to Win in November?" McClatchy Newspapers, February 12, 2010.

Lippman, Thomas W. "Holbrooke Hits Yet Another Snag; Grassley Puts Hold on Nomination in Dispute with State Dept." *Washington Post,* June 26, 1999.

Lockwood, David E., and George Siehl. "Military Base Closures: A Historical Review from 1988 to 1995." Congressional Research Service, October 18, 2004.

Loomis, Burdette A., ed. *Esteemed Colleagues: Civility and Deliberation in the U.S. Senate.* Washington, D.C.: Brookings Institution Press, 2000.

Lott, Trent. *Herding Cats: A Life in Politics.* New York: HarperCollins, 2005.

Lynch, Megan Suzanne. "Unanimous Consent Agreements Establishing a 60-Vote Threshold for Passage of Legislation in the Senate." Congressional Research Service, May 12, 2009.

Mackenzie, G. Calvin. "Nasty & Brutish without Being Short: The State of the Presidential Appointment Process." *Brookings Review* 19, no. 2 (March 1, 2001).

Maclay, William. *Sketches of Debate in the First Senate of the United States, in 1789–90–91.* Edited by George W. Harris, Harrisburg, Pa.: Lane S. Hart Printer, 1880.

Madison, James, Alexander Hamilton, and John Jay. *The Federalist Papers.* 1788, accessed June 12, 2010, http://avalon.law.yale.edu/subject_menus/fed.asp.

Mann, Thomas E. "Examining the Filibuster: Silent Filibusters, Holds, and the Senate Confirmation Process." U.S. Senate Committee on Rules and Administration hearings, June 23, 2010.

Mann, Thomas E., and Norman J. Ornstein. *The Broken Branch: How Congress Is Failing America and How to Get It Back on Track.* New York: Oxford University Press, 2006.

Manning, Jennifer. " Membership of the 111th Congress: A Profile." Congressional Research Report for Congress, February 4, 2010.

Marcus, Ruth. "Be Careful What You Wish For on Filibusters, Democrats." *Washington Post,* January 4, 2011.

———. "Why the Filibuster Is Frustrating but Necessary." *Washington Post,* January 27, 2010.

Mariner, Joanne. "A Good Tool for a Good Fight: In Defense of the Filibuster." *Counter Punch,* November 26, 2002.

Martin, Jonathan. "Tom Daschle to Barack Obama: Meet, Eat, with GOP Leaders." *Politico,* January 16, 2011, accessed January 18, 2011, http://www.politico.com/news/stories/0111/47224.html. [video interview]

Marziani, Mimi. *Filibuster Abuse.* New York: Brennan Center for Justice at New York University School of Law, 2010.

Mascaro, Lisa. "Drive to Alter Filibusters Fizzles as Senate Adopts Modest Fixes." *Los Angeles Times,* January 27, 2011.

Matthews, Donald. *U.S. Senators and Their World.* Chapel Hill, NC: University of North Carolina Press, 1960.

Mayhew, David R. "Supermajority Rule in the US Senate." *PS: Political Science & Politics* 36 (2003): 31–36.

McCann, Anthony J. "The Tyranny of the Super-Majority: How Majority Rule Protects Minorities." UC Irvine: Center for the Study of Democracy, 2002, accessed January 25, 2010, http://escholarship.org/uc/item/18b448r6.

McCarty, Nolan, Keith T. Poole, and Harold Rosenthal. *Polarized America: The Dance of Ideology and Unequal Riches.* Cambridge, Mass.: MIT Press, 2006.

McClure, Jim, and Malcolm Wallop. "Don't Go Nuclear: There Are Other Options for Fighting Democratic Obstructionism." *Wall Street Journal,* March 20, 2005.

McConnell, Mitch. "A Power Grab Democrats Should Avoid." *Washington Post,* January 5, 2011.

McCullough, David. *John Adams.* New York: Simon & Schuster, 2001.

Mellman, Mark S. "A Proposal to End Abuse of Filibuster." *The Hill,* February 23, 2010.

Merkley, Jeff. "Thoughts on the Reform of Senate Procedure." *Washington Post,* November 16, 2010, accessed November 20, 2010, http://voices.washingtonpost.com/plum-line/Senate%20Procedures%20Reform%20Memo.pdf.

Miller, Zell, "Senate Math—41 Is Greater Than 59!" *Wall Street Journal,* March 10, 2003.

Mitchell, George J. "The Not-So-Secret History of Filibusters." *New York Times,* May 10, 2005.

Mondale, Walter F. "Resolved: Fix the Filibuster." *New York Times,* January 2, 2011.

———. "Testimony of Hon. Walter F. Mondale." Joint Committee on the Organization of Congress hearing, July 1, 1993.

Moulitsas, Markos. "Reform the Filibuster." *The Hill,* December 14, 2010.

Murray, Shailagh, and Paul Kane. "Democrats Won't Force War Vote: Effort Halted After GOP Blocks Proposal." *Washington Post,* July 19, 2007.

Nation. "Bring on the Filibuster." February 4, 2010.

———. "Legislative Bomb." April 25, 2005.

New York Times. "Make Them Work." January 25, 2011.

———. "Reform and the Filibuster." January 2, 2011.

————. "The Senate on the Brink." March 6, 2005.

————. "Senators in Need of a Spine." January 26, 2006.

————. "Time to Retire the Filibuster." January 1, 1995.

————. "Walking in the Opposition's Shoes." March 29, 2005.

————. "Who's Filibustering Now?" March 8, 2009.

Nivola, Pietro S., and David W. Brady, eds. *Red and Blue Nation? Characteristics and Causes of America's Polarized Politics.* Vol. 1. Washington, D.C.: Brookings Institution Press, 2006.

————. *Red and Blue Nation? Consequences and Correction of America's Polarized Politics.* Vol. 2. Washington, D.C.: Brookings Institution Press, 2008.

O'Beirne, Kate. "Let 'Em Talk! The Case for Real, Not Fake, Filibusters." *National Review,* February 24, 2003.

O'Connell, Anne Joseph. "Waiting for Leadership: President Obama's Record in Staffing Key Agency Positions and How to Improve the Appointments Process." Center for American Progress, April 21, 2010.

O'Connor, Patrick, and John Bresnahan. "Hoyer to Pelosi: Stand Up to the Senate." *Politico,* February 17, 2009.

O'Donnell, Katy. "Ryan Given New Power Under GOP Rules." *National Journal,* December 29, 2010, accessed December 31, 2010, http://www.nationaljournal.com/member/budget/ryan-given-new-power-under-gop-rules-20101229.

Oleszek, Walter J. "Cloture: Its Effect on Senate Proceedings." Congressional Research Service, December 21, 2006.

————. *Congressional Procedures and the Policy Process.* 8th ed. Washington, D.C.: CQ Press, 2011.

————. "'Holds' in the Senate." Congressional Research Service, May 19, 2008.

————. "Proposals to Reform 'Holds' in the Senate." Congressional Research Service, December 20, 2007.

————. "Self-Executing Rules Reported by the House Committee on Rules." Congressional Research Service, December 21, 2006.

————. "Senate Amendment Process: General Conditions and Principles." Congressional Research Service, February 20, 2001.

————. "Super-Majority Votes in the Senate." Congressional Research Service, February 20, 2001.

————. "Unanimous Consent Agreements in the Senate." Congressional Research Service, May 19, 2008.

Oloffson, Kristi. "Filibusters." *Time,* November 2, 2009.

Oppenheimer, Bruce I. "Changing Time Constraints on Congress: Historical Perspectives on the Use of Cloture." In *Congress Reconsidered,* 3rd ed., edited by Lawrence S. Dodd and Bruce I. Oppenheimer. Washington, D.C.: CQ Press. 1985.

————, ed. *U.S. Senate Exceptionalism.* Columbus: Ohio State University Press, 2002.

Ornstein, Norman J. "Examining the Filibuster: Ideas to Reduce Delay and Encourage Debate in the Senate." U.S. Senate Committee on Rules and Administration hearings, September 29, 2010.

———. "A Filibuster Fix." *New York Times,* August 28, 2010.

———. "Time to Reassess Filibuster to Keep Senate Functioning." *Roll Call,* January 20, 2010.

Ornstein, Norman J., Thomas E. Mann, and Michael J. Malbin. "Abe Fortas Hangs Over Discussion of Judicial Filibusters." *Roll Call,* December 13, 2004.

———. *Vital Statistics on Congress, 2008.* Washington, D.C.: Brookings Institution Press, 2008.

Overby, Marvin L., and Lauren C. Bell. "Filibusters and Filibusterers in the Contemporary Senate: An Examination of the Dynamics and Individual-Level Correlates of 'Extended Debate', 1975–2002." Paper presented at the American Political Science Association, Chicago, 2004, accessed March 15, 2010, http://www.allacademic.com//meta/p_mla_apa_research_citation/0/6/0/2/4/pages 60241/p60241-1.php).

Packer, George. "The Empty Chamber: Just How Broken Is the Senate?" *New Yorker,* August 9, 2010.

Paone, Martin. "Examining the Filibuster: Ideas to Reduce Delay and Encourage Debate in the Senate." U.S. Senate Committee on Rules and Administration hearings, September 29, 2010.

Pappu, Sridhar. "Slumber Party Politics on the Hill: The Democrats Take the Iraq War Strategy to the Mattresses." *Washington Post,* July 18, 2007.

Parker, David. "The Filibuster and Its Discontents: Progressives Want to Get Rid of the Filibuster, the Hold, and Other Minority Protections in the Senate. But Would Strong Majority Control Actually be Better?" *Newsweek,* December 22, 2009.

Pearson, Kathryn, and Eric Schickler. "The Transition to Democratic Leadership in a Polarized House." In *Congress Reconsidered,* 9th ed., edited by Lawrence C. Dodd, and Bruce I. Oppenheimer. Washington, D.C.: CQ Press, 2009.

Pew Research Center for the People and the Press. "Senate Legislative Process a Mystery to Many." January 28, 2010.

Pierce, Emily. "Chambliss' Win Diminishes Democrats' Committee Power." *Roll Call,* December 3, 2008.

Pierce, Emily, and Jessica Brady. "Unhappy Caucus Forces Reid to Rework Strategy." *Roll Call,* November 17, 2010.

Pincus, Walter. "Lott and McConnell Also Have 'Hold' on Holbrooke; Appointment to Election Panel at Stake." *Washington Post,* July 7, 1999.

Pope, Charles. "Ron Wyden and Charles Grassley Fight Senate Secret Holds." *Oregonian,* June 8, 2010.

Posner, Eric A., and Adrian Vermeule. "Legislative Entrenchment: A Reappraisal." *Yale Law Journal* 111 (April 30, 2002): 1665–1705.

Rae, Nicol C., and Colton C. Campbell. *New Majority or Old Minority: The Impact of Republicans on Congress.* Lanham, Md.: Rowman & Littlefield,1999.

Raju, Manu. "Corker Bucks GOP without Regrets." *Politico,* May 5, 2010.

———. "Filibuster Reform Goes Bust." *Politico,* January 28, 2011, http://www.politico.com/news/stories/0111/48325.html.

Raju, Manu, and Scott Wong. "Dems Change Rules; Senate in Chaos." *Politico,* October 6, 2011, accessed October 9, 2011, http://www.politico.com/news/stories/1011/65383.html.

———. "Filibuster Talks to Drive Senate Recess." *Politico,* January 6, 2011, accessed January 6, 2011, http://www.politico.com/news/stories/0111/47186.html.

Rawls, W. Lee. "Examining the Filibuster: Silent Filibusters, Holds, and the Senate Confirmation Process." U.S. Senate Committee on Rules and Administration hearings, June 23, 2010.

———. *In Praise of Deadlock: How Partisan Struggle Makes Better Laws.* Baltimore: Johns Hopkins University Press, 2009.

Redman, Eric. *The Dance of Legislation.* Seattle: University of Washington Press, 2001.

Reedy, George E. *The U.S. Senate: Paralysis or a Search for Consensus?* New York: Crown Publishers, 1986.

Reid, Harry, with Mark Warren. *The Good Fight: Hard Lessons from Searchlight to Washington.* New York: Penguin Group, 2008.

RePass, David E. "Make My Filibuster." *New York Times,* March 1, 2009.

Riddick, Floyd M. Oral History Interview, 1978–1979. Senate Historical Office, U.S. Senate website, www.senate.gov.

Riddick, Floyd M., and Alan S. Frumin, eds. *Riddick's Senate Procedure: Precedents and Practices.* Washington, D.C.: U.S. Government Printing Office, 1992.

Rigdon, Joan Indiana. "Filibuster Reform?" *Washington Lawyer,* September 2010.

Riley, Michael. "Udall Offers Proposal to Clear Senate's Clogged Legislative Pipeline." *Denver Post,* September 29, 2010.

Ritchie, Donald A. *The U.S. Congress: A Very Short Introduction.* New York: Oxford University Press, 2010.

Rogers, David. "The Lost Senate." *Politico,* October 9, 2009, http://www.politico.com/news/stories/1009/27992.html.

Rogers, Lindsay. *The American Senate.* New York: Alfred A. Knopf, 1926.

Rosenbaum, David E. "Clinton Vow to Congress Ends a Threat to His Nominations." *New York Times,* June 17, 1999.

Rotherham, Andrew, and Robert Saldin. "In Defense of the Filibuster." *New York Daily News,* March 3, 2010.

Rove, Karl. "Democrats Can't Filibuster ObamaCare Repeal: The GOP Needs 51 Senate Votes, and a New President, to Get It Done." *Wall Street Journal,* February 10, 2011.

Rudman, Warren B. *Combat: Twelve Years in the U.S. Senate.* New York: Random House, 1996.

Rushing, J. Taylor. "Dem Backers of New Filibuster Rules Undaunted by GOP." *The Hill,* November 13, 2010.

———. "Filibuster Reform Bill Headed for Senate Floor, Faces Uphill Battle." *The Hill,* January 22, 2010.

———. "Harkin Disputes Comparison between Filibuster Reform, 2005." *The Hill,* July 28, 2010.

———. "Levin: Filibuster Reform More Likely After Tuesday's Failed Defense Cloture Vote." *The Hill,* September 22, 2010.

Ryan, Kiki. "Reid Tweets Lady Gaga Over DADT." *Politico,* September 14, 2010.

Rybicki, Elizabeth. "Filling the Amendment Tree in the Senate." Legislative Studies Section, American Political Science Association, January 2010, accessed February 20, 2010, http://www.apsanet.org/~lss/Newsletter/jan2010/Rybick.pdf.

Saar, John. "Paul Tsongas Prepares His Ultimate Weapon on Arms Control: A Senate Filibuster." *People,* April 11, 1983.

Samuel, Terence. *The Upper House: A Journey Behind the Closed Doors of the U.S. Senate.* New York: Palgrave Macmillan, 2010.

Schick, Allen. *The Federal Budget: Politics, Policy, Process.* 3rd ed. Washington, D.C.: Brookings Institution Press. 2007.

Schiller, Wendy J. *Partners and Rivals: Representation in U.S. Senate Delegations.* Princeton, N.J.: Princeton University Press, 2000.

———. "Senate Rule XXII Should Be Amended So That Filibusters Can Be Ended by a Majority Vote: Con." In *Debating Reform: Conflicting Perspectives on How to Fix the American Political System,* edited by Richard J. Ellis and Michael Nelson. Washington, D.C.: CQ Press, 2011.

Schlesinger, Robert. "The Staggering Rise of the Filibuster." *U.S. News and World Report,* February 24, 2010.

Schneider, Judy. "House and Senate Rules of Procedure: A Comparison." Congressional Research Service, April 16, 2008.

———. "Minority Rights and Senate Procedures." Congressional Research Service, August 2005.

Shampansky, Jay R. "Constitutionality of a Senate Filibuster of a Judicial Nomination." Congressional Research Service, December 6, 2004.

Shane, Scott. "Henry Clay Hated It. So Does Bill Frist." *New York Times,* November 21, 2004.

Silver, Nate. "How to Nuke the Filibuster." *Five Thirty Eight: Politics Done Right Blog,* December 14, 2009, http://www.fivethirtyeight.com/2009/12/how-to-nuke-filibuster.html.

Simon, Marsha. "The Real Rules of the Budget Game: Minority Fiscal Decision Making in the United States Senate." PhD diss.,Massachusetts Institute of Technology, 2005, accessed February 23, 2010, http://hdl.handle.net/1721.1/33708.

Sinclair, Barbara. "Examining the Filibuster: Legislative Proposals to Change Senate Procedures." U.S. Senate Committee on Rules and Administration hearings, July 28, 2010.

————. "Individualism, Partisanship, and Cooperation in the Senate." In *Esteemed Colleagues: Civility and Deliberation in the U.S. Senate,*" edited by Burdette A. Loomis. Washington, D.C.: Brookings Institution Press, 2000.

————. "The New World of U.S. Senators." In *Congress Reconsidered,* edited by Lawrence C. Dodd and Bruce I. Oppenheimer. Washington, D.C.: CQ Press, 2009.

————. *Party Wars: Polarization and the Politics of National Policy Making.* Norman: University of Oklahoma Press, 2006.

————. "The 60-Vote Senate: Strategies, Process, and Outcomes." In *U.S. Senate Exceptionalism,* edited by Bruce I. Oppenheimer, Columbus:, Ohio State University Press, 2002.

————. "Tip O'Neill and Contemporary House Leadership" in *Masters of the House: Congressional Leaders Over Two Centuries,* edited by Roger H. Davidson, Susan Webb Hammond and Raymond W. Smock. Boulder, Colo.: Westview Press, 1998.

Smith, Ben, "Pelosi Vents to Obama, Reid on Energy Bill." *Politico,* July 27, 2010.

Smith, Jean Edward. "Filibusters: The Senate's Self Inflicted Wound." *New York Times,* March 1, 2009.

Smith, Steven S. *Call to Order: Floor Politics in the House and Senate.* Washington, D.C.: Brookings Institution Press, 1989.

————. "Senate Rule XXII Should Be Amended So That Filibusters Can Be Ended by a Majority Vote: Pro." In *Debating Reform: Conflicting Perspectives on How to Fix the American Political System,* edited by Richard J. Ellis and Michael Nelson. Washington, D.C.: CQ Press, 2011.

Specter, Arlen. *Passion for Truth.* New York: HaperCollins Publishers, 2000.

Stein, Sam. "DeMint Has Had 'a Standing Hold' on All Legislation for Past Two Years: Dem Senator." *Huffington Post,* September 28, 2010, accessed September 30, 2010, http://www.huffingtonpost.com/2010/09/28/demint-has-placed-a-stand_n_742175.html.

————. "True Test of Senate Compromise Lies Ahead." *Huffington Post,* February 26, 2010, accessed August 1, 2011, http://www.huffingtonpost.com/2010/02/26/durbin-launches-online-pe_n_478225.html.

Stoddard, A.B. "The System Is Broken." *The Hill,* November 17, 2001.

Stolberg, Sheryl Gay. "Senators Who Averted Showdown Face New Test in Court Fight." *New York Times,* July 14, 2005.

Story, Joseph. *Commentaries on the Constitution of the United States.* Vol. 1, 5th ed. Edited by Melville M. Bigelow. Boston: Little, Brown, 1891.

Sununu, John E. "Democrats Err in Bid to Muzzle Senators." *Boston Globe,* January 3, 2011.

Talev, Margaret. "Constant Filibuster Threat Is Tying Senate in Knots." *Seattle Times,* July 20, 2007.

Theriault, Sean M. *Party Polarization in Congress.* New York: Cambridge University Press, 2008.

Theriault, Sean M., and David Rohde. "The Gingrich Senators and Their Effect on the U.S. Senate." Paper prepared for delivery at the American Political Science Association Annual Meeting, July 26, 2010.

Tomasky, Thomas. "The Specter Haunting the Senate." *New York Review of Books,* September 30, 2010.

Tong, Lorraine H. "House Committee Party Ratios: 98th–111th Congresses." Congressional Research Service, March 30, 2009.

———. "Senate Committee Party Ratios: 94th–110th Congresses," Congressional Research Service, November 18, 2008.

Toobin, Jeffrey. *The Nine: Inside the Secret World of the Supreme Court.* New York: Doubleday, 2007.

Tsongas, Paul. "*The Road from Here: Liberalism and Realities in the 1980s.* New York: Alfred A. Knopf, 1981.

Tumulty, Karen. "Doris Kearns Goodwin: 'Let Them Filibuster.'" *Time,* Swampland: A Blog about Politics and Policy, October 21, 2008, http://swampland.blogs.time.com/2010/01/29/doris-kearns-goodwin-let-them-filibuster/.

———. "Sarah Palin in Charge . . . " *Time,* Swampland: A Blog about Politics and Policy, October 21, 2008, http://swampland.time.com/2008/10/21/sarah_palin_in_charge.

Udall, Tom. "Amending the Filibuster Rule." *Politico,* March 5, 2010.

———. "Senate New Year's Resolution: Fixing a Broken Set of Rules." *Washington Post,* January 4, 2011.

U.S. Senate Committee on Rules and Administration hearings. "Examining the Filibuster: History of the Filibuster 1789–2008." April 22, 2010.

———. "Examining the Filibuster: Ideas to Reduce Delay and Encourage Debate in the Senate." September 29, 2010.

———. "Examining the Filibuster: Legislative Proposals to Change Senate Procedures." July 28, 2010.

———. "Examining the Filibuster: Legislative Proposals to Change Senate Procedures." September 22, 2010.

———. "Examining the Filibuster: Silent Filibusters, Holds and the Senate Confirmation Process." June 23, 2010.

———. "Examining the Filibuster: The Filibuster Today and Its Consequences." May 19, 2010.

———. "Requiring Public Disclosure of Notices of Objections ('Holds') to Proceedings to Motions or Measures in the Senate." June 17, 2003.

Viebeck, Elise. "McCain on Lady Gaga: 'I'm Glad She's Paying Attention'." *The Hill,* September 17, 2010.

Wasson, Erik. "Dems Rip Proposed Rule Giving New Power to GOP Budget Chairman." *The Hill,* December 30, 2010.

Wawro, Gregory J., and Eric Schickler. *Filibuster: Obstruction and Lawmaking in the U.S. Senate.* Princeton, N.J.: Princeton University Press, 2006.

————. "Where's the Pivot? Obstructing and Lawmaking in the Pre-Cloture Senate." *American Journal of Political Science* 48, no. 4 (October 2004): 758–774.

Waxman, Henry. *The Waxman Report: How Congress Really Works.* New York: Hachette Book Group, 2010.

Webb, Jim. Interviewed by John King, CNN, at the "Second Annual Washington Ideas Forum," sponsored by the Atlantic, the Aspen Institute, and the Newseum. October 1, 2010, accessed November 1, 2010, http://www.theatlantic.com/politics/archive/2010/10/webb-obama-had-wrong-focus-in-the-beginning/63886/.

Weisberg, Jacob. "Frist's Folly: The Filibuster Is Inherently Conservative. That's Why We Need It." *Slate,* April 20, 2005.

Whalen, Charles, and Barbara Whalen. *The Longest Debate: A Legislative History of the 1964 Civil Rights Act.* Washington, D.C.: Seven Locks Press, 1985.

Wichterman, Bill. "Why Conservatives Should Defend the Senate Filibuster." *Daily Caller,* July 16, 2010.

Wildavsky, Aaron. *The Politics of the Budgetary Process.* Boston: Little, Brown, 1964.

Wilkie, Christina. "Celebrities Enlist Followers in Lobbying Congress on 'Don't Ask, Don't Tell' Vote." *The Hill,* September 19, 2010.

Will, George F. "For Liberals, the Filibuster Is Now the Enemy." *Washington Post,* February 25, 2010.

Williss, G. Frank. "Do Things Right the First Time: Administrative History, the National Park Service and the Alaska National Interest Lands Conservation Act of 1980." U.S. Department of the Interior, September 1985.

Wilson, Woodrow. *Congressional Government: A Study in American Politics.* 15th ed. Cambridge, Mass.: Riverside Press, 1900.

Wolfensberger, Donald R. "Rules, Rules, Rules: Congress Relies on Them." Paper prepared for delivery at the Dirksen Congressional Center Workshop: Congress in the Classroom, Peoria, Ill., July 31, 2007.

Wolfinger, Raymond E. "Filibusters: Majority Rule, Presidential Leadership, and Senate Norms." In *Readings on Congress,* edited by Raymond E. Wolfinger. Upper Saddle River, N.J.: Prentice Hall, 1971.

Wong, Scott. "Three Democrats Demand Filibuster Vote." *Politico,* January 24, 2011, http://www.politico.com/news/stories/0111/48091.html.

Wood, Shelby. "Mt. Hood Runs into a Senator: Oklahoma's Dr. No." *Oregonian,* March 10, 2008.

Zelizer, Julian E. *The Struggles to Reform Congress and Its Consequences, 1948–2000.* Cambridge, UK: Cambridge University Press, 2004.

————. "Why Getting Rid of the Filibuster Is Still a Good Idea." History News Network, May 2, 2005, accessed June 15, 2010, http://hnn.us/articles/11557.html.

INDEX

unemployment insurance extension, 68, 153, 225n1
United Nations, 69, 70, 89
unlimited debate, xvii, 1, 4–5, 6, 8, 11, 12, 18, 20, 23, 24, 27, 54, 56, 58, 68, 70, 75, 77, 78, 84, 85, 94, 128, 140, 154, 157, 162, 177. *See also* debate, extended; filibuster
"up or down" vote, 39, 76, 80, 125, 137, 143, 150, 166

Vandenberg, Arthur, 25–27, 207n31
Vermeule, Adrian, 62
veto, 36, 47, 60, 61; by states, 158; override of, 47, 60
vice president, xiii–xiv, 3, 25, 26, 27, 77, 83, 123, 125, 127, 128–129, 130, 131, 207n38. *See also names of vice presidents*
Vietnam, 42, 69, 169
"vote-a-rama," 114–115, 174–175

Wagner, Robert, 207n31
Wallace, George, 41
Wallop, Malcolm, 84
Wall Street Journal, 84, 110, 143
Walsh, Thomas, 123–124
Walton, Reggie, 37
Warner, John, 46, 106, 211n11, 219n1
Warner-Levin resolution, 106
War Powers Act of 1973, 47, 62

Warren, Francis, 125
Washington, George, 2–3, 4, 63, 139, 154
Washington Post, 29, 40, 74–75, 79, 89, 136, 150, 161, 178, 179, 183
Watergate, xiii, 42, 110; Senate Watergate Committee, 131
Watkins, Charles, 25. *See also* parliamentarian
Watt, James, 165
Watt, Melvin, 138
Wawro, Gregory, 22, 55
Ways and Means Committee, House, 82, 83
Webster, Daniel, 206n19
Weicker, Lowell, 46
welfare reform bill, 113
Wellstone, Paul, 92, 140, 166
Whigs, 20–21
White House, 1, 23, 29, 31, 36, 37, 42, 58, 82, 83, 110, 116, 153, 155, 160, 161, 189
Whitehouse, Sheldon, 143
Whitewater investigation, 38
Wilkins, Roy, 65
Wilson, Pete, 47
Wilson, Woodrow, 22–24, 124
wiretapping, 29
"world's greatest deliberative body," 4, 27, 104, 105, 126–127
Wright, George, 76
Wyden, Ron, 91–92, 184

RICHARD A. ARENBERG served in senior congressional staff positions for 34 years as an aide to Majority Leader George Mitchell and Senators Paul Tsongas and Carl Levin. He currently is an Adjunct Lecturer in Political Science and Public Policy at Brown University, Northeastern University, and Suffolk University.

ROBERT B. DOVE is Parliamentarian Emeritus of the U.S. Senate, having served as the Senate's Parliamentarian and Assistant Parliamentarian from 1966 until 2001. He has provided expert parliamentary advice to legislatures around the world. He currently is an Adjunct Professor at the Georgetown University Law Center, George Washington University, and George Mason University and counsels members of the Patton Boggs law firm on congressional procedure.

★　★　★